The Play of Law in Modern British Theatre

Available or forthcoming titles:
Judging from Experience: Law, Praxis, Humanities
Jeanne Gaakeer

Schreber's Law: Jurisprudence and Judgment in Transition
Peter Goodrich

Living in Technical Legality: Science Fiction and Law as Technology
Kieran Tranter

Imagined States: Law and Literature in Nigeria 1900–1966
Katherine Isobel Baxter

Outlaws and Spies: Legal Exclusion in Law and Literature
Conor McCarthy

Criminality and the Common Law Imagination in the Eighteenth and Nineteenth Centuries
Erin L. Sheley

edinburghuniversitypress.com/series/ecsllh

The Play of Law
in Modern British Theatre

Ian Ward

EDINBURGH
University Press

Edinburgh University Press is one of the leading university presses in the UK. We publish academic books and journals in our selected subject areas across the humanities and social sciences, combining cutting-edge scholarship with high editorial and production values to produce academic works of lasting importance. For more information visit our website: edinburghuniversitypress.com

Edinburgh University Press Ltd
The Tun – Holyrood Road
12(2f) Jackson's Entry
Edinburgh EH8 8PJ

First published in hardback by Edinburgh University Press 2021

Typeset in 11/13pt Adobe Garamond Pro by
Servis Filmsetting Ltd, Stockport,
printed and bound by CPI Group (UK) Ltd
Croydon, CR0 4YY

A CIP record for this book is available from the British Library

ISBN 978 1 4744 5014 0 (hardback)
ISBN 978 1 4744 5015 7 (paperback)
ISBN 978 1 4744 5016 4 (webready PDF)
ISBN 978 1 4744 5017 1 (epub)

Contents

Acknowledgements

I should like to express my gratitude to the editors and publishers of the following journals who have kindly given permission for me to reproduce material. Earlier versions of Chapter 4 appeared in volume 10 of *Law Humanities*, Chapter 5 in volume 29 of *Anglistik*, Chapter 6 in volume 47 of *Contemporary Drama* and Chapter 8 in volume 12 of *Polemos*. I should also like to thank participants at the AIDEL conference, held at the University of Verona in 2015, before whom I presented a preliminary version of Chapter 8. And finally I owe a considerable debt of gratitude to the editor of this series, Bill MacNeil, who made a number of valuable comments and criticisms at various stages during the writing of this book. All very much appreciated.

Introduction

This book is about the interplay of law, politics and history in modern British theatre. There is nothing particularly new about the first part of this aspiration; to contemplate the interaction of law, politics and history. Dramatists have used theatre as a place for political debate since the days of Sophocles. The same is true of historical contemplation. The young Shakespeare built his reputation as a writer of political history; completing two tetralogies during the 1590s, charting English history from Richard II to Richard III. The older Shakespeare might seem to have moved on. But not really. The Jacobean tragedies were still histories, and still political. So too the later 'problem' plays. It was the politics which made them problematic. Writing historical and political drama is not then new. Michael Patterson puts it simply: 'All theatre is political. Indeed, it is the most political of all art forms'.[1] And neither is writing about those who wrote it – racks of books on Shakespeare and history and politics, and Sophocles and classical Greece. And plenty more besides.

Our concern is though with modern drama. The term 'modern' can be loaded, of course; much like its near-relation 'contemporary'. Which means that it can also be a distraction; weeks, months, years spent agonising over the metaphysics of 'modernity'. For the purposes of this book, however, 'modern' is used in the simpler prosaic sense, to provide a chronological frame. The plays which will be discussed in the coming chapters have been written and performed over the previous half-century.[2] They are 'modern' in this sense. And, as such, they invite their audiences to contemplate matters of law and politics which have a certain familiarity. There is nothing new about the areas of legal debate which we will encounter in the coming pages; terrorism,

---

[1] M. Patterson, *Strategies of Political Theatre: Post-War British Playwrights*, (Cambridge UP, 2003), 1.

[2] To an extent, an unavoidably arbitrary determination. By way of comparison, in his 2010 study of 'contemporary' drama, David Lane tracked back fifteen years. See his *Contemporary British Drama*, (Edinburgh UP, 2010).

governance, murder, sexual violence, pornography. But the expressions and the challenges mutate as we will see very shortly when we take a preliminary look at what the coming chapters will entail. First, though, we should pause to contemplate the larger aspiration; the interplay of law, politics and history in modern British theatre.

An obvious place to begin is with Michael Billington's magisterial study, *State of the Nation: British Theatre since 1945*. Starting perhaps with his opening conclusion: 'It is obvious that politics has been a recurrent theme of modern British drama'.[3] Surveying the previous three-quarters of a century, Billington detects a cyclical process; as dramatic attention switches from generation to generation, between matters of public and matters of private politics. It is not, of course, a purely natural cycle; even if hindsight lends a certain inevitability. Shifts in national politics necessarily intrude. Thus, the advance of socialism in the post-war era inspired a raft of plays which contemplated socialist politics; some supportive, some less so. J. B. Priestley's *An Inspector Calls*, which premiered in 1946, is a compelling example of the former.[4] As the 1960s advanced, left-wing political theatre began to mutate; the louder violence of Edward Bond and John Osborne, the quieter violence of Harold Pinter. And then a 'new gang' of radical writers emerge during the later 1970s, once again animated by a palpable shift to the right in national politics. It is here, in a sense, that this book begins, with the work of playwrights such as David Hare, Caryl Churchill and Howard Brenton. The more Thatcherism became entrenched during the 1980s, the richer and more urgent this critique became. Trevor Griffiths referred to a drama of 'strategic penetration'.[5] In the place of idealism comes 'discontent' and disillusion; a different kind of anger.[6]

And a renewed interest in the past. Particularly prevalent, as we will see, in the work of Caryl Churchill. But also apparent in that of Hare and Brenton, and other similarly inclined writers such as David Edgar, and then, a little later, the likes of Mark Ravenhill and Sarah Daniels. Not always because the past needs to be revisited, but because it can provide a context within which the present might be reconceived, and the future perhaps better imagined.[7] A Brechtian impulse, theatre purposed for change. Brenton's *The Romans in*

[3] M. Billington, *State of the Nation: British Theatre Since 1945*, (Faber and Faber, 2007), 3.

[4] A moment similarly seized upon by Simon Shepherd in his account of modern British theatre. See S. Shepherd, *The Cambridge Introduction to Modern British Theatre*, (Cambridge UP, 2009), 11–12.

[5] In Shepherd, *Theatre*, 46.

[6] Billington, *State*, 215–16.

[7] For an extended commentary, see Lane, *Drama*, 157–87.

Britain was perhaps the most arresting, certainly the most controversial, of the genre.[8] Alongside which might be placed the likes of Edgar's *Destiny* and Churchill's *Light Shining in Buckinghamshire*, a play to which we will turn very shortly. But then, as the final decade of the century approached, the cycle turned once again. The private advanced and the past retreated.

There was little time for history in the new 'brutalism' of 'in-yer-face' theatre, which arrived full-throttle in the latter 1990s.[9] The present was far too urgent. Vicious, 'confrontational', distressing, the 'theatre of sensation', as Aleks Sierz called it, at its most violent extreme, calculated to shock and awe.[10] An assault, some surmised, against the authority of text and narrative.[11] Brenton had famously suggested that political theatre should be a place for 'savage insights' rather than 'reasoned discussion'.[12] 'In-yer-face' was something different again. But then it was gone; at least in its more arresting form. The circle turned once more. As the twenty-first century dawned, a new 'world of fear', of crises, domestic and international, inspired a new genre of 'documentary' drama.[13] The contrasts could hardly be more stark. Where the brutalists had written to disrupt and disturb, to confound meaning almost, the 'docu-dramatists' sought to withdraw themselves from the text. Cold reason, and cold history, once again replacing the heat of violent confutation. A different kind of awe, but no less shocking.

There is, of course, a need for caution. Larger histories, such as Billington's, tend to be more broadly-brushed, the narrative coherence lending an almost Whiggish tone. They can also distort; as any revisionist critic will be quick to point out. In his famous essay *The Whig Interpretation of History*, written back in the 1930s, Herbert Butterfield deployed a prescient analogy. Whig

---

[8] Greatest controversy moved around a scene of simulated anal rape. Pressed by organisations such as the National Viewers and Listeners Association, the authorities began criminal proceedings, alleging a breach of the 1956 Sexual Offences Act. The action was withdrawn after a couple of days.

[9] The term 'new brutalism' was sometimes applied to 'in-yer-face' drama; its critics hoping to conjure images of 'new brutalist' architecture from the 1960s and 1970s. To the extent that a number of 'in-yer-face' plays were set amidst the concrete jungles of Britain's inner cities, there is a consonance.

[10] See A. Sierz, *In-Yer-Face: British Drama Today*, (Faber and Faber, 2001), 4–9, 18–19 and also *Rewriting the Nation: British Theatre Today*, (Methuen, 2011), 19, 60–1, 195–200.

[11] See Lane, *Drama*, 28, and also Sierz, *In-Yer-Face*, 208, suggesting that the genre described another of those moments where 'words fail' and the 'language of . . . brutality takes over'. A conclusion that resonates with Richard Weisberg's account of a similar moment, in Vichy France. Weisberg's book, entitled *The Failure of the Word*, is commonly regarded to be one of the founding texts in modern 'law and literature' studies.

[12] Quoted in Patterson, *Strategies*, at 95.

[13] Sierz, *Rewriting*, 71–2.

historians, he supposed, resembled nothing other than 'strolling minstrels' wandering the byways of the past selling romantic ballads to gullible punters.[14] Butterfield was especially bothered by two traits in Whig history, and their consequence; the presumption of progress, and the negation of difference. Concerns shared by progressive dramatists. Theatre, Howard Barker surmised, should be a place of 'healthy confusions'.[15] A defensible position. But also reductive. For the simple reason that anything written is distorted. Writers write to purpose, and they respond to context and to fashion, much as they try to shape it.[16] It is why the history of any theatre might be expected to be cyclical, to turn and return. It is why it might sometimes seem to be progressive, sometimes regressive. Sometimes describing a nation of common purpose, sometimes a 'torn self', as Tim Crouch has put it.[17]

It also why certain voices will, at certain times, seem louder, and quieter. We might here pause to reconceive the idea, and more especially the experience, of theatre. Classical British theatre, as Simon Shepherd suggests, has always tended towards text. It is a 'readable tradition', a 'Whig tradition' indeed.[18] But whilst it is 'consciously written', it is also consciously performed. It assumes a visibility and an audibility. It invites us to look and to listen.[19] The gesture edits the text; moderating what Phyllis Nagy terms the 'zeal for the literal'.[20] So too the voice; and not just the voice which appears on stage. Acknowledging the particular need for political theatre to resist 'disciplinary' sclerosis, Baz Kershaw refers to a strategy of 'ensnaring' the audience.[21] Helen Nicholson motions similarly, to a theatre of 'reflexive participants'.[22] Progressive theatre serves no purpose if the only change takes place on stage.

Unless, of course, we re-think what is we mean by stage. A sentiment

---

[14] H. Butterfield, *The Whig Interpretation of History*, (Bell and Sons, 1931), 11–13, 39–41, 64.

[15] Quoted in Patterson, *Strategies*, 85. A contemporary of Hare and Brenton, Barker identified himself with what he called the 'theatre of catastrophe', taking its lead from the work of early twentieth century continental dramatists such as Artaud. As such, he was perhaps more in step with some of the 'in-yer-face' drama of the 1990s.

[16] A sentiment with which Billington closes his study of post-war British theatre. See *State*, 410–11.

[17] In Sierz, *Rewriting*, 228.

[18] Shepherd, *Theatre*, 119, 189.

[19] On the relation of text and performance, see Patterson, *Strategies*, 3, and Lane, *Drama*, 7–13.

[20] Quoted in Sierz, *In-Yer-Face*, 242.

[21] B. Kershaw, *The Radical in Performance; Between Brecht and Baudrillard*, (Routledge, 1999), 31.

[22] H. Nicholson, *Applied Theatre: The Gift of Drama*, (Palgrave, 2005), 10.

which likewise encourages another more prosaic kind of movement, away from more familiar theatrical 'institutions'; into schools and shopping centres, parish halls and political assemblies.[23] Different audiences, different stages; we will come across examples of both in the coming chapters. It would be a mistake to diminish the continuing authority of text and writing.[24] But it would be no less a mistake to neglect the evolving dynamics of performance and reception. Innovation nurtures progression.

The politics of 'critical dissent' is then mutable, in a variety of ways.[25] Urgencies differentiate; amongst writers, amongst actors and amongst audiences.[26] There were different kinds of 'angry young men' during the 1960s, just as there were different kinds of angry young women. And there still are. Historical drama assumed various guises, 'in-yer-face' writing different expressions of violence, different 'feasts of filth', as one disgruntled reviewer put it. And there are, as we will see, all kinds of 'docu-drama' too; some more 'docu' than others. Moreover, a particular context further sharpens the critical eye. As its title infers, this book is more especially about the writing and presentation of legal issues on the modern British stage; something which necessarily invites us to contemplate the relation of legal and theatrical performance.[27] It also invites us to focus further on particular areas, and controversies, in law, which we will also do. Some will be familiar, even vintage; such as the need to reform legal education and criminal procedure, to reinvest the idea of the rule of law and the independence of the judiciary. Others, whilst hardly unknown to history, have assumed a renewed vitality, and notoriety; the 'war' against terrorism, the idea of restorative justice, the challenges, and abuses, of technology. We will encounter each of these in the coming chapters.

The practice, and theory, of law then directs our critical attention more closely. And there are other contextual dynamics. Amongst the most obvious, in the context of this book at least, are those of gender. Here there is an especially rich critical literature to be discovered. And some more coincidences; which, as is so often the case, are not really coincidences at all. According to Elaine Aston, 'women dramatists' have, over the previous quarter-century,

---

[23] In a later chapter we will come across a play written for schools, performed in Parliament. For broader commentaries on alternative 'theatres', see Shepherd, *Theatre*, 52–9, and Sierz, *Rewriting*, 34–45.

[24] See Lane, *Drama*, 189.

[25] See Billington, *State*, 410.

[26] See here Zierz, *Rewriting*, 7.

[27] See N. Rogers, 'The Play of Law: Comparing Performances in Law and Theatre', 8 *Queensland University of Technology Law and Justice Journal* 2008, 438, 443.

provided the vital 'energising force' in modern British drama.[28] Something which coincides with a perceived 'crisis of masculinity', ever more apparent as the twentieth century drew to a close.[29] And which further coincides with the evolution of critical legal thinking; a distinctive critical legal feminism rising from the embers of the Critical Legal Studies movement. Another particular voice gaining strength across intellectual and political disciplines. Only this time it is a voice which has not hitherto been much heard, in the theatre, in history, or in the law.

The place of politics in modern drama has not then gone unnoticed; nor the history. And there is consonance in these histories of dramatic history too. Much the same course charted by Billington can be found in Michael Patterson's *Strategies of Political Theatre* and Aleks Sierz's *Rewriting the Nation*. The same continuities, the same subversive dis-junctures. A landscape both settled, and not. Within which we need to locate, as closely as possible, the place of law. We should sketch out what is to come.

Eight chapters in total, presented in three sets. The first contains two chapters. Both are concerned with what we might term testamentary, or 'documentary' drama, a genre which is especially concerned with the raising of voices and the capacity for nurturing communicative engagement. An aspiration which, of course, has long lain at the heart of 'law and literature' scholarship. Whilst they share a common theme, the two chapters examine very different expressions of 'voice'. The first revisits David Hare's play *Murmuring Judges*, which premiered in 1991. The second part of Hare's renowned 'state of the nation' trilogy, *Murmuring Judges* was written as an excoriating attack on legal practice, prejudice and process. The moment, as we will see, was anyway consonant. For much of the 1980s, scholars on both sides of the Atlantic had been busy developing a distinctive genre of 'critical legal scholarship' to the same political purpose; to uncover the politics and the prejudice of legal education and practice. Later mutations of this scholarship would, as we have already noted, include critical legal feminism. And also 'law and literature' and 'law and humanities'. Another coincidence then, and another reason to start our book here.

The second of these 'testamentary' chapters is concerned with a more recent species of 'docu' or 'verbatim' drama. Plays which, as we will see,

---

[28] E. Aston, *Feminist Views on the English Stage: Women Playwrights 1990—2000*, (Cambridge UP, 2003), 1, and also 169. Patterson gestures to the same in his *Strategies*, at 156–7.

[29] As we will see, it is often suggested that much of the 'in-yer-face' drama of the 1990s can be interpreted as a specific response to this 'crisis of masculinity'. Though, at a variant, Mark Ravenhill has suggested, that it might be more closely comprehended as a 'crisis' of 'hetero-sexuality'. See Sierz, *In-Yer*-Face, 180, and also *Rewriting*, 19, 186.

commonly revisit legal or quasi-legal institutions or inquiries. The audience serving as a kind of jury, or 'witness', as Simon Shepherd puts it.[30] Intrinsically jurisprudential, and so peculiarly consonant once again, to our particular purpose. The origins of this genre are commonly traced, in the critical literature, to the writing and performance of Richard Norton-Taylor's *The Colour of Justice* at the very end of the 1990s. Its particular subject was the judicial inquiry which sought to uncover the truth behind the flawed investigation into the murder of Stephen Lawrence. Norton-Taylor has since written a series of further documentary plays, many of which were conceived in response to the so-called 'war on terror'. Whilst we will review the broader genre, our primary concern will be with one of the later of these plays, entitled *Called to Account*. It imagines the trial of the former British Prime Minister Tony Blair on various charges relating to breaches of international law.

The second set of chapters investigates the writing of history in modern British drama. The first two return to what Charles Dickens liked to call the 'great seventeenth century time'. The third is a prospective history, which also takes us back into the nineteenth century. The closer focus of the first of these three chapters is the work of Caryl Churchill, one of the most influential voices in the political theatre of the later 1970s and 1980s. A contemporary of Hare, as well as fellow left-leaning dramatists such as Howard Brenton and David Edgar, the younger Churchill commonly used history to stimulate reflection on the 'condition' of women in contemporary society. We will take a more particular look at two of these early plays, *Vinegar Tom* and *Light Shining in Buckinghamshire*. The former revisited the notorious witch-hunts of the early seventeenth-century, whilst the latter reconceived the birth of English radicalism.

The remaining two chapters in this second set are about kings; both, by odd coincidence, called Charles. The first is Howard Brenton's *55 Days*, first performed in 2012. The king is Charles I and the fifty-five days to which the title refers are those which preceded his execution on 30th January 1649, a period which encompassed one of the most dramatic trials in English history; of the King himself, on charges of high treason. The purpose of Brenton's play is to investigate the nature of monarchy, the performance of government, and the often strained relation of the personal and the public in the exercise of power. The same concerns, not surprisingly, animate the second of our kingship plays. Mike Bartlett's *King Charles III* is, though, very different. And for an obvious reason. His king is prospective, his play an exercise in virtual history. *King Charles III* imagines the days and weeks which follow

---

[30] Shepherd, *Theatre*, 38.

the death of Queen Elizabeth II. So again, a muse on the place of monarchy in twenty-first century Britain. But haunted by different spectres. Various Shakespearean kings perhaps most obviously, but also that of the Victorian constitutionalist Walter Bagehot. A century and a half have passed since Bagehot published his *English Constitution*. In the opinion of some, still the definitive commentary on what a monarch can do, and not do. Bartlett wonders.

If the second set of essays might be termed 'histories', the third might, following the same Shakespearean conceit, be termed 'tragedies'. Matters of high politics and constitutional controversy are replaced with contemplations of private and personal tragedy. More particularly, contemplations of violence and violation which engage matters of gender and criminal jurisprudence; in turn touching on the experiences of rape and sexual assault, child murder, and 'revenge' pornography. The first revisits one of the most controversial play performed on the British stage in the last three decades. Sarah Kane's *Blasted* is commonly acclaimed as a definitive contribution to the 'in-yer-face' drama which created such a critical stir in the 1990s. No play distressed the critics, and perhaps the audience, more than *Blasted*; one of two plays in which Kane addressed head-on the experience of rape and violent sexual assault. Whilst the status of Kane as a prospectively feminist writer remains a matter of critical debate, the urgency of her writing does not.

The second of our 'tragedies' contemplates a different violence. Few crimes animate greater popular revulsion than child murder. It is, perhaps, the incomprehensibility of the crime. Representing, as Mark Ravenhill put it, 'a tear in the fabric' of our humanity. There have, in recent years, been a number of dramatic engagements with the related subjects of paedophilia and child murder; Denis Harrower's *Blackbird*, Dennis Kelly's *Taking Care of Baby*, Rob Evans's *A Girl in a Car with a Man*, Bryony Lavery's *Frozen*. The later piece of writing will be our closer focus. In large part because Lavery's play introduces a further jurisprudential dimension. *Frozen* explores the merits and demerits of 'restorative' justice as an alternative strategy for addressing the trauma of violent crime. Advocates of 'restorative' justice commonly base their case on the inherently communicative nature of the process. *Frozen* tests the veracity of this claim.

The final chapter in the book addresses a different violence again. Theatre, ancient and modern, has long touched on questions of pornography, sometimes critically and sometimes in performance. Particular histories are though shorter. The advance of the internet has nurtured a range of new mutations and challenges to a more familiar experience of violence and violation; amongst which can be counted what has become known as 'revenge porn', a peculiarly vicious, commonly gendered, species of cyber-harassment.

The text around which the chapter moves is Evan Placey's *Girls Like That*, first performed in late 2013. It is notable that Placey's play was written explicitly for student theatre. As such, it engages a pedagogic aspiration shared by both progressive theatre and cross-disciplinary 'law and literature' scholarship.[31] Whilst it does not deny the value of legal regulation, *Girls Like That* confirms that an effective response to species of 'revenge' pornography will require more than the mere drafting of new legal regulations. It will require a significant adjustment in patterns of cultural behaviour. Which is what, in a sense, progressive political theatre is for.[32]

---

[31] For a commentary on the educative aspiration of progressive theatre see Shepherd, *Theatre*, 216–17.

[32] See Lane, *Drama*, 147, reaching the same conclusion.

1

Murmurings

Our first play takes us to the very heart of the 'law and literature' enterprise. David Hare's *Murmuring Judges* was first performed in 1991. The second of a trilogy of plays which examined the 'condition' of British public life in the late twentieth-century, *Murmuring Judges* took a more particular look at the complacency and corruption of the justice system. It was intended to shock and disturb. And also educate. And it is this latter aspiration which resonates. Literary jurisprudence is not solely about teaching. But it is principle amongst its various 'strategies'. It hopes that the deployment of literary texts might enhance a law student's appreciation of the human dimension of legal practice. In these terms, Richard Weisberg referred to its 'poethical' ambition. In its 'attention to legal communication' and by enhancing our sensitivity to the 'plight of the other', such a jurisprudence can 'revitalize the ethical component of law'.[1] The capacity of literature to engage the student audience is enhanced, for very obvious reasons, where it touches upon issues which import an experiential dimension. Very often this process of textual importation has to be massaged, most obviously by the classroom teacher. A seminal 'law and literature' text such as *The Merchant of Venice*, for example, has to be made to matter. Whilst it has a collateral value in teaching students about the treatment of Jews in late Elizabethan England or the practice of late medieval usury regulation, its greater value lies in demanding engagement with larger issues of justice and the ethical treatment of the 'other'.[2] Which is precisely what *Murmuring Judges* does. Except that it does require much massaging. *Murmuring Judges* is front-on about the law.

More especially, it is about what self-styled 'critical' lawyers like to term the 'law job'. What is it, who does it, and why? And with what consequence?

---

[1] R. Weisberg, *Poethics: And Other Strategies of Law and Literature*, (Columbia UP, 1992), 46.

[2] The critical literature on these various issues in *The Merchant of Venice* is unsurprisingly vast. For an introduction, see I. Ward, *Shakespeare and the Legal Imagination*, (Butterworths/Cambridge UP, 1999), 115–41.

In the first part of this chapter, we are going to take a closer look at this 'critical' scholarship. We will see, once again, that it was driven by a particular concern regarding legal education; a coming generation of law teachers unpersuaded that it was enough to just describe the law. And not only 'not enough', but also dishonest. The law, they surmised, was a political instrument wielded to political purpose. And law students needed to know this. At which point, we will also notice a coincidence. It was this same scepticism which animated Hare. He too wanted to strip away the pretences of the 'law job'. And he wanted to do so at pretty much the same moment. A history of the 'critical legal studies' movement might start at some point towards the end of the 1970s, and run through to the end of the century. Some might write the history slightly longer, some perhaps slightly shorter. But most would admit that if there was a high-point, it was probably around the turn of the 1980s into the 1990s. Precisely when Hare was putting the finishing touches to *Murmuring Judges*. We will turn to Hare and his play in the second part of this chapter. In doing so, we will encounter a range of issues regarding legal practice and the legal profession, which are no less tendentious today than they were three decades ago. And then, in the third, we will return to the didactic aspiration. Conceiving the 'law job' has changed in the last thirty years, and the 'law and literature' movement has played a key role in this process.

The Critical Lawyer

A history of the 'critical legal studies' movement, which swept through North American, and later British law schools, during the 1980s and 1990s, evolves through disciplines. It starts in the later 1970s, with a number of left-leaning socio-legal scholars. By the mid-1980s, the pace has gathered, and the movement has assumed a more aggressively political position. Mark Kelman talked of 'trashing' the legal establishment.[3] The alleged mythologies of liberal legalism appeared to stimulate a particular frustration; providing, according to Mark Tushnet, a mask for systemic social and political inequalities.[4] Karl Klare worried about the alienating consequence of a 'liberal rights consciousness'.[5]

By the end of the 1980s, however, it is possible to discern both greater variety and greater subtlety. The political critique is hardly diminished; though the idea that only the liberals are to blame begins to look rather crude. The

---

[3] M. Kelman, 'Trashing', 36 *Stanford Law Review* 1984, 1987.
[4] M. Tushnet, 'Critical legal studies: a political history', 100 *Yale Law Journal* 1991.
[5] K. Klare, 'Labour law as ideology: towards a new historiography of collective bargaining law', 4 *Industrial Relations Law Journal* 1981, 479.

impulses of continental 'post-modernism' catch the eye. It is even possible to espy particular variants, including a 'liberal' postmodernism. Fragmentation becomes fashionable. Some are tempted to reinvest more traditional ethical questions, approached from alternative academic disciplines, including the literary and linguistic. Sub-species of 'critical legal studies' begin to flower; critical legal history, critical race theory, critical legal feminism, kinds of law and 'humanities' scholarship, including 'law and literature'. We will encounter each of these in the coming pages, on more than one occasion. For which reason, we do not need to look more closely into this history now. But we do want to look more closely at a particular feature which is not only common to these various flowerings but which also played a defining role in stimulating the intellectual evolution.

The 'law job' was never simply the job done by lawyers. At least as important, if not more, was the 'job' done by legal teachers. Kelman famously dismissed the traditional law school lecture as an exercise in 'patently unstable babble'.[6] Provocative, of course. But then 'trashing' was never about conciliation. Duncan Kennedy was of a similar mind. In a 1982 article entitled 'Training for Hierarchy', he concluded that most of what law students are taught is 'nonsense'. But 'biased and motivated rather than random error'. In other words, 'nonsense with a tilt'. And, critically, it goes largely unnoticed; at least amongst the supplicant students. Hierarchy 'with a vengeance'. Students are taught to respect without question, not just what they are taught, but who teaches them; itself predictable enough, mostly 'white, male and middle class'. An attitude of 'deference' which will equip them nicely for life as professional lawyers. They will learn a 'language' and a set of behavioural habits, 'a plethora of little p's and q's for everyone to mind', ranging from how they speak to how they dress to how they 'gesture' in court, and out. The unquestioning attitude, moreover, adds a dimension of 'complicity'. Students 'act affirmatively within the channels cut for them, cutting them deeper, giving the whole a patina of consent'.[7] And then, when they leave University and go on to the next stage of training, it is the same again, only worse. In such a way, the legal hierarchy perpetuates itself, from one generation of law student to the next.

The matter of legal education, and its inadequacies, was famously revisited in 'Roll Over Beethoven'; an iconic CLS 'conversation' piece published just a couple of years later in the *Stanford Law Review*. The discussants, Peter Gabel and Duncan Kennedy, borrowed from Jack Finney's cult-fiction

---

[6] Kelman, 'Trashing', 322.
[7] D. Kennedy, 'Legal Education as Training for Hierarchy', in D. Kairys (ed) *The Politics of Law: A Progressive Critique*, (Pantheon, 1982), 40–2, 53–7.

novel *The Body Snatchers*, in order to cast an image of 'podded' law students; trained to function as emotionless instruments of the legal establishment.[8] The idea that someone might do a job more effectively if they strip away their emotions was not, of course, new. Two centuries earlier, Robert Owen referred to his factory workers as 'animate mechanisms'; which, he inferred, was a good thing. In their 'conversation', Gabel and Kennedy went on to chart the 'weird dissociation' which every law student experiences, as they are transformed 'without realising' it, from being human beings into lawyers. No longer is it 'enough to have good politics; you've got to be able to make good legal argument'; something which requires the law student to recast their 'real existential feelings that led them to become political people into an ideological framework that coopts them into adopting the very consciousness they want to transform'.[9]

Of course, it is not just a matter of alerting students to what might be happening to them. It is also a matter of devising strategies of re-attachment to overcome the 'false consciousness'. To reinvest a sense of 'solidarity', as so many 'crits' liked to term it. Roberto Mangabeira Unger urged fellow law teachers to adopt strategies of 'transformative possibility' in the classroom, to make students appreciate their responsibilities as 'active and conscious participants' in the life of their community.[10] At this point, we approach a thicker idea of legal 'ethics'; a subject to which we will return later in the chapter when we will discover that there are thinner versions too. As to the kinds of strategies which law teachers might adopt, amongst others, Unger recommended experiential 'storytelling'.[11] Allan Hutchinson has done much the same. Such a strategy impresses upon students the fact that the 'law job' is essentially participatory and performative, and therefore creative too. 'We are never not in a story', Hutchinson argues. Because 'History and human action only take on meaning and intelligibility within their narrative context and dramatic settings'.[12] It is here that the didactic aspirations of 'critical' legal scholarship come into alignment with those of a 'poethical' jurisprudence. It is here too that the thicker species of legal 'ethics' begins to conjure the possibilities of a different kind of jurisprudence, of the emotions, of 'kindness' and 'critical compassion'; rather more 'love', as Unger puts it, and rather

---

[8] The novel was dramatized into an equally iconic Hollywood film, directed by Don Siegel, in 1956.

[9] P. Gabel and D. Kennedy, 'Roll Over Beethoven', 36 *Stanford Law Review* 1984, 26.

[10] R. Unger, *The Critical Legal Studies Movement*, (Harvard UP, 1986), 112–13, and also *Law in Modern Society: Toward a Criticism of Social Theory*, (Free Press, 1976), 206–7.

[11] R. Unger, *Passion: An Essay on Personality*, (Free Press, 1984), 84.

[12] A. Hutchinson, *Dwelling on the Threshold*, (Carswell, 1988), 13–14, 21–2.

less law.[13] We will return to this thought in due course. But first, Hare and *Murmuring Judges*.

The State of the Nation

The Hare Course

David Hare is one of the most influential and most controversial of contemporary British dramatists. The influence tends to attract the controversy. In Hare's case, it is exacerbated by his oft-stated belief that the theatre is a suitable place in which to press political arguments; a 'unique forum in which society can discuss itself', a place of judgement indeed.[14] In *Writing Left Handed*, a quasi-autobiographical reflection on the art, and responsibility, of the playwright, published in 1991, Hare concluded in ringing terms: 'A good play, in the truest sense, ventilates democracy'.[15] Which necessarily means making ethical arguments too. There can be no political good without moral good; an argument which Hare adopts, approvingly, from the philosopher Raymond Williams. 'I tend to write about whether there is any such thing as personal morality, and if there is whether it makes any difference, whether there is such a thing as living and behaving well', Hare confirmed in an interview given in 1999. Politics written in 'personal terms', concerned with what seems to be right and wrong in particular instances and moments.[16]

An overtly 'political' writer then, by his own admission. Like many of his generation choosing 'drama in the hope of using it to advance political ends'.[17] And so prejudiced, which only makes for more controversy. Left-leaning; far enough to annoy those on the right, but not far enough to convince those further to the left. It comes as no surprise to discover his support for the 'New' Labour project associated with former Prime Minister Tony Blair; the beginning of whose tumultuous fall from power we will chart in the next chapter. And no surprise to discover plenty of acerbic metaphorical jibes. If ever there was an example of the consummate 'champagne socialist', critics liked to aver, it is David Hare. Perhaps. But then all writers write from somewhere else. In his novel *Dombey and Son*, Charles Dickens famously appealed for a 'benignant spirit' who might, from above, peer into the darker

[13] Unger, *Passion*, 219–22.
[14] In R. Boon, *About Hare: the playwright and the work*, (Faber and Faber, 2003), 39. For similar comments, see Hare, *Obedience*, 4 and also 114, confirming that 'Judgement is the heart of theatre'.
[15] D. Hare, *Writing Left Handed*, (Faber and Faber, 1991), 53.
[16] In Boon, *Hare*, 90–1. See also Hare, *Obedience*, 161–2.
[17] Hare, *Obedience*, 1, 23, 140.

heart of middle-class England.[18] But until one came along, he would do it. That was 1847, and Dickens was about to embark on his own investigation into the 'condition' of Victorian England; the great trilogy of first *Bleak House*, then *Hard Times* and *Little Dorrit*.

Our immediate moment is the late 1980s; the end-game of Thatcherite Britain. A decade during which, according to Michael Billington, Hare had consolidated his position as a 'spokesman for a generation', more especially a generation which set itself against the political philosophy of the Conservative Prime Minister Margaret Thatcher.[19] There were various aspects of Thatcher's conservatism against which Hare, and fellow left-leaning playwrights, such as Caryl Churchill and David Edgar, complained. High on the list was the commercialisation of the theatre. Interpreted as a conscious attempt to impoverish a medium of opposition; all the more critical in the relative absence of any other kind.[20] Nearly as high was a perceived attempt to revive a spirit of Victorian 'values' in both public and private life; especially felt by playwrights who wanted to use the stage in order to interrogate, and challenge, a variety of gender and sexual prejudices.

And the longer that Thatcher had stayed in power, and the more often that her Conservative party had continued to win elections, the greater the urgency, and the loathing. Early expressions of Hare's particular discontent with Thatcherism could be perceived during the first part of the 1980s. Most obviously perhaps *Pravda*, co-written with Howard Brenton, a caustic commentary on Thatcherite economics, and then again in *The Secret Rapture*.[21] With hindsight the arrival of the latter, in 1988, can be taken to represent a significant moment; when, it has been supposed, Hare decided to 'deal with Thatcherism' on a 'personal' level.[22] A strategy which would find 'epic' projection in a trilogy of plays which he composed over the following five years; *Racing Demon*, *Murmuring Judges*, and *Absence of War*. Each focus on a familiar institution; in turn, the Church, the law, and the political party.

---

[18] C. Dickens, *Dombey and Son*, (Penguin, 2002), 702.

[19] M. Billington, *The State of the Nation: British Theatre Since 1945*, (Faber and Faber, 2007), 262, and also 269. For further commentary on the political context of the late 1970s and 1980s and its impact on the theatre, see K. Dorney, *The Changing Language of Modern English Drama*, (Palgrave, 2009), 165–8.

[20] Replaced, it seemed, by a dawning age of sparkly musicals. Such that the name of Andrew Lloyd Webber was treated with almost the same degree of loathing as that of Thatcher herself. Lloyd Webber's stated admiration for Thatcher doing nothing to assuage the contempt.

[21] See L. Taylor, 'In opposition: Hare's Response to Thatcherism', in R. Boon (ed) *The Cambridge Companion to David Hare*, (Cambridge UP, 2007), 49–50, 53–5.

[22] D. Pattie, 'The Common Good: The Hare Trilogy', 42 *Modern Drama* 1999, 366, 368.

The Dickensian parallel is immediate not just in terms of strategy, but of conception. The 'state of the nation' examined through the lens of the 'all the people who are actually dealing' with the consequences of Thatcher's 'ideological assault'.[23] All those 'trying to survive' in an increasingly demoralised institutional environment; like, of course, the theatre itself.[24] Hare had written about the interplay of the institutional and the individual plenty of times before; an 'abiding interest', as one critic affirmed.[25] But not on such a scale. Nurtured, he later recalled, by a 'pervasive feeling' of both 'personal' and 'national despair', Hare eschewed the 'existential' for the 'organisational', and the possibility, however elusive, of a reinvested 'social justice'.[26]

Critics have tended to suggest that the first of three plays was perhaps the most compelling. Hare had undertaken a considerable amount of field research before writing *Racing Demon*, which went into production in 1990. Visiting East End parishes, talking with clergymen and lay, even attending General Synod.[27] And he had been impressed, rather more than he had expected. Here at least were people who seemed to care, whose sense of morality and 'way of life was genuinely valuable'.[28] The plot, set in an inner-city parish, moved around the relationship between an old-fashioned liberal vicar and his evangelical curate. A microcosm of the larger debate which was, at the time, being argued within the Anglican church. And of course within the nation. At one point, Hare's increasingly exasperated Bishop complains that the incessant political, as well as theological, bickering had 'turned' the Church 'into a ghastly parody of government'; 'You've politicised everything'.[29] In a sense, the arguments, theological and constitutional, were familiar enough, and could be tracked back into the eighteenth century. But the challenge of Thatcherism had brought them back into a sharper focus. As indeed did challenge of the Church itself, which assumed an increasingly critical voice during the 1980s; expressed most contentiously in its 1985 report on inner-city deprivation, *Faith in the City*.[30] There were various

23 In Billington, *State*, 327, 329–30.
24 In Pattie, 'Trilogy', 363.
25 See Wade, 'Hare's trilogy', 64, and also Boon, *Hare*, 6 and 23, and Pattie, 'Trilogy', 366.
26 Hare, *Obedience*, 48–9, Pattie, 'Trilogy', 364, and also Wu, *Dramatists*, 109, quoting Hare's later affirmation that 'British society needs not to abolish its institutions, but to refresh them'.
27 With, as he later admitted, at the time 'no other motive but curiosity'. In Pattie, 'Trilogy', 363.
28 Whilst never going so far as to embrace the metaphysics of Christianity. See Wade, 'Hare's trilogy', 67, 70. And Hare's own comments, in *Obedience*, at 231–2.
29 D. Hare, *Racing Demon*, (Faber and Faber, 1996), 77.
30 The Church had also refused to provide any moral support for the Falklands 'war', two years

reasons for the spiritual, and social, crisis which appeared to have spread across so many British cities. But mainly, the report concluded, it was because of Thatcher and her government.[31]

In terms of Hare's career, the writing of the trilogy was evidently significant. A 'mid-career capstone', according to one critic.[32] Genuinely 'remarkable', according to another.[33] Particular reviews tended to be mixed. *Racing Demon*, as we have inferred, was generally well-received. The characters were relatable, their struggles admirable. Less so *Murmuring Judges*, which came next in 1991. Too earnest some supposed, too little to like. We will reserve further judgement for now. The third and final play, *The Absence of War*, was in many ways the most urgent of all. Unsurprising, given Hare's political affinity. The immediate inspiration was the unsuccessful Labour party election campaign of 1992, under the leadership of Neil Kinnock. And it could be read narrowly. Kinnock bemoaned that Hare had made him look like an 'arsehole'. But the reach of the play was much wider and longer, than the fate of one politician and one election.[34] The failure of the Labour Party was enduring, and it stretched far beyond the election booth. Billington recalled a conversation with Hare, in which the playwright intimated that *Racing Demon* had also really been about the 'current state of the Labour Party'.[35] *Murmuring Judges* might be conceived similarly; the same fundamental tensions, between conservative nostalgia and progressive idealism. And it was not just about the Labour Party, as Hare observed. If that was the perception, the play had 'failed'.[36] *Absence of War* simply crystallised a deeper malaise in British politics and society. A politics of 'mendacity', as Hare put it, geared by focus groups and spin doctors and 'fake' news.[37]

Some things change, some stay the same. Margaret Thatcher was removed from office, by her own party, in late 1990. Normality reinvested, the hand-bag wielding Britannia replaced by a mild-mannered accountant from Huntingdon named John Major. Who then defeated the Labour Party

---

earlier; which had gone down just as badly. For a commentary on the context of the play, see Homden, *Hare*, 203–6.

[31] See Taylor, 'Thatcherism', 60–2.

[32] L. Wade, 'Hare's trilogy at the National: private moralities and the common good', in in R. Boon (ed) *The Cambridge Companion to David Hare*, (Cambridge UP, 2007), 64.

[33] Duncan Wu, in *Six Contemporary Dramatists*, (St Martins Press, 1995), at 109.

[34] For a commentary here, see Homden, *Hare*, 221–3.

[35] Billington, *State*, 332.

[36] See Homden, *Hare*, 223–4.

[37] In Boon, *Hare*, 111. Hare's concerns regarding the 'culture' of 'new' journalism are well-documented. An 'arrogance' that promotes the condemnation of everything except itself. See Hare, *Obedience*, 134–6.

once again, in 1992. 'You know what I think?' Hare's defeated Labour leader observes in *Absence of War*, 'I think, let's all be Tories. After all, they always win'. Eventually, though they lost; in a sense. In 1997 a 'New' Labour Party came to power, under the leadership of Tony Blair. Some espied a re-branded Thatcherism. But there would be reform, social and constitutional. A Human Rights Act in 1998, successive devolution statutes, a Freedom of Information Act in 2000, and then, a little later, the 2005 Constitutional Reform Act. We will encounter some of its provisions shortly. Reform then. But not necessarily that much change; at least not under the surface. A decade and a half on, Hare looked back to the extended moment when he wrote his 'state of the nation' trilogy. In tones variously angry and despairing. The Church has descended further into 'farce', the political classes into a renewed 'vindictiveness'.[38] For which reason, the need to continue writing political plays has never been more urgent. Which Hare has, of course, done. Some domestic, such as the privatisation of the railways in *The Permanent Way*, the state of the public services in *Skylight*. But about matters of international politics too. *Via Dolorosa* took a look at the Israel-Palestine conflict, *Stuff Happens* and *The Vertical Hour* the so-called 'war on terror'. We will revisit this 'war', and these plays, in the next chapter.

A Forward Looking Bar

Murmuring Judges introduced a range of particular abuses in order to present a picture of broader demoralisation in the legal system. Which, in turn, was representative of the still broader demoralised 'condition' of 1980s Britain. It might, in this sense, be viewed as an essentially political critique. Which it is. But it is also something more because the interplay of the personal and the political again gives *Murmuring Judges* an ethical edge. The 'key question' in the play, as Les Wade suggests is that of 'moral responsibility, the difficult and clouded situation of acting in an ethical manner', which makes for argumentation. The title of the play is instructive, gesturing to a state of mutual discontent, between the legal profession and its critics. In a different context, he referred to 'background murmurings' as commentaries, sometimes veering towards the 'derogatory'.[39] It fits.

Another indent: *Murmuring Judges* is animated by two intersecting plot-lines. The first moves around Gerard, who is convicted of abetting a robbery. Gerard had driven a get-away van, apparently unaware of what his 'accomplices' were actually doing. His greater offence though, is being 'kind of Irish' (31).[40] It

---

[38] Hare, *Obedience*, 219–21.

[39] Hare, *Obedience*, 1.

[40] All internal references are taken from D. Hare, *Murmuring Judges*, (Faber and Faber, 1993).

transpires that the police have 'planted' Semtex in Gerard's flat. The plot-line had a particular resonance in the 1980s, as questions were raised regarding the convictions of the so-called 'Birmingham Six' and 'Guildford Four'; similarly based, it was widely supposed, on planted 'evidence'. The play is not though written in the tradition of 'trial' literature, as Carol Homden points out. Gerard's case is incidental to the broader 'appeal'.[41] All the cases seem incidental. That is the problem. A 'trivial affair', Gerard's barrister observes of the case, taken at the last minute as a 'favour' to a colleague who had gone to the races. For which reason, the loss should not be counted against his 'bowling average' (3). A life might be ruined. But not, thankfully, a career.

A complacency which brings us to the second plot-line; contemporary debates regarding the mooted reform of the legal profession, in particular the Bar. The argument that the legal profession should be modernised was hardly new. A Royal Commission on Legal Services published a *Final Report* just as Thatcher came to power in 1979. It concluded, not only that there was no need for substantive change, but that there should be a regulatory framework put in place to protect the Bar from the ravages of the market. Which was precisely what the incoming Thatcher government did not intend to do. Various 'anachronisms' were irritating; the shady process with which judges were chosen, and barristers granted 'silk', the determination to continue wearing wigs and silly clothing, commonly identified in a hostile press. But what Thatcher really wanted was to open the legal profession, like the theatrical, to market-forces.[42] The contention here moved around the idea that rights of audience might be granted to solicitors; themselves under pressure to relinquish their monopoly of conveyancing practice. Only marginally less controversial was the proposal that there might be a more open appointment-process for judges, that the Bench might moreover be populated by other than barristers. Some espied a slippery slope; what next, more diversity, more women, more judges from different ethnic backgrounds, more lawyers from the wrong schools and the wrong universities?

All of which meant that Thatcher and Hare arrived, incongruously perhaps, at a very similar place.[43] Not that Hare was so bothered by the market. But he too was convinced that the innate conservatism of the Bar was representative of the broader recalcitrance of the English ruling elite. And directly causative of the kind of complacency evinced in Gerard's case.

---

[41] See Homden, *Hare*, 209.

[42] See R. Abel, 'The Politics of Professionalism: The Transformation of English Lawyers at the End of the Twentieth Century', 2 *Legal Ethics* 1999, 131–3, and also J. Creaton, 'Modernizing the courts and the legal profession', 9 *Contemporary Politics* 2003, 117–20.

[43] See here Pattie, 'Trilogy', 366–7.

The English legal profession was interested in itself, and only itself. And he was, in the main, right. All professions, as Richard Abel observed, tend to be inward-looking and viscerally 'conservative'.[44] But none quite so excessively as the legal. The Bar dug in. Realising that wig-wearing might not itself be a sufficiently persuasive cause around which to rally public support, it made recourse to various cherished constitutional principles, such as that of an independent judiciary, and, by insinuation, an independent Bar. Hare's Judge Cuddeford does exactly this in conversation with a prospectively reformist Home Secretary. It is not, the Judge hastens to confirm, simply a matter of preference. It is a question of 'constitutional' propriety (52). Cuddeford and his fellow barristers are thoroughly appalled at the prospect of having to modernise. Busy raising a fighting-fund, they have already raised a million pounds in just four days.

The tone of *Murmuring Judges* tends to move with place. The scenes set in prison with Gerard, and in a local police station are bleaker. Gerard is coming to terms, not just with his sentence, but with a life lived in constant fear. A young policewoman is battling prejudice and her conscience. The station is full of prospective 'criminals' to be processed, her colleagues swamped with 'directives'. Exhaustion and abuse is pervasive, in both environments. The 'system' is on the verge of collapse (70, 75). Conversely, the scenes set in and around the Inns of Court seem, on the surface at least, to be slightly lighter. There is comedy here, albeit of the uncomfortable kind. Here again, Hare had done a considerable amount of fieldwork before writing *Murmuring Judges*, talking with barristers, getting himself invited to dinner at the Inns. *Murmuring Judges* is not a verbatim play of the kind which we will encounter in the next chapter, but there is a pleasing suspicion that much of what is said on stage is derived from what had been said over a glass of port or three.

The temptation to think so is greatest in the scene at the beginning of the second Act, where the Home Secretary has accepted an invitation to dine at Lincoln's Inn. Like his creator, doing a spot of fieldwork, hoping to gauge the likely reaction to his mooted reforms; whilst also making a plea for the judges to stop sending so many criminals to prison. The mood is hostile, the plea a bargaining chip. But the evening is convivial all the same, the dinner lovely, if a bit fatty. The 'silver cutlery and the silver tongues', as Carol Homden puts it, 'are on full display'.[45] The Gilbert and Sullivan tone is set from the out, as the Toastmaster reads out the variously improbable names of attendant guests, and the Home Secretary is invited to 'drink in

---

[44] Abel, 'Politics', 131.
[45] Homden, *Hare*, 210.

the atmosphere' (50–1). The main course is 'Roast Venison Baden-Baden' (53). The subject of dinner allows Hare to deploy a familiar curiosity; the habit of requiring a would-be barrister to 'eat' so many 'dinners'. Necessary, Judge Cuddeford observes, in order to avoid the kitchens running at a loss. But also to perpetuate the culture of the Bar. The Judge continues: 'The law is a college. We meet. We talk. A judge perhaps has a word with a barrister. He says nothing overt. Nothing critical. Maybe only a look, a chance remark. And yet all the time . . . there are hints. Thanks to these a barrister is learning. The social *is* the political'. And 'How do you put a true price on that?' (54)

Richly ridiculous. But insidious too. And the Judge is not finished. Bristling at the suggestion that the Bar might have become 'hidebound', he presses on: 'Small chance of that . . . Remember, all the time judging brings you in touch with ordinary people. In our courts. We see them every day. Ordinary, common-as-muck individuals. Some of them quite ghastly, I promise you that . . . This makes us alert to public opinion. We're closer to it, perhaps, than you think' (55). Just as ridiculous, and just as insidious. For all the chatter about 'constitutional proprieties', the 'independent judiciary' being 'perhaps the most important bulwark against chaos this country has', is to miss the point (56). Detachment breeds dislocation. The Bar, as Sir Peter admits, is an exclusive 'club', operating to its own normative and behavioural patterns.[46] Sporting metaphors recur. The law is a 'game', a contest of unequals (70). 'You see, the thing is' the clerk of Chambers explains to Irina, a newly arrived barrister, 'the point is, it's a team. There's a lot of latitude. But you play in a team. You want to start inside, not outside' (11). A young policewoman is given precisely the same advice by her senior officer in the parallel plot-line: 'Didn't they tell you? It's a team game' (33).

Irina is another of Hare's 'secular saints'.[47] A former Commonwealth scholar who knows precisely what it is like to be an 'other'. And who also knows that if she wants to stay in the game, 'tricky' as it is, she must accommodate the 'judgements' and the 'prejudice' to which the 'other' is invariably subjected (84,90). Wearying and 'demeaning', but for now at least necessary (94). Early in the play she makes the mistake of appearing in court in a green dress and is quickly advised that she must change into black. Ridiculous again. On other occasions, the inference is more troubling. When the head of Chambers, Sir Peter Edgecombe QC, introduces Irina to Judge Cuddeford, he cannot resist an insinuation. She 'seems to have all the

---

[46] As Hare confirmed, discussing the play, in interview. In Boon, *Hare*, 130.

[47] Arriving from Antigua. A rather obvious parallel might be made with Shakespeare's Portia, who descends on Venice from the fresher 'air' of Belmont in *The Merchant of Venice*. For further comment, see Wade, 'Hare's trilogy', 72.

assets we need in a forward-looking bar'; to which Cuddeford responds 'Yes. I see those. Most clearly' (6). A bit of banter perhaps. But also a species of 'abuse'.[48] Hare's stage-direction continues 'She is black, in her mid-twenties, neat, well-presented, open-faced, with a quiet politeness which is hard to interpret'. Different then; at least from all the white, male, middle-class barristers who make up the rest of the 'team'. Irina is later persuaded to go to the opera with Sir Peter. Because that is what 'well-presented' young female barristers are for; to add a little glamour to the lives of boring old male ones. Why not? He is a 'decent man', as Woody the clerk confirms, 'Why put his back up?' (11)

But it is, of course, this culture of hierarchy and deference which facilitates the petty racism and myriad misogynies. We might contrast two Enlightenment philosophers. According to Jean-Jacques Rousseau, there could be no true liberty without an appreciation of mutual, and equal, respect. Nor could there be a public morality without an appreciation of sentiment as well as sense. Respect is felt as well as thought.[49] It has been suggested that Hare militates towards a kind of 'post-modern' ethics; a 'primal' kind of justice founded on feeling and sentiment.[50] There was, by way of contrast, no such tolerance of such 'softheartedness' in the jurisprudence of Rousseau's great antagonist, Immanuel Kant.[51] Sentiment should never be allowed to intrude upon the reason of law. Feelings corrupt. As indeed does a wearying concern with what might seem 'right' or wrong. What feels 'right', as Sir Peter explains, had 'got' nothing 'to do' with the law. It is not his duty to be 'soggily compassionate' (93). It is his duty to be exactly the opposite.

Except, of course, that we can never excise feeling from judgement; nor indeed a sense of what is right. It is just harder, as Amartya Sen famously supposed, to make the case for justice in a world of 'rational fools'.[52] It is here that Irina's 'other-ness' presents, perhaps, its greatest challenge. It is not what she wears that really threatens the complacencies of life in Sir Peter's Chambers, nor the colour of her skin. It is her willingness to care. 'Yes I've been worried, and yes, I'm a lawyer', she observes in conversation with Gerard, 'The two things can go together, you know' (39). Towards the end

---

[48] As Duncan Kennedy confirms. See his *Sexy Dressing etc. Essays on the Power and Politics of Cultural Identity*, (Harvard UP, 1993), 131, 147. Similar instances of casual sexual and racial abuse occur in the parallel plot of the play, set in the local police station.

[49] See here M. Nussbaum, *Upheavals of Thought: The Intelligence of Emotions*, (Cambridge UP, 2003), 350–1.

[50] Wade. 'Hare's trilogy', 75–6.

[51] Kant's *Doctrine of Virtue*, quoted in Nussbaum, *Upheavals*, 358.

[52] A. Sen, *Choice, Welfare, and Measurement*, (MIT Press, 1982).

of the play, the audience learns that Gerard's appeal has resulted in a reduc-
tion in his sentence by six months. Here again, it was part of the 'game', a
'lame-dog' appeal pleaded on the grounds of 'clemency', a young family and a
first offence (86–7, 100). Barely a success, and certainly not enough to satisfy
Irina. She will continue, plotting a further appeal, moving to a more 'radical'
set of Chambers, joining the John Wilkes Society to fight for better prison
conditions. A glimmer again.

Perhaps. In the final line, Sandra decides to have a 'word' with her Chief
Superintendent (109). But we do not know for sure what she will say. Or
what he will say. Or what, if anything, will be done. Still less if anything much
will change. Looking back, Hare has, once again, struck a rather depressive
note. The 'shocking travesties of justice' about which he wrote in *Murmuring
Judges* should have led to a 'fitting humility' amongst judges and politicians.
But they did not. On the contrary. If anything debates regarding the possible
'reform' of criminal procedure, and indeed 'the criminal', have assumed an
'ever-cruder vindictiveness'. The 'bloodlust' of right-wing 'editorial-writers'
appears to be insatiable.[53]

A Happy Picture?

As we noted earlier, there would be some essentially superficial reforms to
the legal profession and legal practice. A Courts and Legal Services Act was
passed in 1990. The Bar had lobbied intensely to minimise its impact. The
House of Lords rang to familiar referents; Magna Carta, the Bill of Rights,
the independence of the judiciary, the separation of powers. 'Loss of freedom
seldom happens overnight', the Lord Chief Justice, Lord Lane, sagely warned,
'Oppression does not stand on the doorstep with a toothbrush moustache
and a swastika armband. It creeps up insidiously; it creeps up step by step;
and all of a sudden the unfortunate citizen realizes that it has gone'.[54] Judge
Cuddeford would have been proud. But appalled all the same. For, regardless, the Act did end the monopoly on rights of audience.[55] And it would
get worse. The incoming Labour government issued a White Paper in 1998,
worryingly entitled *Modernizing Justice*. It suggested a raft of new measures
intended to further increase competition in the market for legal service.
Simply 'unconstitutional', Lord Steyn advised his fellow peers in familiar

---

[53] Hare, *Obedience*, 219–20.

[54] In Creaton, 'Modernizing', 119.

[55] It also established an office of Legal Services Ombudsman, to oversee complaint-handling
mechanisms, and required the professional bodies to seek the approval of the Lord
Chancellor before making any significant changes to training regulations and codes of conduct.

tones.[56] But again to little avail. The 1999 Access to Justice Act granted rights of audience to all lawyers, without exception.

Acts of Parliament can, however, only do so much. And it can rarely do much about market-forces or indeed the force of cultural prejudice. The greater fears of the Bar never really came to fruition. Licensed conveyancers struggled anyway to compete with solicitors on the high street, which meant that fewer solicitors were to be found clamouring for rights of audience. The position in regard to professional diversity, moreover, would only slowly, and barely, change. The 2005 Constitutional Reform Act shifted much of the responsibility for selecting prospective judges away from the Lord Chancellor, and to a new Judicial Appointments Committee. But still, diversification in the senior judiciary 'remains painfully slow'; unsurprising perhaps, given that the judiciary is now left to select itself.[57] And all the wealthy, white men seem to prefer selecting lots of other wealthy, white men. It remains the case that there are far more male judges than female, and far fewer from ethnic minorities. And graduates of certain universities, namely Oxford and Cambridge, continue to enjoy dramatic over-representation at all levels. A snap-shot of the British Supreme Court in late 2018 tells its own story; twelve justices, nine men, three women, all white, all we can safely assume 'comfortable', three-quarters from Oxbridge.[58] Representative of something perhaps, but certainly not the nation. As for the Lord Chief Justice and the Master of the Rolls; both male, both white, both Oxbridge. If we dumb-down a fraction and take a glance at the Court of Appeal there is not much to surprise; forty-one judges, thirty-three male, eight female, just one BAME (British Asian Minority Ethnic). The relevant Justice Department website which lists senior judges does not provide all the educational details for Appeal judges.[59] But we can make a pretty confident guess as to the *alma mater* of the overwhelming majority.

---

[56] In Creaton, 'Modernizing', 121.

[57] See G. Gee, 'Rethinking the Lord Chancellor's role in judicial appointments', 20 *Legal Ethics* 2017, 6, and also 9–10. The Lord Chancellor retains a marginal role in the selection process. In the first eight years, all but 4 of the 4000 JAC recommendations were accepted. Otherwise the judges select each other, determining job specifications, writing references, designing 'texts', sitting on selection panels.

[58] The exceptions being some of the token Northern Irish and Scottish justices, and one graduate of Durham University. The make-up of the Court changed in January 2019, with the retirement of Lord Sumption, who was replaced by Lord Justice Sales. Oddly enough male, white and Oxbridge; in fact, educated at both Oxford and Cambridge. So not that much of a change then.

[59] See <https://www.judiciary.uk/about-the-judiciary> (last accessed 26th June 2020) and <https://www.judiciary.uk/about-the-judiciary/who-are-the-judiciary/diversity/judicial-diversity-statistics/judicial-diversity-statistics-2018/> (last accessed 26th June 2020) .

The proportion of women and ethnic minority judges increases further down the line. But it is only at the level of magistrate the women finally outnumber men. The percentage of BAME judges bobs along in low single figures until it reaches the same point. It is possible to put a positive spin on some of the numbers. At least a decent number of women and BAME give it a go. More than 50 per cent of UK law students are female; and 60 per cent of newly enrolled solicitors. As Lord Neuberger observed in his 2012 Upjohn Lecture. Legal training 'has much to be happy about so far as women are concerned and not that much to be unhappy about with regard to ethnic minorities'. Thereon though it is nothing like such a happy picture.[60] Somehow all the women, and most of the BAME, seem to struggle to progress. At least the profession and the government is aware of the problem and has put measures in place. And a committee. The Judicial Diversity Committee, the same Justice department website announces, has already agreed 'steps' to 'reach out to a more diverse pool of lawyers'. Fingers crossed; but not too tight.

And what is true of the Bar is true of the larger City law firms, and the smaller; mostly run by men, mostly white, mostly rich. Here again, there is an awareness. A recent report commissioned by the Solicitor's Regulatory Authority, published in 2017, threw up some predictable statistics.[61] In 1970, just 10 per cent of newly enrolled solicitors were female. In 2016, as we have just noted, it is 60 per cent. And the figure for BAME solicitors is now just under 20 per cent; from next to nothing. But then, once again, they all seem to disappear. Two-thirds of partners in larger City firms are men; 75 per cent are white men. Women, the report concludes, 'may be disadvantaged' as they try to climb the career ladder. Well indeed. The SRA further supposes that current 'plans' to 'reform' legal training will also help diversification. The stimulus here was provided by the Legal Education and Training Review (LETR), which reported in 2013. It though was less concerned with diversity than with making legal education more responsive to the evolving demands of the 'marketplace'.[62] The abolition of the Qualifying Law Degree will certainly change this landscape. But it is not clear how it will ensure a greater proportion of female and BAME sat in the Supreme Court or round the boardroom of 'magic circle' City firms; unless it is supposed that far more

---

[60] Lord Neuberger, 'Reforming legal education', 47 *Law Teacher* 2013, 13–14.

[61] *Mapping Advantages and Disadvantages: Diversity in the Legal Profession in England and Wales*, available at <https://www.sra.org.uk/sra/how-we-work/reports/diversity-legal-profession/> (last accessed 26th June 2020).

[62] See P. Leighton, 'Back from the future: did the LETR really prepare us for the future?', 48 *Law Teacher* 2014, 88.

lawyers who know rather less about the law will somehow help. Doubtful. Some things change; but mostly not much.

As Hare probably sensed. Duncan Wu has referred to a 'deep scepticism' in Hare's political writing during the early 1990s.[63] The lack of assurance certainly troubled reviewers of *Murmuring Judges*. The feeling that not much, in the end, has changed; or indeed is likely to.[64] The tone bothered some too. Too 'information-heavy', according to Billington.[65] Too much to learn, too little to feel. As a result, failing to 'engage the audience in anything beyond a level of mild interest'.[66] The focus on an alleged miscarriage of justice was, Billington suggested, a distraction. There was a bigger argument. The crime rate had risen by 40 per cent during the 1980s; a consequence of enduring economic recession and cut-backs in public services. But Hare had missed it or avoided it. Ultimately though it just seemed colder. And quieter. Too much 'murmuring', not enough anger; as Carol Homden concluded. 'To be above the battle', as Hare suggested, 'To allow all points of view'.[67] Commendable, in a sense. The same metaphor which Dickens conjured in *Dombey*. But the studied tone can be enervating. Where Dickens seemed angered, Hare seems despairing. The Bar has repelled pesky reformers for centuries. It can brush away a pesky playwright. The stats prove that.

Re-thinking the Other

The political impulse of 'critical' legal scholarship has sometimes appeared to overwhelm the ethical. But a revitalized ethics always has, as we noted earlier, been there; an ultimate aspiration indeed for those most interested in law teaching. The idea of 'legal ethics' has, moreover, become more broadly fashionable in recent years; something that appears to be of concern to the profession itself, rather than just a few scattered law teachers. As we insinuated earlier, though, this interest can assume a rather thinner aspect; a concern with little more than ensuring the proper disclosure of documents, and being a bit more polite in court. And a thicker aspect.

Legal 'Ethics'

It might seem rather incongruous to align the words 'legal' and 'ethics'. It is certainly rare in legal literature. Morally upstanding lawyers rarely stride

---

[63] Wu. *Dramatists*, 97.

[64] See Boon, *Hare*, 47, and Homden, *Hare*, 215, both wondering what, if anything, is actually achieved by the end of the play; certainly nothing assured.

[65] Billington, *State*, 330.

[66] Homden, *Hare*, 216.

[67] In Homden, *Hare*, 216.

across anyone's stage. More likely a few slippery ones are flitting about in the shadows. Charles Fried famously wondered if the very nature of the profession made it impossible for a 'good lawyer' to be a 'good person'.[68] It was a rhetorical question, of course; to which the answer was a kind of affirmative. But still, it had to be asked. Not least because there is an influential strain of jurisprudence which is keen to stress a sharp distinction between matters of law and matters of morality. The 'is' of law, generations of legal positivists have soberly affirmed, must always be distinguished from the 'ought'. Lawyers look after the first, vicars and busy-bodies the latter. The odds, historical, cultural and jurisprudential, appear then to be stacked against the ethically-inclined lawyer.

But recently all that has started to change. It has become fashionable to suppose that there might be such a thing as 'legal ethics'. Though not so recent, or so fashionable, that it could persuade Hare's bent copper, Barry. 'I don't take lectures on ethics from lawyers', Barry responds when Irina presumes to challenge his integrity (102). And we are entitled to wonder just how much Hare might be convinced today. Probably not much. It might be that a coming generation of lawyers has suddenly decided that it is time to take ethics seriously; or it might be that the demands of a reconfigured profession, customer-facing, market-driven, has made them. As Richard Abel famously insinuated.[69] The Legal Services Act 2007 intimated the the Solicitors Regulation Authority in England and Wales should assume a rather more credible strategy for dealing with client complaints regarding allegations of professional misconduct.[70] Four years later, the SRA introduced an 'outcomes' approach purposed for 'managing risk'. Necessary for 'business to do business'.[71] A year earlier, the Chair of the Legal Services Board had made a number of suggestions for the reform of legal education, of which 'ethics' was 'first and foremost'. Before rather spoiling it by confirming that 'ethics' matters because it is what the modern 'consumer' wants.[72] And the recent

---

[68] C. Fried, 'The Lawyer as Friend: The Moral Foundations of the Lawyer-Client Relation', 85 *Yale Law Journal* 1976, 1060.

[69] R. Abel, 'Between Market and State: The Legal Profession in Turmoil', 52 *Modern Law Review* 1989, 317.

[70] Statistics are damning. It was noted in 1999, that there was a backlog of 17,000 complaints waiting to be investigated by the Office for the Supervision of Solicitors. Richard Abel recorded that between 1973 and 1979 the Law Society fielded 43,031 complaints, which resulted in proceedings being taken against just 333 solicitors. See also P. Baron and L. Corbin, 'The unprofessional professional: do lawyers need rules?', 20 *Legal Ethics* 2017, 164.

[71] See Baron and Corbin, 'Rules', 164, 168.

[72] D. Edmonds, 'Training the lawyers of the future: a regulator's view', 45 *Law Teacher* 2011, 10.

proposals of the Legal Education and Training Review (LETR) reinforce the same. The 'primary objective' of the LETR was to ensure that the provision of legal training recognises 'particularly the need to protect and promote the interests of consumers'.[73]

Not then the highest of moral grounding. But still, the 'rise' of legal ethics warrants a closer look, not least because it has stimulated a considerable amount of didactic reflection. Ethics, it is assumed, does not come naturally; or at least not professional ethics. It must be taught. 'Ethical concerns', according to William Twining, 'are central to the role of lawyers as educators'.[74] Recent proposals for the radical reform of legal education in England and Wales has elevated the subject of 'legal ethics' to a kind of quasi-core; even if, in real terms, its teaching remains a 'marginal' activity in many law schools.[75] At which point, the argument as to the thickness of the prospective ethics arises; how far should the teacher of 'legal ethics' venture into the moral maze? Go too far, the sceptic cautions, and the lawyer starts to assume the guise of a moral activist. Thinner is safer. It might just mean impressing upon students the importance of being a bit nicer to each other, in court and in the classroom.[76] And turning up neat; and not in green. Leading the ethically-driven law teacher to explain the arts of polite conversation and sartorial discretion; but not perhaps much else. Abel is one of many who wonders if the 'legal profession's chronic regulatory crisis can be solved by reformulating' a set of 'ethical rules'.[77]

Or law teachers can contemplate something a little thicker. Or perhaps a lot. Donald Nicholson has suggested that law teachers should look to reinvest a sense of 'altruism' in their prospective lawyers.[78] Few go quite so far. A number have militated towards Bernard Williams's deceptively simple question: 'how should one live?' Which can then be refined to purpose, leaving the legal ethicist to ask; 'how should the lawyer practice?' The concession has obvious attractions. It eschews deeper metaphysical contemplation and more rigorous metaphysical injunction too. It admits context: 'Laws do not exist in

---

[73] In Neuberger, 'Reforming', 7.

[74] W. Twining, 'Professionalism in legal education', 18 *International Journal of the Legal Profession* 2011, 168.

[75] See D. Nicholson, 'Calling, Character and Clinical Legal Education: A Cradle to Grave Approach to Inculcating a Love for Justice', 16 *Legal Ethics* 2013, 40.

[76] See Baron and Corbin, 'Rules', 156–7, 171, noting the rise of codes of conduct in a number of US state bars, and also R. Abel 'The Professional is Political', 11 *International Journal of the Legal Profession* 2004, 145–51.

[77] Abel, 'Professional', 145.

[78] Nicholson, 'Calling', 37–9.

the air; they apply to real people in real circumstances'.[79] And contingency. And thus a measure of utilitarian discretion; intimating that the greater end might, on occasion, permit a more questionable means.[80] Alice Woolley thus supposes that a lawyer may be able to shape an ethically 'meaningful' professional life, even if on occasion it falls short of stricter moral injunction or ethical practice.[81] Thicker then, but in the absence of a more determinative metaphysical template, not perhaps that thick.

Charles Fried ended up at a similar point; albeit taking a slightly different route. What, he wondered, should a 'decent' lawyer do if faced with vying duties to clients and the wider public interest. Various such dilemmas might be conjured. It might be the recommendation of tax avoidance schemes or using statutes of limitations to defeat a debt claim. Or it might be concealing contrary evidence or seeking to frighten or humiliate witnesses in court. The ethical challenges which criminal lawyers encounter can seem more urgent.[82] Either way, when push comes to shove, Fried concluded, the client comes first. There are 'limits' of course, and the lawyer should not do 'wrong'. But they are free to exploit a 'wrong of the system'. And should do so. Because if the lawyer does not do their best for a client, then the system itself fails and becomes 'unjust'.[83] The client with the more scrupulous lawyer is more likely to lose. Tim Dare reaches the same conclusion.[84] Here, of course, determining the 'limits' is absolutely critical. Bullying rape victims in a courtroom seems more reprehensible than advising a client as to how they might minimise tax liability. But if determination is just seeming, there is a contingency to be reconciled.

Which, in a sense, is fine; because that is what life is. If ethics is about personal relations, then contingency is inevitable. The legal profession will always be inhabited by men like Judge Cuddeford and Sir Peter Edgecombe and women like Irina Pratt; because, once again, human nature is variable, human experience more so still. The purpose of a 'legal ethics' training will always be to trim around the edges. Rules can help to do this, setting limits as to what lawyers can do, by law and by convention. But a rule-determined

---

[79] See A. Woolley, 'Context, Meaning and Morality in the Life of the Lawyer', 17 *Legal Ethics* 2014, 2–4, 10, and also 'Forum: Philosophical Legal Ethics', 13 *Legal Ethics* 2010, 172.

[80] See D. Markovits, *A Modern Legal Ethics: Adversary Advocacy in a Democratic Age*, (Princeton UP, 2008), 35, 47–8, 106–16

[81] See Woolley, 'Context', 18–22.

[82] See E. Cape, 'Rebalancing the Criminal Justice Process: Ethical Challenges or Criminal Defence Lawyers', 9 *Legal Ethics* 2006, 57, 70–9.

[83] Fried, 'Lawyer', 1066.

[84] See his contribution to 'Forum: Philosophical Legal Ethics', at 182.

'legal ethics' can only enhance the feeling that legal practice is a kind of game. A thicker ethical aspiration, appreciating the inevitability, and desirability, of human contingency, focusses on asking questions rather than preempting resolutions. Most importantly, it invites engagement, intellectual and sentimental. It seeks to nurture more Irinas and fewer Sir Peters. We should take a closer look at this possibility. Not least because it chimes so evidently with the aspirations of literary jurisprudence. But before we do, we should recall the other 'other'; which tends to get neglected in the 'legal ethics' literature.

Aside from the external 'other', there is the internal; those who work within the legal environment. The lack of diversity in the legal profession is not just a sociological problem, a matter of weighing statistical underrepresentation. It is also ethical, perpetuating exclusion, altering the culture and temper of legal practice.[85] The treatment of 'others' within has an immediate impact on the treatment of 'others' without. It is, as we noted earlier, no coincidence that Irina feels a greater affinity with Gerard, than does Sir Peter. And very likely a far greater affinity with Gerard than she does with Sir Peter. Irina, if we recall, is an 'other' for at least three reasons; black, female and foreign. It would be difficult to be much more outside. Or to be made to feel more outside; as Patricia Williams put it, an identity 'casually inscribed' by the varying 'definitional demarcations' of others.[86]

And the legal profession is still very much a 'club'; even if the membership criteria might have relaxed just a fraction over the last decade or so. The right schools, the right university, the right banter; still the pre-requisites of a successful legal career.[87] And there is, of course, absolutely nothing in the LETR proposals which makes mention of any of this. The gender dimension takes us neatly into the final part of this chapter. There is a considerable literature which supposes that because she is female, Irina is naturally disposed to 'person oriented reasoning'; a supposition commonly related to the work of early 'second wave' feminist writers such as Carol Gilligan.[88] And there is a considerable literature which is wary of the inherent stereotyping. Thus Drucilla Cornell prefers a 'post-modern' feminism, arguing that a genuine concern with the fate of the 'other' demands an essential appreciation of 'her

---

[85] See Edmonds, 'Training', 13–14.
[86] P. Williams, *The Alchemy of Race and Rights: dairy of a law professor*, (Harvard UP, 1991), 10.
[87] See H. Sommerlad, 'The Commercialisation of Law and the enterprising legal practitioner: continuity and change', 18 *International Journal of the Legal Profession* 2011, 73–108.
[88] See H. Sommerlad, 'The Ethics of Relational Jurisprudence', 17 *Legal Ethics* 2014, 284. The classic Gilligan work here is *In a Different Voice*, (Harvard UP, 1982).

difference and singularity'.[89] If Irina feels a greater compassion for Gerard, it is not simply because she is female. It is because she is different, better socialised, and probably better educated. She has learnt to think about justice as well as the law. And something else. She cares.

Justice and Compassion

Which might seem rather whimsical. But it is only so because it has become unfamiliar. It was there, as Costas Douzinas suggests, in the 'promise' of Enlightenment.[90] In his *Treatise of Human Nature*, David Hume confirmed that:

> No quality of human nature is more remarkable, both in itself and in its consequences, than that propensity we have to sympathise with others, and to receive by communication their inclinations and sentiments, however different from, or even contrary to our own.[91]

Adam Smith suggested much the same in his *Theory of Moral Sentiments*. Justice is about fairness, but not just fairness. It is also about 'pity and compassion'.[92] The Enlightenment was not just about building steam-engines and working out profit-margins. Or writing positive jurisprudence. It was about inculcating 'sentiments of sociability', as Rousseau put it in his *Social Contract*.[93] About making better people, kinder, more compassionate, more thoughtful; not just more efficient and more dutiful. About 'painting a picture', as Oliver Wendel Holmes put it, not just 'doing a sum'.[94] The spirit of romance tempering that of reason. Spreading what John Stuart Mill termed the 'contagion of sympathy'.[95] The metaphor is prescient.

Sympathy is a natural sentiment. But, like justice, it needs a culture, and it needs sustenance. Which is where the writing of 'sad and sentimental stories' might come in, as the philosopher Richard Rorty suggests. Rorty envisages much the same kind of human rights 'imaginary' as Douzinas,

---

[89] D. Cornell, *The Philosophy of the Limit* (Routledge, 1992), 62.

[90] C. Douzinas, *The End of Human Rights: Critical Legal Thought at the Turn of the Century*, (Hart, 2000), 17–19, 33, 255–9.

[91] D. Hume, *A Treatise of Human Nature*, (Oxford UP, 1978), 316.

[92] A. Smith, *A Theory of Moral Sentiments*, (Oxford UP, 1976), 9. For a commentary on Smith's theory of 'judicious' empathy, see M. Nussbaum, *Love's Knowledge: Essays on Philosophy and Literature*, (Oxford UP, 1990), 338–45.

[93] See M. Nussbaum, *Political Emotions: Why Love Matters for Justice*, (Harvard UP, 2013), 45.

[94] In M. Nussbaum, *Poetic Justice*, xix.

[95] J. Mill, 'Utilitarianism', in J. Mill and J. Bentham (eds) *Utlitarianism and Other Essays*, (Penguin, 1990), 110.

sustained by a political culture of 'friendship' and 'kindness'.[96] Here again, the insight is not new. Mill, following Comte, wondered the possibility of a 'religion of humanity' in these terms. So did his contemporary, George Eliot. According to Eliot, the best means of investing a proper sense of humanity is through an 'extension of our sympathies', through the 'picture of human life such as a great artist can give'.[97] The kind of artistry might vary. Roberto Unger warned against the 'lush particularism' of some forms of 'literary art', but likewise recommended the 'transformative' potential of experiential 'storytelling'.[98] There is something in this.

As Martha Nussbaum avers, in her manifesto for a 'reformed' liberal education, *Cultivating Humanity*. Educational practice is undoubtedly enriched by 'stories of real people's diversity and complexity'. It can indeed 'cultivate' the 'ability to think what it might be like to be in the shoes of a person different from oneself to be an intelligent reader of that person's story, and to understand the emotions and wishes and desires that someone so placed might have'.[99] And it need not be limited to personal experience. There is a place for the 'narrative imagination' too. For 'we always bring ourselves and our own judgements to the encounter with another; and when we identify with a character in a novel, or with a distant person whose life story we imagine, we inevitably will not merely identify; we will also judge that story in the light of our own goals and aspirations'. 'Intelligent citizenship' is both experienced and imagined.[100] Thus it is suggested that a 'legal ethics curriculum' which invited students to revisit famous trial scenarios, in fact or fiction, might help to produce more 'ethically literate' students.[101]

The same sentiment recurs across a series of writings in which Nussbaum has pressed the case for a more 'literate' political ethics. In *Love's Knowledge* recommending literature for the simple reason that it 'speaks about us, about our lives and choices and emotions'.[102] Not instead of philosophy necessarily, or history, but as well as. And again, at the outset of *Poetic Justice*, declaring, in unambiguous terms, 'I defend the literary imagination precisely because it seems to me an essential ingredient of an ethical stance that asks us to concern

[96] See R. Rorty, *Contingency, Irony, and Solidarity*, (Cambridge UP, 1989), 186.

[97] G. Eliot, *Selected Essays, Poems and Other Writings*, (Penguin, 1990), 110.

[98] Unger, *Passion*, 84.

[99] M. Nussbaum, *Cultivating Humanity: A Classical Defence of Reform in Liberal Education*, (Harvard UP, 1997), 10–11.

[100] Nussbaum, *Cultivating*, 11.

[101] See S. Mercer and C. Sandford-Couch, 'Legal Ethics in the Trial of Oscar Wilde', 16 *Legal Ethics* 2013, 120–3.

[102] Nussbaum, *Love's Knowledge*, 171.

ourselves with the good of other people whose lives are different from our own'.[103] Here again, there is nothing especially original in the aspiration. Aristotle assumed that 'good' people are defined by their determination to secure the 'good' of their community. Something which demands engagement, and 'perception', as well as the exercise of 'practical' judgement.[104] Richard Weisberg gestured in the same direction in his *Poethics*, supposing that 'Stories about the "other" induce us to see the other, and once we do so, we endeavour consistently to understand the world from within the other's optic'.[105] Nussbaum deploys the same metaphor. In *Political Emotions* conjecturing various 'cultures of empathy' which can nurture a critical 'ability to see the world through the eyes of others and to recognize their individuality'.[106]

But it is not, of course, just recognition. It is, as Nussbaum repeatedly argues, also about engagement, which means conversation and 'voice'.[107] Listening to those 'silenced' by 'opprobrium'.[108] To those 'voices', as Ariel Dorfman puts it, which otherwise remain 'hidden, at the bottom of the rivers of silence of humanity'.[109] Literature is good at this, better perhaps than philosophy. Because it cherishes 'particularity' rather more, it makes us listen harder.[110] In the final part of *Poetic Justice*, Nussbaum interrogates Walt Whitman's aspiration, in his poem *Song of Myself*, to attest 'sympathy':

> Through me many long dumb voices
> Voices of the interminable generations of prisoners and slaves,
> Voices of the diseased and despairing and of thieves and dwarves . . .
> And of the rights of them the others are down upon . . .
> Through me forbidden voices,
> Voices of sexes and lusts, voices veil'd and I remove the veil . . .[111]

We will come across plenty more 'forbidden voices' in the coming chapters. And we will come across Nussbaum again, arguing the same case for a 'compassionate' jurisprudence in the most straightened of circumstances. Sufficient, in the darkest of moments, to 'awaken a larger sense of the human-

---

[103] Nussbaum, *Justice*, xvi.
[104] See Nussbaum, *Love's Knowledge*, 28, 36–44, 69–73, 166, and 216, discussing various strategies of imaginative engagement and the 'politics of perception'.
[105] Weisberg, *Poethics*, 46
[106] Nussbaum, *Political Emotions*, 198.
[107] Nussbaum, *Political Emotions*, 52, 157.
[108] In Nussbaum, *Justice*, 119.
[109] A. Dorfman, *Other Septembers, Many Americas: Selected Provocations 1980–2004*, (Pluto, 2004), 232.
[110] Nussbaum, *Love's Knowledge*, 165, 189.
[111] W. Whitman, *The Complete Poems*, (Penguin, 1996), 85, 87.

ity of suffering'.[112] The invocation of compassion takes us a little further. More than mere sympathy, a compassionate politics is an 'outgrowth of empathy'; a reaching out to the 'other' impelled by a sense of sadness for their suffering. Here again, much depends on strategies of sustenance. And here again, we can spot a metaphorical resonance. Like Mill, Nussbaum refers to an 'emotional contagion', to be nurtured by a 'political culture' of free 'conversation' and 'vivid imagining'.[113] Not easy, of course. Patricia Williams refers to the 'hard work of listening across boundaries'.[114] The darker moments make us fearful, and fear encourages us to detach ourselves, to concede to suspicion and hatred. The existential threat stretches our moral integrity. And indeed our legal, as we will shortly see. Just as we can only test our moral fibre when there is a pressing temptation to be cruel, so too can we only test the mettle of our jurisprudence when the cases are 'hard'. Dealing with this, though, is the marrow of a genuine legal ethics.

[112] M. Nussbaum, 'Compassion and Terror', in J. Sterba (ed) *Terrorism and International Justice*, (Oxford UP, 2003), 231, 234.

[113] Nussbaum, *Political Emotions*, 155.

[114] P. Williams, *The Rooster's Egg: On the Persistence of Prejudice*, (Harvard UP, 1995), 200.

2

Thinking the Unthinkable

For the vast majority of us, it is difficult to imagine quite what went through the minds of the pilots who flew the jets that they had hijacked into the Twin Towers in New York on 11th September 2001. It is likewise difficult to imagine what went through the minds of those who planted bombs in London on 7th July 2005, or more recently those who launched their attacks on various sites in Paris in November 2015. In a prosaic sense, this is a good thing. It should not be ordinary or readily comprehensible. At the same time, there is a case for somehow trying to understand. As Martin Amis does in his essay *The Second Plane*, trying to imagine more precisely what was going through the mind of the pilot who flew the second plane on 9/11.[1] We shall return to Amis's essay in due course. The alternative to thinking hard is to accept a situation of what Amis, elsewhere, termed 'gangrenous futility'.[2] The modern state cannot, of course, seem indifferent. There has to be a counter-terrorist response. During the last decade and a half successive UK governments have accordingly passed a series of anti-terrorist statutes.[3] The fact that each has been triggered by expressions of judicial disquiet is a testament to just how hard countering terrorism, within the bounds of law at least, has proved to be. Counter-terrorism then is not easy, especially if we are prepared to ask ourselves the harder questions; questions not about terrorists, or at least not just about terrorists, but questions that are about us.

This chapter is about asking hard questions, and more particularly about the role that literature might play in helping us to frame our interrogation. It is about how we might overcome the 'explosion of silence' which so com-

---

[1] M. Amis, *The Second Plane*, (Jonathan Cape, 2008).

[2] Comments made in the *Guardian Review*, 19th May 2007, at 4.

[3] From detentions orders to control orders to TPIMs, the successive statutes which established these regulatory regimes being the 2001 Terrorism Act, the 2001 Anti-Terrorism Crime and Security Act, the 2005 Prevention of Terrorism Act and the 2011 Terrorism Prevention and Investigative Measures Act.

monly follows the explosion of the terrorist bomb.[4] It will require us to think further on the relation of law and literature, and its aspiration. In the previous chapter, we explored the potential for 'law and literature' to 'revitalise' the ethics of law and justice. We also supposed that the aspiration is peculiarly well-suited to the 'theatrical context'.[5] Quite how far these 'strategies' can be taken remains a matter of contestation. Some, as we noted, prefer to simplify the ambition; to a capacity to humanise prospective lawyers. The aspiration is no less compelling for being more simply conceived. The prospective reach of 'poethics' is, of course contingent, on both discipline and moment. Certain areas of legal practice lend themselves more readily to 'poethical' reflection. And certain experiences impel closer consideration of what it means to be human. There is not much 'poethical' scholarship on the law of international secured transactions. There is conversely a lot on criminal justice and the law of evidence. And in recent years there has been more and more on what might, for want of something better, be termed counter-terrorist 'law'.

We will start this chapter with a closer look at the poetics, and poethics, of terror. After which we will move on to examine a particular genre of drama which has evolved, in considerable part, as an expression of this poetics. As we will see, documentary, or verbatim, drama did not originate as a response to the 'war on terror'. But it did seem to offer itself as a peculiarly suitable medium with which to promote broader public reflection. In the final part of this chapter, we will focus our attention more particularly still on the work of Richard Norton-Taylor, one of the leading contemporary docu-dramatists. Norton-Taylor has written a series of plays exploring various aspects of this 'war on terror'. But none has, perhaps, generated quite such controversy as *Called to Account*; an imaginary enactment of the 'trial' of the former British Prime Minister, Tony Blair. Of course, the fact that the trial is fictive, even if the testimony is not, raises questions; not just about the reach, and integrity, of documentary drama, but about the nature of a trial.

The Poetics of Terror

At the more contentious edge of what has become familiar as terrorist 'studies' is the temptation of the counter-intuitive; it comes with the asking of

---

[4] See here U. Beck, 'The Terrorist Threat: World Risk Society Revisited', 19 *Theory, Culture and Society* 2002, 39.

[5] See H. Derbyshire and L. Hodson, 'Performing Injustice: Human Rights and Verbatim Theatre', 2 *Law and Humanities* 2008, arguing, at 198, that the 'formality and practicality that tend to characterise legal discourse can be balanced by the imaginative, emotional response to the experience of others that is made possible by its articulation within a theatrical context'.

harder questions. In a sense, the counter-intuitive is a dangerous gambit. We are not supposed to think it. We are not really encouraged to ask difficult questions. Such questioning breaches what former US Secretary of Defence Donald Rumsfeld liked to term 'message discipline'.[6] But we need to all the same. The terrorist counter-intuitive takes two prominent forms, the first of which finds expression in Amis's *The Second Plane*; daring us to imagine the mind of a terrorist. What makes this controversial is the possibility that imagination might lead to understanding, even empathy. The second expression of the counter-intuitive is more familiar to historians of terrorism. It challenges the supposition that terrorism is something that terrorists do. History, to the contrary, shows that terrorism is more commonly what states do. We need to concentrate a little more closely on these counter-intuitions and their implications. We will start with the latter.

Historians like to conjure the origins of terrorism. It is not easy. It is, however, easier to identify the moment when political theorists started talking about it as a political strategy. That moment was 1790, the year in which Edmund Burke published his *Reflections on the Revolution in France*. Famously Burke identified terrorism as a peculiarly aesthetic political strategy, an expression indeed of the 'metaphysical sublime'; a subject which he had previously treated on a number of occasions, most substantively in his *Philosophical Enquiry*. Here he had concluded that the 'ruling principle' of the 'sublime' might be defined as that which 'fitted in any sort to excite ideas of pain' or 'terror'.[7] In *Reflections*, it assumed a very dark expression and a distinctly murderous one too. It was an expression of the 'false sublime', a 'monstrous tragic-comic scene'; today we might call it a politics of 'shock and awe'.[8] At its heart, of course, could be found the famous and fanciful depiction of the storming of Versailles and the 'rape' of Marie Antoinette.[9] Burke and his compatriots viewed the events of 6th October 1789 with the same horror that we might view those of 9/11 or 7/7; and the need to depict the violence, and the sexual violation, readily overcame any countervailing

---

[6] In R. Jackson, *Writing the War on Terrorism*, (Manchester UP, 2005), 26.

[7] E. Burke, *A Philosophical Enquiry*, (Oxford UP, 1990), 36–7, 53–4, 113. For a discussion of the nihilistic tendency in Burke's 'existential sublime', see P. Crowther, *Critical Aesthetics and Postmodernism*, (Oxford UP, 1993), 128–9.

[8] E. Burke, *Reflections on the Revolution in France*, (Penguin, 1986), 92. For a commentary on 'shock and awe', see J. Butler, *Precarious Life: the Power of Mourning and Violence*, (Verso, 2006), 148–9.

[9] Burke, *Reflections*, 164. For commentaries on this scene, and its rape imagery, see I. Kramnick, *The Rage of Edmund Burke: Portrait of an Ambivalent Conservative*, (Basic Books, 1977), 31, and also T. Furniss, *Edmund Burke's Aesthetic Ideology: Language, Gender and Political Economy in Revolution*, (Cambridge UP, 1993), 115–16, 122.

concern regarding the veracity of the depiction.[10] Burke was unashamed. He was a poet, not a chronicler. He wrote so that his audience might be 'alarmed into reflexion', so that it might be 'purified by terror and pity', so that 'tears might be drawn from me, if such a spectacle were exhibited on stage'.[11]

The fact that Burke confirmed a peculiar relation between political terror and dramatic art is hugely important. It is possible to craft similar conjunctions, between art and liberalism, and Marxism, and conservatism and so on. But rarely is the affinity quite so dependent and so blatant. Reaching a little further back in history, Terry Eagleton has identified the same intrinsic relation in classical Athenian drama, in plays such as Euripides's *The Women of Troy* and *The Bacchae*.[12] So too Anthony Kubiak, who notes that 'whilst terrorism is not theatre, terrorism's affiliation with political coercion as performance is a history whose first impulse is a terror that is theatre's moment, a terror that is so basic to human life that it remains largely invisible except as theatre'.[13] Four years after Burke published *Reflections* Robespierre had hosted a Festival of the Supreme Being in the Champs de Mars in Paris. The designer was Jacques Louis David. The violence of 'terror', Robespierre declared to the assembled masses, was a necessary sacrifice to the 'cult of sensibility'; which was why they were all having a party, singing songs and writing revolutionary poetry.[14]

The Burkean counter-intuitive is occasionally contemplated today. John Gray has suggested that both the modern terrorist and the modern counter-terrorist can be best appreciated as 'disciples' of Robespierre and his Jacobin associates.[15] It is present too in Jean-Paul Sartre's notorious preface to Frantz Fanon's *The Wretched of the Earth*, a caustic damnation of French colonialism and its consequence published in 1961. According to Sartre, France had 'sown the wind', and the freedom fighter or terrorist, the descriptor being nothing more than a matter of prejudicial perspective, 'is the whirlwind', the 'child of violence, at every moment he draws from it his humanity'.[16] More recently still, and no less arresting, are the words of the Syrian poet Nizar Qabbani: 'I am with terrorism/ If it is able to free a people/ From tyrants and

---

[10] See here Furniss, *Aesthetic Ideology*, 139–41 and I. Ward, *Law, Text, Terror*, (Cambridge UP, 2009), 39.

[11] Burke, *Reflections*, 175.

[12] T. Eagleton, *Holy Terror*, (Oxford UP, 2005), 5–27.

[13] A. Kubiak, *Stages of Terror: Terrorism, Ideology and Coercion as Theatre History*, (Indiana UP, 1991), 2.

[14] See S. Schama, *Citizens: A Chronicle of the French Revolution*, (Penguin, 1989), 831–6.

[15] J. Gray, *Black Mass: Apocalyptic Religion and the Death of Utopia*, (Penguin, 2007), 27.

[16] J-P. Sartre, 'Preface', to F. Fanon, *The Wretched of the Earth*, (Penguin, 2001), 18–20.

tyranny.'[17] Terrorists do not spring from the womb fully formed. They are created by circumstance, commonly fuelled by experiences of resentment and suffering, by what Ted Honderich terms their 'bad lives'.[18] And they tend to be responsive, as Burke, Fanon and Qabbani in their differing ways suggest. The state violates; the violated respond. It is not always so perhaps. But it is often so.

And they can be created by the time they are twelve, as Richard Soans attests in his verbatim play *Talking to Terrorists*. He records the observations of one Bethlehem schoolgirl of that age, as she comments on the experience of 'seeing one of the girls in the form below me, Christine' shot by an Israeli army sniper. It was the 'saddest' of many sad days. She continued 'When I first saw the Twin Towers on television, I felt sorry. But now I feel happy that they died. It's their turn to suffer. I could see many thousands of them die. I wouldn't feel a thing'.[19] Soans's play might be categorised as a testament of dispossession too. We will contemplate the peculiar 'strategies' of documentary and verbatim drama shortly. It is supposed to make us more sensitive to the plight of others, and in so doing encourage us to better understand why they might do certain things which we otherwise find incomprehensible.

In her essay *Terror and Compassion*, Martha Nussbaum takes this insight a step further. We glanced briefly at this essay in the previous chapter, and more extensively at Nussbaum's idea of 'political emotion'. According to Nussbaum, it is not simply a matter of better rationalising. It is also a matter of better feeling, of empathetic and compassionate engagement. This is the second of our counter-intuitive temptations. It resonates with the call of human rights lawyers such as Costas Douzinas, Conor Gearty and Martha Minow, who have variously argued that the formal discourse of rights should be tempered by a more sensitive dialogue of suffering and compassion.[20] Nussbaum, as we noted, developed the idea of a compassionate ethics across a series of writings, commonly drawing on classical and Enlightenment theories of political 'friendship', the 'sentiments of sociability' Rousseau termed

---

[17] In Tariq Ali, *Bush in Babylon: the Recolonisation of Iraq*, (Verso, 2003), 12–13.

[18] T. Honderich, *Terrorism for Humanity: Inquiries in Political Philosophy*, (Pluto, 2003), 109–11, 147, and *After the Terror*, (Edinburgh UP, 2002), 72–3, 85, 125, 136–7.

[19] R. Soans, *Talking to Terrorists*, (Oberon, 2005), 96–7.

[20] The relative weight placed on compassion and suffering varies. In *Can Human Rights Survive?* (Cambridge UP, 2006), 46, Gearty expresses a preference for compassion. The case for 'suffering' finds its strongest defence in Upendra Baxi's *The Future of Human Rights*, (Oxford UP, 2002), at 17. For an influential critique of formal human rights, more broadly engaged, see M. Minow, 'Interpreting Rights: an Essay for Robert Cover', 96 *Yale LJ* 1987), especially 1860–2, 1897–1910.

them.[21] And it is this same sentiment which pervades *Terror and Compassion*, at the conclusion to which Nussbaum returns to the same place as Eagleton, to classical Athens, in order to conjure what 'good' might come of the otherwise horrific experiences of terror:

> As Euripides knew, terror has this good thing about it: it makes us sit up and take notice. It is not the endpoint of moral development, and it may be a trap, hooking our imaginations on drama rather than leading us towards a new attention to the daily. But terror can at least be the beginning of moral progress.[22]

It might be, she continues, that the 'experience of terror and grief' of 9/11 was 'just that, an experience of terror and grief'. But it might also denote something more. It might help us to 'cultivate a culture of critical compassion', one that 'can awake a larger sense of the humanity of suffering' and 'a patriotism constrained by respect for human dignity and by a vivid sense of the real losses and needs of others'. Ultimately, as Euripides realised, it is a matter of challenging 'ourselves, again and again'.[23]

Testaments and Trials

There is little space for compassion in legal process and practice. Compassion is left to the poets. It is, of course, this divide which literary jurists such as Nussbaum and Weisberg try to bridge. This is not to say that the law disdains literature. Indeed, recourse to poetry and high rhetoric tends to be more apparent on those occasions where law is struggling most. A good example is the case of *A (no. 1)*, more familiar as the 'Belmarsh detainees' case, in which Lord Hoffman waxed lyrically on the 'life of the nation' and the threat which indefinite detention without trial presented, and Lord Scott sought recourse to the origins of 'terror' in suggesting that such measures were 'the stuff of nightmares, associated whether accurately or inaccurately with France before and during the revolution' as well as 'Soviet Russia during the Stalinist era'.[24] Similar rhetoric might be found in the various agonies articulated by particular Justices on the US Supreme Court in cases such as *Hamdi* and *Padilla*.[25] Whimsy lurks; even in the most austere and hallowed of judicial halls.

---

[21] M. Nussbaum, *Political Emotions: Why Love Matters for Justice*, (Harvard UP, 2013), 45.

[22] M. Nussbaum, 'Terror and Compassion', in J. Sterba (ed) *Terrorism and International Justice*, (Oxford UP, 2003), 251.

[23] Nussbaum, 'Terror', 251.

[24] *A, X and Y v Secretary of State for the Home Department*, [20102] EWCA Civ. 1502, paras.97 and 155.

[25] One of the most obvious examples perhaps being Justice Stephen's invocation of the Star

At the same time, however, it remains true that the law does not readily admit a lot of poetry. Nor does it tend to welcome interlopers, those who might otherwise wish to engage simply by means of expressing a passing interest or a desire to empathise. There are rules of evidence to prevent interlopers and random sympathisers. In this way law is more precise and functionally effective; if effectiveness means efficiency. If however effectiveness means justice, then it is possible to conceive of different ways of reaching judgement. Such a conclusion is reached by those who, in certain circumstances, recommend alternative modes of quasi-jurisprudential investigation, such as Truth Commissions. Here too, as Archbishop Desmond Tutu famously advised at the opening of the South African Truth and Reconciliation Commission, the larger purpose is to listen to stories in order to promote the 'healing of a traumatised and wounded people', rather than hold judicial inquiries into who might be held to blame for the myriad offences committed by all parties during apartheid.[26] Over the course of seven years, between late 1995 and 2002, the South African TRC listened to hundreds and hundreds of such stories.[27] Half a century ago, Albert Camus sensed that the twentieth century might be one characterised by 'fear'. 'We live', he projected, 'in terror because dialogue is no longer possible', because we can no longer discern 'beauty in the world and in human faces'.[28] Bodies such as the South African TRC are established to confound such pessimism. They are in this sense gestures of defiance.

It might thus be concluded that TRCs lie at the margins of law and literature; part trials, part theatre. And the same can be said of a particular species of contemporary drama, which has appeared to lend itself especially to the peculiar experiences of terrorism.[29] Here again the quasi-jurisprudential resonance is immediate. Verbatim or documentary drama has become an increasingly common recourse for a number of playwrights who, in recent years, have wanted to focus our attention on what governments do in situa-

Chamber and the 'ideals symbolized' in the American flag in *Padilla*. For a discussion see J. Martinez, 'Jose Padilla and the War on Rights', 80 *Virginia Quarterly Review* 2004, 56–67, and also Ward, *Law*, 154–5.

[26] D. Tutu, *No Future Without Forgiveness*, (Ebury Press, 1999), 86–7.

[27] For a compelling commentary on the way the TRC worked, see A. Krog, *Country of My Skull*, (Vintage, 1999), particularly 259 and 278–9.

[28] A. Camus, *Between Hell and Reason*, (Wesleyan UP, 1991), 117–8.

[29] Both Nicholas Kent and David Edgar have commented on the comparative relation of truth and reconciliation commissions and 'restorative' drama. See their comments in 'Verbatim Theatre', *The Tricycle: Collected Tribunal Plays 1994–2012*, (Oberon, 2014), 38–9, and also D. Edgar, 'Unsteady States: Theories of Contemporary New Writing', 15 *Contemporary Theatre* 2005, 307.

tions where they feel the need to act beyond the boundaries of legality.[30] As a species of theatre it acquires an enhanced urgency for reason of its peculiar compositional genre. The distinction between the two lies in the fact that verbatim drama exclusively deploys the attested statements of original parties, whereas documentary drama can import other 'primary' sources.[31] But what both species of 'docu-drama', as it is often termed, share is an intrinsically judgemental aspiration, and tone. In effect, what such plays do is reconvene courts, inviting audiences to assume the role of investigative jurors.

At the same time, they make so-called 'public' inquiries genuinely public.[32] There is a distinctly Brechtian resonance here, the purpose of political theatre being to 'put living reality in the hands of living people'.[33] David Hare has intimated the same. In 'an age where politics is marked by mendacity' theatre is the one 'place where society can go to take a sober account of itself, and see itself more truly'. It is the 'best court society has'.[34] Norton-Taylor, to whose particular work we will shortly turn, refers to the 'special scrutiny' that political theatre can bring to bear.[35] Michael Billington has appraised the genre in very similar terms, suggesting that it has sprung 'from a profound popular disillusion with both politics and the media'. It is moreover a generic 'resurgence' rather than an inauguration, for not only can isolated examples of docu-drama be identified earlier in the history of post-war theatre, but so too might a common aspiration be traced still further back. The ambition of classical drama was just the same; that of 'peeling off layers of deception'. Ultimately, the reason we need documentary drama is the same as the reason

---

[30] See Derbyshire and Hodson, 'Injustice', 191–211, and also L. Ben-Zvi, 'Staging the Other Israel: The Documentary Theatre of Noah Chilton', 50 *Drama Review* 2006, at 45 commenting on the 'explosion' of verbatim drama in the decade leading up to 2006.

[31] The distinction is not always clearly made even by practitioners. See here M. Luckhurst, 'Verbatim Theatre, Media Relations and Ethics', in N. Holdsworth and M. Luckhurst (eds), *A Concise Companion to Contemporary British and Irish Drama*, (Blackwell, 2008), 205–6. The precise term 'verbatim' was first deployed as a theatrical genre by Derek Paget in his 'Verbatim Theatre: Oral History and Documentary Techniques', 3 *New Theatre Quarterly* 1987, 317–36.

[32] See the comments of Nicholas Kent in 'Verbatim Theatre', 9.

[33] See Derbyshire and Hodson, 'Injustice', 206. For a discussion of the many and myriad species of political drama which have populated the British stage during the last half century, see J. Reinelt, 'Selective Affinities: British Playwrights at Work', 50 *Modern Drama* 2007, 305–24.

[34] In R. Boon, *About Hare: the playwright and the work*, (Faber and Faber, 2003), 79 and 111, and also D. Hare, *Obedience, Struggle and Revolt*, (Faber and Faber, 2005), 114.

[35] 'Verbatim Theatre', 11.

we need any drama. It both 'enriches our theatre and enhances our under-standing of the world we live in'.[36]

Hare has made his own particular contribution to the genre, *Stuff Happens*, an uncompromising critique of the 'war on terror' and the consequences which follow when 'lethal unreason and opportunism' overcome the fragile bounds of international law.[37] The consonance between docu-drama and the 'war on terror' is striking. Soans's *Talking to Terrorists* is another prominent example, as are the plays of Richard Norton-Taylor. At the same time, it should be noted that the relationship is certainly not exclusive. Documentary drama was flourishing well before 9/11, as we shall see Norton-Taylor had already written three pioneering contributions during the 1990s.[38] Moreover, subsequent plays, written by different documentary dramatists, have focussed public attention on events such as the Hutton Inquiry, the Israeli-Palestine conflict, and more latterly the 2011 riots in north London.[39]

And the composition can vary too. Not all are so obviously juridical in style. Soans's *Talking to Terrorists* is rather more fragmentary and reflective. Neither is it so overtly political as Hare's, nor as closely focussed on the immediate consequence of the 'war on terror'. And it may not seem to be quite so overtly angry either. It is, however, no less urgent. Another example of documentary theatre inspired by the consequences of the so-called 'war

---

[36] See M. Billington, 'Introduction', to *The Tricycle: Collected Tribunal Plays 1994–2012*, (Oberon, 2014), 2–3. The same suggestion in regard to classical origins is made by David Edgar, in 'Verbatim Drama', at 38, suggesting that Aeschylus's *The Persians* might be regarded as one of the very earliest examples of documentary drama. For further commentary on this, and the broader supposition that documentary drama has re-emerged as a consequence of popular disillusionment with both political, and media, culture, see Derbyshire and Hodson, 'Injustice', at 198 and 207. For a discussion of earlier verbatim plays produced by Max Stafford-Clark's Joint Stock Company during the 1970s and 1980s, see D. Lane, *Contemporary British Drama*, (Edinburgh UP, 2010), 59–60.

[37] See here Hare, *Obedience*, 193, and also E. Kuti, 'Tragic Plots from Bootle to Baghdad', 18 *Contemporary Theatre Review* 2008, 465–6.

[38] *Half the Picture* in 1993, *Nuremberg* in 1996, and *The Colour of Justice* in 1999.

[39] Being respectively *Justifying War* by Norton-Taylor, *My Name is Rachel Corrie*, edited by Alan Rickman and Katharine Viner, and *The Riots* written by Gillian Slovo. The latter play was prompted by Nicholas Kent, who had made contact with Slovo within days of the British Government confirming that there would be no public inquiry into the police shooting of Mark Duggan, or its consequences. *My Name is Rachel Corrie* was edited from Corrie's personal diaries and email correspondence. It has had, perhaps endured, a controversial performance history, following its initial production at the Royal Court Theatre in London in 2006. A New York production was cancelled at short notice following concerns expressed by the local Jewish community; itself a testament to its emotional and political force. It finally opened off-Broadway at the end of 2006.

on terror' is Vera Brittain and Gillian Slovo's *Guantanamo: 'Honor Bound to Defend Freedom'*. There has been no more obvious abuse of jurisprudential process than at the camp which the US government established at Guantanamo Bay in order to detain alleged terrorists, initially without judicial process; no more obvious abuse and no more chronically misjudged too. If it is difficult to imagine what went through the mind of the second pilot on 9/11, it is just as difficult to imagine what went through the mind of whoever decided that images of shackled cowering teenagers dressed in orange-jump suits would somehow dampen the anger of militant jihadi youth peering at TV screens in Benghazi and Baghdad.[40]

In splicing together the commentaries of inmates, their lawyers and their captors in *Guantanamo*, Brittain and Slovo did at least three things. The first, articulated in the voice of the British lawyer Gareth Peirce, is to emphasis the peculiar relation of the ordinary and the extraordinary; ordinary young men placed in an extraordinary situation, not just as personal experience, but as a matter of jurisprudence.[41] The absence of law is the second thing which the play emphasises. *Guantanamo* is framed by excerpts from Lord Steyn's renowned Mann Lecture, in which he excoriated the presence of the camp as an 'utterly indefensible' affront to the precepts of international justice, and a jurisprudential 'black hole'. In such a circumstance, plays such as *Guantanamo* perform an essential role in bringing to the 'bar of international opinion' those who must be held accountable.[42] And the third thing which such a play can do is insinuate once again the possibility, and the virtue, of compassion. As one of the relatives of a 9/11 victim admits, if anyone held at Guantanamo was indeed innocent, and it seems that many if not most probably were, then 'they deserve all our sympathies and all of our efforts to sort of make sure they do actually get the justice they deserve'.[43]

Critics have applauded this evident poethical capacity. Janelle Reinelt, for example, has praised the particular 'explanatory power' of documentary drama to 'shape ideas, question truth claims, sway public opinion,

---

[40] See here Dame Mary Arden regretting the fact that Guantanamo 'constitutes one of the most enduring images of President Bush's war on terror'. In her 'Human Rights in an Age of Terrorism', 121 *Law Quarterly Review* 2005, at 621

[41] The paradox is noted by David Edgar in his contribution to the 'conversation' on 'Verbatim Drama', at 32–3.

[42] J. Steyn, 'Guantanamo Bay: The Legal Black Hole', 53 *International and Comparative Law Quarterly* 2004, 1–15. For further commentary on the extra-judicial nature of Guantanamo, see D. Dyzenhaus, *The Constitution of Law: Legality in a Time of Emergency*, (Cambridge UP, 2006), 1–3, 202–10, and also Ward, *Law*, 148–59.

[43] V. Brittain and G. Slovo, *Guantanamo: Honor Bound to Defend Freedom*, in *The Tricycle: Collected Tribunal Plays 1994–2012*, (Oberon, 2014), 552.

and construct an aesthetics that sometimes functions as an epistemology'.[44] Wendy Hesford recommends a dramatic genre which possesses a peculiar facility to encourage our contemplation of 'ethical and moral questions raised by the repetition of trauma and the violation of human rights'.[45] David Lane recommends a stage for 'unheard stories'.[46] There are still concerns. The genre is constraining. Documentary drama tends to the arid.[47] And oddly limiting as a consequence. Necessarily excising, as Steve Waters has put it, those 'moments of private reflection, moments of immediate choice' which otherwise make theatre human.[48] *Hamlet* without the personal reflection would have been a duller production. Precision is not always a good thing. Nor veracity, the particular claim to which is also contested. The material might be primary, verbatim or otherwise, but the writer still gets to choose what is said and what is not said, to play the role of editor.[49] And documentary dramatists are sensitive to this criticism. Nicholas Kent is quick to confirm that in the case of Tribunal plays there was a 'rule' that they would never 'jump the chronology' of witnesses.[50] But there has to be some editing, as Norton-Taylor confirms, for reasons of pragmatism if nothing else. There is only so much time and some testimony just better 'encapsulates' the 'story'.[51]

Responding to the suggestion that a verbatim dramatist uses the same literary license as any other kind of dramatist David Hare has countered with the suggestion that the 'process' of writing documentary or verbatim drama is 'akin to sculpture. You find the driftwood on the beach, but you carve the wood and paint it to make it art'.[52] David Lane reaches a similar conclusion, appreciating a necessary paradox. Verbatim theatre 'cannot present an objective truth or it would not succeed as art' but 'it must succeed as art to be effective as theatre'.[53] There is then reason for caution. However, it is not

---

[44] J. Reinelt, 'Towards a Poetics of Theatre and Public Events', 50 *Drama Review* 2006, 72.

[45] W. Hesford, 'Staging Terror', 50 *Drama Review* 2006, 39.

[46] Lane, *Drama*, 66.

[47] See here Luckhurst, 'Theatre', commenting on the necessary 'tension' between the 'facts' and the lure of 'artistic representation', 203–5.

[48] In N. Rogers, 'The Play of Law: Comparing Performances in Law and Theatre', 8 *Queensland University of Technology Law and Justice Journal* 2008, 436.

[49] For a sense of this unease, see Lane, *Drama*, 66–77, and S. Bottoms, 'Putting the Document into Documentary', 50 *Drama Review* 2006, 56–68.

[50] 'Verbatim Theatre', 13. It was not always followed by other documentary dramatists. Moreover, Norton-Taylor broke it himself in *Justifying War*, when the final word was given to Mrs Kelly, who had not even given evidence at the original inquiry. There is no strict chronology to follow in the essentially fictive *Called to Account* either, as we will shortly see.

[51] 'Verbatim Theatre', 14.

[52] Hare, *Obedience*, 29.

[53] Lane, *Drama*, 77.

a reason to question the value of documentary drama. It is simply a matter of calibrating expectation. A verbatim account of a judicial inquiry is not the same as the inquiry itself, and other documentary drama, which still more obviously splices verbatim commentaries together in order to create particular narratives of injustice, imports a still greater element of creative imagination. This is not a bad thing. It is just something.

The Trials of Richard Norton-Taylor

No documentary dramatist has played a more significant role in the develop-ment of the genre than Richard Norton-Taylor.[54] An investigative journalist by training, Norton-Taylor began writing docu-drama during the mid-1990s. In reflective moments he has expressed a certain consequential confusion, being 'not sure whether I'm a playwright or a journalist'; though 'David Hare tells me I'm a playwright'.[55] In a recent roundtable, he confessed to being a 'journalist, principally', but 'also a compiler, or a playwright, the editor of tribunal plays'.[56] The political motivation is certainly unarguable, and there is again a distinctly Brechtian tone in his observations regarding 'real' theatre; that there is something 'extraordinary about real people saying real things about extraordinarily important events'.[57] More pertinently, however, it is perhaps the forensic skills of the professional editor which makes journalists such as Norton-Taylor so peculiarly well-suited to 'writing' verbatim drama.[58]

Norton-Taylor has written seven documentary plays, beginning with *Half the Picture* in 1994 and *Nuremberg* in 1996. The production of his account of the Macpherson Inquiry, entitled *The Colour of Justice*, in 1999, is commonly recognised as a watershed moment in the history of contemporary documentary drama.[59] Four more recent plays have focussed on terrorism or more closely state responses to terror. The setting of *Bloody Sunday*, first produced in 2005, is Northern Ireland and the Saville Inquiry. The remain-ing three, *Justifying War*, *Called to Account* and *Tactical Questioning*, each

---

[54] Norton-Taylor began work at the *Guardian* in 1975, specialising in the investigation of perceived abuses of governmental power. In 1986 he won the Freedom of Information Campaign Award for Journalism.

[55] In Luckhurst, 'Theatre', 205.

[56] 'Verbatim Theatre', 4, and at 7–8, adding that he was a 'frustrated journalist' too.

[57] Quoted in Derbyshire and Hodson, 'Injustice', 199.

[58] See Nicholas Kent's comments in 'Verbatim Theatre', at 34, recommending an ability to 'make a story very brief, very concise', and concluding that Norton-Taylor, along with fellow docu-dramatist Gillian Slovo might be regarded as 'two people who were not play-wrights' by training but became 'consummate playwrights, in a rather wonderful way'.

[59] According to Hare the play was 'rebuke to the British theatre for its drift towards less and less important subject matter'. In Lane, *Drama*, 61.

address the more recent consequences of the 'war on terror'.[60] In each case, there is accordingly a peculiarly jurisprudential intensity to go along with the Burkean insinuation, lots of legal language, and lots of lawyers. And a particular style of directorship and staging. Each was first produced at the Tricycle Theatre in Kilburn under the directorship of Nicholas Kent.[61] The Tricycle became synonymous with docu-drama, critics noting the particular suitability of its austere decoration and the stripped-back staging character-istic of Kent's direction. In *Called to Account*, the actors simply sit around a table; a staging which rather obviously resembles the setting of an American grand jury.[62]

This austerity does not preclude emotional intensity. On the contrary, as the same critics noted, some of the evidence articulated in plays such as *Called to Account* could leave an audience variously angry and tearful.[63] The calibra-tion of emotional response is something every dramatist has to contemplate. But inviting audiences to embrace the particular responsibilities that come with the 'collective act of bearing witness' does ask particular questions, as Norton-Taylor admitted in his 'Editor's note' to *The Colour of Justice*; the need to present 'as fair, balanced and rounded a picture as possible' whilst also engaging the empathies of the audience.[64] And there is always and unavoidably, of course, the matter of editorial 'compression', essential to the crafting of a coherent dramatic narrative.[65]

And in the case of *Called to Account*, there is something else too. For whilst *Justifying War* and *Tactical Questioning* revisit particular judicial inquiries, *Called to Account* is a piece of 'virtual' verbatim drama.[66] It pretends to establish a court to hear 'The Indictment of Anthony Charles Lynton Blair for the Crime of Aggression Against Iraq'.[67] It is pretence because, in reality,

---

[60] The Saville Inquiry was tasked with re-investigating the circumstances surrounding the shooting of thirteen civilians by British soldiers in Londonderry on 30th January 1972. *Justifying War* revisited the Hutton Inquiry into the death of the Home Office scientist David Kelly. *Tactical Questioning* revisited the Baha Moussa Inquiry, which investigated the alleged mistreatment, in one case fatal, of Iraqi citizens held by British troops at Basra.

[61] Notable exceptions include *Stuff Happens* which was first staged at the National Theatre in 2004 and *Talking to Terrorists* which received its premiere at the Royal Court in 2005.

[62] See <http://www.nytimes.com/2007/01/08/theater/08blai.html> (last accessed 26th June 2020).

[63] On the capacity of docu-drama to inspire emotional responses, see Hare, *Obedience*, 76–7.

[64] See Norton-Taylor's own comments in *Tribunal Plays*, at 293, and also C. Megson, '"This is all theatre": Iraq Centre Stage', 15 *Contemporary Theatre Review* 2005, 371.

[65] Quoted in Luckhurst, 'Theatre', at 207–8.

[66] Something which, according to Susannah Clapp in the *Observer Review*, left the play open to the 'charge of tendentiousness'. See her review of 29th April 2007.

[67] A 'dream', in the words of the reviewer in the *Evening Standard*, which is likely 'cherished

there has been no such indictment and no such court. And there probably never will be. There is no likelihood of any domestic proceedings and very little prospect of Blair being indicted before an international tribunal.[68] The crime of aggression was created at the Nuremberg Trials and subsequently defined by the UN in 1974, but only as a crime committed by states. As a consequence the International Criminal Court does not presently exercise jurisdiction over crimes of aggression; for which reason if Anthony Charles Lynton Blair is to be brought before a court of justice to answer the indictment, for now at least it is going have to be in Kilburn rather than in Rome.[69]

The 'evidence' upon which the indictment rests is derived from a series of interviews conducted with various 'witnesses' in early 2007; in sum, twenty-eight hours of evidence taken from fourteen witnesses.[70] Not all of the evidence was used in the indictment.[71] Compression was inevitable, as was an element of aridity. The reviewer in the *Evening Standard* craved a little 'passionate emotion'. But the same reviewer also acknowledged that the dominant 'legal tone' was 'always cool, clear and shocking', and in the end necessary.[72] Paul Taylor in the *Independent* reached the same conclusion, appreciating the need for a tone which reflected the 'dogged, methodical' nature of jurisprudential inquiry.[73] It is not the place, Michael Billington confirmed in the *Guardian*, for loud 'voices'. The atmosphere of sobriety added to the sense of gravity, according to the reviewer in the *New York Times*, making the play more 'gripping' still.[74] Unsurprisingly editorial prejudice coloured some reviews. *Variety* regretted the 'unwelcome bias', the *Socialist Review* rather relished it.[75]

---

by hundreds of thousands'. See <http://www.standard.co.uk/goingout/theatre/blair-put-on-trial-over-iraq-7394628.html> (last accessed 26th June 2020).

[68] Though the former Prime Minister might be wise to exercise a little discretion in regard to where he should holiday in the future. Certain countries, such as Germany, have enacted domestic statutes intended to facilitate the prosecution of crimes of aggression against individuals.

[69] A decision which was reached, according to Kent, in conversation with the renowned international lawyer Philippe Sands, who provided much of the impetus for the play. See 'Verbatim Theatre', 26.

[70] The first interviews were held at Matrix Chambers in London. But when Blair's wife, Cherie Booth discovered what was going on in her own chambers, they had to be moved to a merchant bank in the City. See 'Verbatim Theatre', 26.

[71] Unused material is published in an appendix to the text.

[72] See <http://www.standard.co.uk/goingout/theatre/blair-put-on-trial-over-iraq-7394628.html> (last accessed 26th June 2020).

[73] See P. Taylor, 'Between Iraq and a Hard Place', the *Independent*, 26th April 2007

[74] See <http://www.nytimes.com/2007/01/08/theater/08blai.html> (last accessed 26th June 2020).

[75] See <http://variety.com/2007/legit/reviews/called-to-account-1200559867/> (last accessed

But then theatre is always going to be biased, even the documentary kind.

Called to Account is divided into two Acts, preceded by opening statements from both the prosecution and the defence. The former presents the formal 'indictment', under powers conferred by Article 15 of the Rome Statute.[76] It advances four questions, or 'facts':

> One, what was Mr Blair's true purpose in using force against Iraq: was it regime change or the elimination of WMD? Two, when did Mr Blair commit himself to use force: was it in March 2003, or was it earlier, in March 2002? Three, did Mr Blair manipulate the presentation of the evidence on WMD, and did he wilfully disregard evidence and advice that would have been unhelpful in his case, including the legal case? Four, what was Mr Blair's true state of knowledge as to the legality of the use of force? (667)[77]

In reply, the defence stressed that the 'case' is 'about law', and not 'about politics'; that the evidence must be 'hard' and 'cogent'; and that the prosecution must prove that Blair 'intended to act in breach of international law' (668). The 'key issue', as Norton-Taylor subsequently confirmed, is the veracity of the Attorney-General's advice regarding the legality of military action in Iraq; and much of *Called to Account* moves around this particular investigation.[78]

Early draft advice, passed by the Attorney-General Lord Goldsmith to the Prime Minister in February 2003, confirmed that UN Resolution 1441 'did not expressly authorise the use of force' in Iraq. There were only three ways in which war could be justified in international law; in self-defence, for reasons of pressing 'humanitarian' circumstance, or in pursuit of a UN Resolution mandating intervention. And none were presently credible, for which reason the 'safest legal course' would be to seek a fresh UNSC Resolution. By 7th March the Attorney-General's position had begun to shift. In a legal opinion delivered to Cabinet, he now suggested that there was a 'reasonable' case for war, but that the converse opinion was also still true. Ten days later, on the 17th, he furnished Cabinet with a one-page Parliamentary answer which stated that, in the light of evidence that Iraq was in 'material breach' of Resolution 1441, under the terms of Resolution 678

26th June 2020) and <http://socialistreview.org.uk/314/blair-dock> (last accessed 26th June 2020).

[76] The Rome Statute establishes the International Criminal Court. Article 15 defines the 'preliminary' investigative powers of the prosecutor'.

[77] All in internal references are from *The Tricycle: Tribunal Plays 1994–2012*, (Oberon, 2014).

[78] In <http://socialistreview.org.uk/314/blair-dock> (last accessed 26th June 2020).

military action could be taken without the need to seek a fresh Resolution. The much longer thirteen-page version, it was later discovered, was withheld from Cabinet. It was more equivocal again.[79] Goldsmith later claimed that his opinion had shifted following a series of discussion with various intelligence experts on both sides of the Channel. But for many, the essential question remained to be answered: was the revised advice given in good faith, or was it adjusted to meet political imperatives? In such a circumstance, it was commonly agreed, the Attorney-General is in a 'difficult' position (690, 705). But his constitutional responsibilities are clear and bear no equivocation. The Attorney-General must provide legal advice that is politically impartial.

The Attorney-General is an off-stage presence; as of course is his Prime Minister. *Called to Account* is written instead around the testimony of eleven other witnesses. Five of these are introduced in the first Act. The first, Shirwan al-Mufti, was invited to provide testimony on the internal condition of Iraq in the years leading up to the war, and more particularly on whether there was a 'humanitarian' crisis of the kind which might have justified military intervention.[80] It is not obvious that there was, or at least it is not obvious that the situation was worse in 2003 than it had been during the previous decade. The theme shifts more closely to that of dissimulation with the testimony of the second witness, Scott Ritter, who served on the UN Special Commission on Iraq. In his opinion, Blair's statement on the subject of 'weapons of mass destruction' or WMD, made to Parliament in September 2002, was 'absurd' and 'deliberately misleading' (678). The surmise is of course challenged by defence counsel, on the grounds that Ritter is prejudiced, and that Parliamentary inquiries had exculpated Blair. The same strategy is adopted in regard to a number of prosecution witnesses. The third witness is the journalist Michael Smith, who first broke the 'story' of the so-called Downing Street Memo, in which the head of MI5 Sir Richard Dearlove had concluded that 'intelligence' was being manipulated by the government in order to justify going to war; that it was being 'fixed to match up to the policy' (684).[81] The Memo was just one of eight leaked documents, a number of which provided further evidence that Blair, in line with senior members of the Bush administration, was already talking of 'regime change' as a reason for war,

---

[79] As Lord Lester confirms in testimony not used in the play but appended to the published text. The shortened version and the longer were 'completely different' (751).

[80] The obvious parallel being the situation in Kosovo a decade earlier, which had prompted NATO intervention.

[81] Smith was working for the *Daily Telegraph* and the *Sunday Times* during the period in which he received the documents. In 2006 he was won a British Press Award for his work on the story.

regardless of the strictures of international law (682–3). The fourth witness is Sir Murray Stuart Smith, Commissioner for the Intelligence Services.[82] His purpose is to attest to the veracity of the 'intelligence' presented by his predecessor, and more particularly to doubt how the Prime Minister might have reached an 'unequivocal' view as to whether Iraq was in breach of UN resolutions (689–90).

The final witness in the first Act is the former International Development Secretary, Clare Short, from whose evidence two very clear points emerged. First, Blair treated Cabinet discussion as nothing more than a series of 'little chats' (694). Second, he lied a lot. Most obviously, he continued to tell senior colleagues that no decision had been reached in regard to war when it had. It was 'just straightforward deceit' (695). And delusion too, as Short insinuated: 'He doesn't see it as lies, but I'm afraid it is lies' (696). And the same suspicion colours her evidence in regard to the Attorney-General's advice to Cabinet on 17th March, which suggested that war against Iraq was, in the end, legal. It was 'stunning' and, in her opinion at least, 'completely dishonourable' (699). Short's opinion in regard to both the deception and the delusion is echoed in the subsequent evidence of the lawyer and MP Bob Marshall Andrews, in whose opinion Blair had 'deliberately misled' Parliament in March 2003, and very probably 'himself' too (725). The testimony given by both Short and Marshall Andrews is damning, and the fact that the former's evidence is deployed as the structural pivot of the play is certainly no coincidence.

A different kind of delusion characterises the evidence with which the second Act opens, that of Michael Mates, former Tory Minister of State and member of Lord Butler's intelligence committee. Here it is not just a failure to appreciate right and wrong, but an inability to accept responsibility for the consequences. It was probably just a 'cock-up', Mates concluded. It 'nearly always' is (704). If the Attorney-General's advice was a bit 'contrived' that was 'neither here nor there' (706). No one takes parliamentary answers at face value, even those given by senior law officers. Five further witnesses follow. The first is Edward Mortimer, director of communications for the Secretary-General of the UN. His evidence concluded with the supposition that, in the event of war, Blair was determined that Britain should 'be in it' (717). Next is Juan Gabriel Valdes, Chilean ambassador to the UN. His evidence confirms the same perception, that whilst the UK might have preferred a fresh UNSC Resolution, it was prepared to proceed without. He further confirmed that the UN weapons inspectors had found no evidence of Iraq's 'material

---

[82] In his own words, in effect a 'one-man judicial review of the Secretary of State's power to issue warrants to bug people' (687).

breach' of the conditions written into existing Resolutions (719–20). Valdes' testimony is followed by that of Marshall Andrews, and then finally Richard Perle, former US Assistant Secretary of Defence, and Sir Michael Quinlan, a former senior civil servant at the Ministry of Defence. Perle testifies to the frustrations felt in the Bush administration in regard to the UN weapons inspectorate and holds to his belief that the Iraq war was, in the circumstances, 'legitimate' if not strictly 'legal' (735). In his comparatively brief evidence, Quinlan, though preferring to suppose that the Prime Minister did not act with 'deliberate mendacity', assumes the opposite view (740).

Blair, as we noted before, is an off-stage presence. But *Called to Account* is ultimately about him, what he thought and what he said; all the charm and all the 'lies'.[83] At best, his behaviour, like that of his Attorney-General, was 'odd' (693). But it probably gestured to something more. 'Something happened', Marshall Andrews supposes, and 'what happened came from the Prime Minister' (727).[84] And it is not just the manipulation of legal advice. There were also the 'deliberately misleading' statements made to Parliament (678). As critics generally agreed, Norton-Taylor's Blair emerges as a 'messianic' zealot who was allowed to get away with it all far too easily; for which reason, if there is any guilt to be attributed it might just as readily be directed towards those who failed to hold him to 'account' (702).[85] Blair may have 'manipulated the law' in order to justify an illegal war, as the prosecution alleges in its closing statement (742). But the failure of accountability was collective, cultural and institutional.

It was also rhetorical and jurisprudential.[86] Evasive political language nurtures evasive politicians, to an extent indeed that they eventually become self-deluded.[87] And in much the same way evasive legal language nurtures evasive law. For regardless of the ethical issues involved, it is evident that there is, in the end, no clear breach of international law; for which reason the audience is entitled to wonder quite what the point of international law might be if it is not to hold politicians like Blair to account. The reason, as Shirwan al-Mufti confirms, is simple. UNSC Resolutions are so 'elastic' that

---

[83] As Norton-Taylor put it in the roundtable conversation published in the collected Tricycle Plays. See 'Verbatim Theatre', 28.

[84] A view which is again echoed by Lord Lester in his appended testimony (753).

[85] See <http://www.standard.co.uk/goingout/theatre/blair-put-on-trial-over-iraq-7394628.html> (last accessed 26th June 2020).

[86] See here, speaking to the genre more broadly, Derbyshire and Hodson, 'Injustice', 203–4.

[87] The insight is common to each of the Tribunal plays, and it might be ventured to all documentary drama. See Kuti, 'Plots', 465, commenting on Hare's ability in *Stuff Happens* to translate the 'tragedy of war into a tragedy of language and talk', and also See Norton-Taylor's observations, at 'Verbatim Theatre', 20.

they can be interpreted 'in any way you like' (675). Blair may have lied to his own Parliament, his own people, the international community indeed, but in strictly legal terms he is guilty of little more than breaching ancient conventions of Parliamentary etiquette. Little wonder, as Short concludes, that the British people have 'lost faith' in their political and legal institutions (702).

But then the play was never really about guilt, as Nicholas Kent confirmed. The 'premise' was never to find Blair 'guilty'. It was to ensure that the 'whole thing' was properly 'aired'.[88] *Called to Account* is an investigative inquiry, not a trial. And it is a poethical inquiry too, concerned with the ethical consequence of corrupted 'legal communication'. Reinelt refers to documentary drama as a 'demonstration of caring, engagement, and commitment', as a 'gesture' of concern, of 'revolt' even.[89] Documentary drama shows that we are bothered. *Called to Account* does. At its heart lies a very big question; whether the launching of a war which devastated the lives of thousands of mostly innocent Iraqis was morally, as well as legally, justified.[90] It should concern us. And so should all the smaller questions regarding the practice of modern British government. At the same time, of course, the imaginary nature of Norton-Taylor's tribunal invites particular caution. Whilst it is possible to seek recourse to Hare's defence, that documentary dramatists simply exercise a little more discretion in the driftwood they collect and which they make into art, in this case, the discretion is considerable and the art peculiarly speculative. The driftwood is, however, the same. And so is the achievement. Moreover, the peculiarly 'forensic' and 'punctilious mirroring of legal process' in *Called to Account* might be said to lend a compensatory fidelity; serving 'to emphasise and implicitly decry the absence of actual legal proceedings'.[91]

There is finally the question of audience. What can a play like *Called to Account* do? Such a question has an especial urgency in regard to a species of drama which is so concerned with judgement and with raising public awareness. The potential is undoubted. Richard Levy suggested that *Guantanamo* 'should be seen by 30 million Americans'; if it was, it 'could really make a difference and change their understanding'.[92] But it was not, of course, seen by 30 million Americans. It is always difficult to calibrate a reasonable

---

[88] See <http://www.nytimes.com/2007/01/08/theater/08blai.html> (last accessed 26th June 2020) and also 'Verbatim Theatre', 28, admitting that he did not think that they had anyway found Blair 'guilty of the crime of aggression'.

[89] Reinelt, 'Poetics', 82–3.

[90] See here Derbyshire and Hodson, 'Injustice', 202.

[91] Derbyshire and Hodson, 'Injustice', 201.

[92] In Derbyshire and Hodson, 'Injustice', 210.

expectation in such circumstances, for which reason it is just as difficult to assess the real difference that theatre has made or can make.[93] It might well be that more attend the theatre than commonly attend judicial inquiries. But it may not be that many more.[94] There again it might be the more that matters.[95] Moreover, it is hard to see how things would be better if the genre of documentary drama had never evolved. If nothing else, plays such as *Called to Account* help to transcend the 'explosion of silence'. They show that we, as a society, care about what our governments do, and more pertinently perhaps what they should not do.

[93] On the difficulty of assessing 'the longer-term effects – ideological or otherwise – that performance actually might have on its audience', see B. Kershaw, *The Politics of Performance: Radical Theatre as Cultural Intervention*, (Routledge, 1992), 21.

[94] It has been surmised that up to 25 million may have seen a Tricycle Tribunal play, either in theatre or critically on the television. The supposition was made by Joan Bakewell, writing in the *Independent*, 17th March 2006. It can be no more than surmise.

[95] As Derbyshire and Hodson observe, the fact that so many documentary dramas were 'produced at theatres with a high degree of cultural prestige, attracting audiences largely from the educated, professional classes, and thereby assisting a group of well-informed and critically engaged citizens to contribute to debate in the public sphere' might seem to be rather 'elitist', but in a pragmatic sense has its 'upside'. See their 'Injustice', 207. The same is intimated in the *British Theatre Guide* review of *Called to Account*, available at <http://www.britishtheatreguide.info/reviews/calledaccount-rev> (last accessed 26th June 2020).

3

Churchill's Wars

Caryl Churchill has established herself as one of the foremost dramatists of her generation; her name commonly spoken alongside those of
contemporaries such as David Hare, David Edgar and Howard Brenton. It
is esteemed company, and it imports inferences. It suggests most obviously
that Churchill is a political playwright, perhaps even a radical playwright.
Her 'voice' is 'oppositional' by inclination.[1] It is also confessedly 'feminist';
for which reason the parameters of her company shift, to include the likes
of Pam Gems, Phyllis Nagy and Sarah Daniels.[2] Her early association with
Monstrous Regiment, in the mid-1970s, is commonly seen as a pivotal
moment in the shaping of contemporary feminist theatre. Janelle Reinelt has
recently referred to the 'feminist praxis' which has 'accompanied' Churchill's
'artistic journey'.[3] Such a reputation, of course, begs immediate questions,
not just in regard to what radical, and still more what radical feminist writing
might be, but also in regard to what a feminist theatre might be thought to
represent. Much the same argument moves around the writing of a feminist
history or, as it is sometimes distinguished, women's history. We shall take a
look at these particular species of writing in due course. They shape a necessary context within which Churchill's writing, and that of many other 'feminist' playwrights, must be considered.

The acclaim which attends to Churchill's writing is in part a testament to
political consequence. Plays such as *Cloud Nine*, *Top Girls* and *The Skriker* are

---

[1] E. Aston and E. Diamond, 'On Caryl Churchill', in E. Aston and E. Diamond (eds) *A Cambridge Companion to Caryl Churchill*, (Cambridge UP, 2009), 1.

[2] For Churchill's testamentary comment see Janelle Reinelt 'Caryl Churchill and the politics of style', in E. Aston and J. Reinelt (eds) *The Cambridge Companion to Modern British Women Playwrights* (Cambridge UP, 2000), 174, adding that in her own opinion Churchill is 'arguably the most successful and best-known socialist-feminist playwright to have emerged from Second Wave Feminism'. Elaine Aston agrees. Her writing was 'enormously important' in the development of feminist theatre in the later twentieth century. See her *Feminist Views on the English Stage*, (Cambridge UP, 2003), 18.

[3] See here Reinelt, 'On sexual and feminist politics', 19–20.

just as commonly recognised as being definitive pieces of modern 'feminist' drama. It is also a testament to prolificity. Over the course of half a century, Churchill has written in excess of fifty plays. But it is also a testament to compositional range.[4] *Cloud Nine* and *Top Girls* are overtly ironic and political. *The Skriker* is dense and allusive, poetic, even mystical.[5] A different kind of poetry informs the later *Serious Money*, a verse play written in rhyming couplets. In sharp contrast, much of the earlier *Fen* is written in vernacular. *This is a Chair* is different again, a series of surreal postmodern farces likened by some critics to Magritte on stage. Similar is her recent 2012 play *Love and Information*, comprising over fifty short scenes, none longer than twenty-five seconds in performance. And then there are the notable translations, of Strindberg's *A Dream Play* and Seneca's *Thyestes*. *The Lives of the Great Poisoners* is a libretto, incorporating dance as well as music. *A Mouthful of Birds*, the inspiration for which evisited Euripides's *The Bacchae*, was co-written with the choreographer David Lam. A Churchill play can assume many forms.[6]

But whilst few modern playwrights evidence quite such a compositional as well as thematic range, there are discernible threads in the canon. A first is, of course, political urgency, more especially a pressing concern with the 'condition' of women. A second is history. *Top Girls*, arguably Churchill's most acclaimed play, raises a serious of figures from women's history, some more mythic than others; and invites them to dinner.[7] *Cloud Nine* is set, or at least partially set, in late Imperial Britain. The 1984 *Softcops* revisits the regulatory state of nineteenth-century France. A lot of Churchill's plays deploy particular historical moments.[8] The two plays which will provide the closer focus of this chapter are both historically situated. Indeed, they both reach back to the same historical 'moment', for *Vinegar Tom* and *Light Shining in Buckinghamshire* are both set in mid-seventeenth-century England. Critics as a consequence commonly term them 'revolutionary' plays. Moreover, the coincidence of composition insinuates further affinities. Both plays were written in 1976, for which reason it is likewise supposed that they might be read

---

[4] Sarah Daniels has referred, in admiring tones, to Churchill as a 'Picasso' of theatre. See Aston, *Stage*, 19, and also Rebelatto, 'On Churchill's Influences', in Aston and Diamond, *Churchill*, 164.

[5] Of all Churchill's plays, Aston surmises, the one which 'the critics least understood and were most hostile to'. In *Stage*, 29.

[6] See here Reinelt, 'Churchill', 186–9.

[7] For the seminal importance of this particular play in the evolution of modern feminist theatre in England, see Aston, *Stage*, 20–3.

[8] For the significance in Churchill's use of history, see Aston, *Stage*, 18–19.

as companion pieces. We shall do so. But first, we must dig a little deeper into these shared contexts, starting with the very idea of writing history that is both dramatic and feminist.

Performing History

There have been histories of women and indeed women historians for centuries. But there have not been many. The academic discipline of history has in general been a male preserve; as have most academic disciplines.[9] Whig historiography is an obviously male art-form; men writing about other men doing famous things. Even the critique of Whig historiography has been written, in the main, by men.[10] Any woman, such as Catharine Macaulay, who dared to intrude were commonly dismissed for 'adopting Masculine opinions'.[11] In the same way, any famous women who appear in these grander narratives tend to be esteemed as often as not for their peculiar masculinity; Boadicea, Elizabeth I, Margaret Thatcher, even Florence Nightingale. Being a famous nurse might seem to be a more obviously female vocation. But Nightingale is usually appraised less for her ability to mop fevered brows than for her capacity for organising stuff; much more the brusque Health Trust CEO than the harassed A&E night nurse. And there is of course a particular irony in the fact that the emergence of a distinctive 'women's history' in England during the 1980s owed so much to a shared antipathy towards Thatcherite politics.[12]

Women's history is, of course, prejudiced too; all history is prejudiced. And it is controversial. For some, it is an expression of a larger battle for 'political power', an avowedly feminist enterprise.[13] Others are less sure, trou-

---

[9] And still largely is. See variously K. Gleadle, 'The Imagined Communities of Women's History: current debates and emerging themes, a rhizomatic approach', 22 *Women's History Review* 2013, 526–7, H. Smith, 'Women Intellectuals and Intellectual History: their paradigmatic separation', 16 *Women's History Review* 2007, 354–5, and from the slightly different perspective of 'men's history', T. Ditz, 'The New Men's History and the Peculiar Absence of Gendered Power: Some Remedies from Early American Gender History', 16 *Gender and History* 2004, particularly 1–7. The debate as to the gendering of history is nowhere fiercer, perhaps understandably, than in the historiography of the suffrage movement. See here J. Purvis, 'Gendering the Historiography of the Suffragette Movement in Edwardian Britain: some reflections', 22 *Women's History Review* 2013, 576–90.

[10] M. Spongberg and C. Tuite, 'The Gender of Whig Historiography: women writers and Britain's pasts and presents', 20 *Women's History Review* 2011, 673–4.

[11] For a commentary on Catharine Macaulay, and the hostility with which she was met by male contemporaries, see Spongberg, 'Gender', 676–7.

[12] see K. Cowman, L. Davidoff and J. Rendall, 'Twenty Years On: remembering the origins of the Women's History Network', 22 *Women's History Review* 2013, 673–84.

[13] See Gordon, 'History', 20.

bled by spectres of categorisation and diminishment. Aligned uncertainties continue to move around the relative merits and demerits of a distinctive species of 'her-story'.[14] Controversies aside, the intellectual prejudices militate towards the revisionist and the sceptical; and, at its poetic edge, towards the deconstructive too.[15] Written out of the grander narratives, it looks to different kinds of literature and different kinds of writers.[16] Maria Edgeworth matters as much as Edward Gibbon. Jane Austen's *Northanger Abbey* tells us more about early nineteenth-century England, and its historians, than Lord Macaulay and his vast and vastly over-wrought *History of England* ever could. It embraces the novel, and the poem, and the myriad species of testamentary literature, letters, diaries, memoirs.[17] It is an avowedly 'discursive' history.[18] As such, it enjoys an evident affinity with the 'return to history' movement in literary criticism. History is re-sited; radically 'decentred'.[19] Borrowing from post-war left-wing historiography, it prefers to write its 'history from below'.[20] And at the edges, because that is where the female voice, more often than not,

---

[14] The controversy here being the fear that 'her-story' only serves to categorise and, in creating a victim-type, diminish the place of women in history. In other words it inheres the same kind of 'totalizing tendencies' which characterise other predominantly male historiographical traditions. At a tangent, concern is expressed in regard to women's history having somehow, almost without noticing, entered the 'mainstream'. On these controversies see variously S. Johansson, 'Herstory as History: A New Field or Another Fad?' in B. Carroll (ed) *Liberating Women's History*, (Illinois UP, 1976), 400–5, 410–16, L. Gordon, 'What's New in Women's History', in T. de Laurentis (ed), *Feminist Studies/Critical Studies*, (Macmillan, 1988), 20–4, and also Gleadle, 'Imagined', 525.

[15] Kathryn Gleadle has recently suggested that it might be termed 'rhizomatic'; a term familiar to botanists and intended to infer a multiplicity of shifting connections. See her 'Imagined', 524–40. The argument, albeit without the same metaphor, can be found in Gordon, 'History', at 25–8, and also C. Smith-Rosenberg, 'Writing History: Language, Class and Gender', in T. de Laurentis (ed) *Feminist Studies/Critical Studies*, (Macmillan, 1988), 31–2.

[16] See here C. Hill, *Liberty Against the Law: Some Seventeenth-Century Controversies*, (Penguin, 1996), 3–18.

[17] See here Spongberg, 'Gender', 674–5, 678–84, K. Barclay and S. Richardson, 'Performing the Self: women's lives in historical perspective', 22 *Women's History Review* 2013, 180–1, and also P. Summerfield, 'Concluding Thoughts: performance, the self, and women's history', 22 *Women's History Review* 2013, 350–1.

[18] See here Smith-Rosenberg, 'Writing', 31–8.

[19] According to Natalie Zemon Davis. See her 'Decentering History: local stories and cultural crossings in a global world', 50 *History and Theory* 2011, 530.

[20] The borrowing is not without controversy of course; in part because it is a borrowing in many cases from a radical historiography the frame of which has already been set by previous generation of male historians, but also because it seems to condone the repositioning of women's history as a kind of sub-species of 'social' history. See Cowman, 'Twenty Years On', 676, and also Hill, *Liberty*, 4.

is to be found.[21] Militating away from the heroic and the agonistic, it seeks out voices that are quieter or quieted, and 'moments' that are particular.[22] Its preference is for a history which, to follow Levi-Strauss and more recently the likes of James Chandler and Kathryn Gleadle, might be termed 'anecdotal' as well as 'personal'.[23]

And the same is just as true of those 'histories' which are written in dramatic form. The desire to 'close the gap between the personal and the political' is an animating feature of Churchill's writing.[24] It is what, according to critics such as Janelle Reinelt, aligns Churchill's writing with the idea of 'her-story' which was so popular in the 1970s and 1980s.[25] The determination to raise quieter voices, from both past and present, is definitive of modern feminist drama. So too is the shared appreciation that the history of women is, to borrow from Judith Butler's influential thesis, 'performative' as well as dialogic, a history of 'individual and collective identities' variously 'framed and reiterated' in a multitude of 'public' spaces.[26] The theatre offers itself as such a place; a reason indeed why the historical 'staging' of women was for so long so contentious.[27] Feminist writers have, conversely, long appreciated the strategic potential of theatre, cherishing its facility for consciousness-raising and 'resistance' and through the necessary fluidity of dramatic performance its capacity to nurture critical self-reflection.[28]

Of course, the relation between 'feminist' theatre and plays about women is again arguable; not least because the term feminist is itself unstable and contentious.[29] A 'feminist' reading of a play does not necessarily make a play feminist, nor does the intention of the writer.[30] It is why a Sarah Kane play might be read as feminist despite the author's express denial; a paradox we

---

[21] See here D. Gabbacia and M. Maynes, 'Gender History Across Epistemologies', 24 *Gender and History* 2012, 535–8.

[22] Linda Gordon recommends a strategy of 'good historical listening'. See her 'History', at 29.

[23] See here Gleadle, 'Imagined', 533–4, and J. Chandler, *England in 1819: The Politics of Literary Culture and the Case of Romantic Historicism*, (Chicago UP, 1998), 4–5, 39–40, 67–74. For the same allusion to 'anecdote' in the more particular case of women's history, see Spongberg, 'Gender', 675.

[24] See Aston, *Stage*, 36.

[25] Reinelt, 'On feminist and sexual politics', 21, 24 .

[26] See here J. Butler, *Gender Trouble: feminism and the subversion of identity*, (Routledge, 1990), 25, and also Barclay, 'Performing', 178, and Gabaccia, 'Gender', 521–2, 525.

[27] On the importance of the theatre as a place of female conversation, see Aston, *Stage*, 11–16.

[28] See G. Harris, *Staging Femininities: performance and performativity*, (Manchester UP, 1999), 6–8, and also S. Shepherd, *The Cambridge Introduction to Modern British Theatre*, (Cambridge, 1009), 197–9.

[29] See Shepherd, *Theatre*, 196–7, and also Aston, *Stage*, 9–10.

[30] Harris, *Staging*, 7, 22–3.

will explore in a subsequent chapter. Caryl Churchill, in contrast, identifies herself as a feminist writer; but it does not mean that her plays are necessarily feminist, certainly not all the time.[31] That is as much a matter of interpretation and reception. Even so, and despite the various definitional variables, it can still be supposed that the affinity between women's history and 'feminist' theatre is sufficiently conspicuous.[32] They arrived at much the same time, inspired by the resurgence of 'second wave' feminism during the 1970s and were nurtured by the same common antipathy through much of the 1980s and early 1990s; towards a Thatcherite conservatism which assumed a distinctively masculinist hue.[33]

Here again, particular 'moments' have proved to be especially suggestive in the dramatic writing of women's history; both in terms of setting and composition. The seedier side of eighteenth-century London, and more especially the lives of its prostitutes, has, for example, attracted the attention of Timberlake Wertenbaker and April de Angelis.[34] The late nineteenth and early twentieth century have an obvious appeal too. Recent years has seen a revival in the tradition of 'suffrage plays'; a genre which found an original voice between around 1907 and the outbreak of the Great War in 1914.[35] The modern revival can be dated to Sheila Rowbotham's 1980 *Friends of Alice Wheeldon*, which tells the story of the Derbyshire suffragette who was accused of trying to assassinate David Lloyd George. More recent contributions include Rebecca Lenkiewicz's *Naked Skin* in 2008 and Sally Sheringham's *The Sound of Breaking Glass* in 2009. At a slight variant, the campaign to unionise women factory workers in south London at the turn of the century is the subject of Sarah Daniels's acclaimed 1998 play *Gut Girls*.

Twelve years earlier, Daniels revisited a different historical 'moment' in her play *Byrthrite*. *Byrthrite* contemplated more closely the sexual and reproductive rights of women. It was also set in seventeenth-century England. There were lots of battles during the English revolution, not the least significant of which were intellectual. It was a moment of questioning and contention; and

---

[31] Acknowledging the centrality of feminism in her work, alongside that of socialism, Churchill has confirmed 'I feel strongly about both and wouldn't be interested in a form of one that didn't include the other'. In Aston, *Stage*, 18.

[32] See Summerfield, 'Thoughts', 346.

[33] See Shepherd, *Theatre*, 193–200, and Aston, *Stage*, 3–4.

[34] In the latter instance in the form of an adaptation of John Cleland's *The Life and Times of Fanny Hill*. Wertenbaker revisits much the same themes in her 1985 play *The Grace of Mary Traverse*. And the same 'moment' has attracted the attention of Mark Ravenhill too, albeit at a slight tangent, his 2001 play *Mother Clap's Molly House* revisiting 'gay' 1720s London.

[35] The production of Elizabeth Robins's *Votes for Women* at the Royal Court Theatre in 1907 is generally taken to be the starting point for the 'suffrage play' genre.

has, for this precise reason, proved to be a popular recourse for female, and feminist, playwrights. Helen Edmundson has revisited seventeenth-century Ireland in order to encourage the same kind of comparative reflection. The violence inflicted by Cromwell's troopers on the native population in her 1993 play *The Clearing* imported an obvious contemporary resonance. Bryony Lavery, whose play *Frozen* will be the focus of a later chapter in this book, revisited the same historical moment in her earlier play *Witchcraze*. The title is again suggestive. The history of witchcraft, in England as elsewhere, presumes a peculiar susceptibility. Women are given to demonic madness, and only the god-fearing perspicuity of English men can save the 'chosen' people from their satanic clutches.

Plays about witch-hunts are not the exclusive domain of the female dramatist. Arthur Miller's *The Crucible* disproves any such assumption. But the consonance between the particular subject-matter, of witches and their hunting, and the aspiration of modern feminist drama is unarguable. The seventeenth-century 'moment' becomes critical in a sense that is both semiotic and semantic. And it is of course precisely this moment which attracted Caryl Churchill's attention in 1976. Indeed the first of her two 'revolutionary' plays *Vinegar Tom* is, as we shall see, about witchcraft. But before we take a look at *Vinegar Tom* and at *Light Shining in Buckinghamshire*, we must take a still closer look at their broader historical and intellectual context; at both the semiotics and the semantics.

The World Turned Upside Down

The first English civil war ended in May 1646, when King Charles I surrendered himself to the Scottish Covenanter army at Newark. The last remaining Royalist armies had been destroyed at the battles of Naseby and Langport the previous summer. The rest of 1646 was spent in an increasingly indecorous series of negotiations with Covenanter and Parliamentarian delegations. Then, in January 1647, the King was, to all intents and purposes, sold to Parliament. The scene is renowned. A troop of the New Model Army arrived at Holdenby House in Northamptonshire, where Charles was being held. When told that he was being taken into custody, Charles famously asked by what 'commission'. The Cornet in command merely gestured to his troop. Charles nodded his assent. It was a 'fair commission, and as well written as I have seen a commission in my life'.[36] It was far too late, but finally, Charles

---

[36] Cornet George Joyce, formerly a tailor in civilian life, had a reputation for being something of a firebrand, certainly happy to articulate radical Leveller opinions. At the same time correspondence suggests that he was acting with Cromwell's approval. See Royle, *Civil War*, 399–401.

had come to realise what was happening. The English commonwealth was turning upside down.[37]

God hath not been with us

Summer 1647 was spent much like summer 1646; in a state of confusion, and incessant negotiations. Autumn arrived. The harvest failed, the army threatened mutiny, and there was yet another rebellion in Ireland. On October 18th Fairfax and Cromwell were presented with copies of a new tract entitled *The Case of the Army Truly Stated*. It was stimulated, in an immediate sense, by the various frustrations and anxieties which had accompanied attempts to negotiate a settlement with the King during the summer.[38] There were, however, deeper grievances. Matters were coming to a head; which for Fairfax and Cromwell meant that they had to be headed-off. And so ten days later, a General Council of Officers was summoned at a church hall in Putney.[39] There were to be walk-on parts for a smattering of priests and civilian radicals, but the principle actors were military.[40] Whilst the immediate concern was to somehow address the concerns of the *Case*, without actually conceding much of what was demanded, the debates were underpinned by two broader questions. A first touched on the matter of politics and constitutions. A second touched on the matter of God. The mood was febrile, as might be expected. Much was at stake; after all, this was God's 'chosen people' building a 'new Jerusalem'.

As a consequence of its likely authorship, the *Case* is generally presented as a Leveller tract.[41] Historians, of both Whiggish and Marxist hue, have been variously tempted to write romantic histories of Levellerism, of brave early-day socialists valiantly arguing the case for what might today be termed a social-democratic constitution. More recent revisionist accounts are however

---

[37] *The World Turned Upside Down* was the name of a popular ballad of the 1640s, ironically sung as a protest against Parliament. Its modern familiarity might be traced to the publication, under the same name, of Christopher Hill's influential collection of essays on mid-seventeenth-century radicalism.

[38] Radical sections in the New Model were most immediately troubled by the *The Heads of the Proposals* which had been submitted by senior officers to the King in June 1647. See here E. Vernon and P. Baker, 'What was the First *Agreement of the People?* 53 *Historical Journal* 2010, 49–50.

[39] Where the Army was stationed.

[40] Including Wildman, who pronounced himself the 'mouth' of the rank-and-file Army radicals. See Woodhouse, *Puritanism*, 10.

[41] The most likely candidates being either Edward Sexby or John Wildman, or indeed both. The extent to which the *Case*, which was written as an internal army document, can be properly termed Leveller remains a matter of debate. See Gentles, 'Army', 144–6.

cautionary, suggesting that the landscape of English radicalism in the later 1640s was a bit more fragmentary and lot more prosaic.[42] Indeed it is now supposed that radical Levellerism was as much a consequence as a cause of the Putney debates.[43] The *Case* is perhaps indicative. On the one hand, it spoke of the 'grievances, dissatisfactions and desires of the Army' that had been ignored these 'many months', and the need for 'more speedy and vigorous actings'. It spoke of wages and pensions unpaid, and regiments disbanded 'before satisfaction or security is given'. But it also spoke to larger concerns, of the 'infamy of Parliament' and the neglect of the people's 'just rights and liberties'; the kinds of concerns which would not be addressed by any negotiated settlement with the King.[44]

These latter constitutional concerns founded the first *Agreement of the People* which, following hot on the heels of the *Case*, was presented on the first morning of the Putney Council. Again, for reasons of authorship it too has assumed a fabled place in Leveller history, not uncommonly as a kind of incipient Bill of Rights.[45] Like the *Case*, the *Agreement* was rooted in the same appreciation of 'interests' shared, and the determinative principle of 'equal distribution'.[46] The implicit affinity between proprietary and political inter-

---

[42] Morrill notes the presence of an 'implicitly anti-army' tone of much Leveller writing in 1646 and early 1647. Whilst the respective parties would come closer together over the following two years, it suggests some disagreement amongst radical factions at the time. See his *The Nature of the English Revolution*, (Longman, 1993), 321–4.

[43] See Blair Worden, 'The Levellers in History and Memory c1660–1960', in M. Mendle (ed) *The Putney Debates of 1647: The Army, the Levellers and the English State*, (Cambridge UP, 2001), 262–82. Morrill argues that Leveller idealist detached themselves from Army radicals who, after Putney, assumed however reluctantly a more pragmatic caution. See his *Revolution*, 325–9, and also in J. Morrill and P. Baker, 'The Case of the Armie Truly Restated', in Mendle, *Putney Debates*, 103–24. An earlier revisionist account of the same can be found in M. Kishlansky, 'The Army and the Levellers: the roads to Putney', 22 *Historical Journal* 1979, 795–824. For a more recent appraisal see Vernon and Baker, '*Agreement*', 42–7 and 59, and also E. Vernon, 'A Firme and Present Peace; Upon Grounds of Common Right and Freedome: The Debate on the *Agreements of the People* and the Crisis of the Constitution 1647–59', in P. Baker and E. Vernon (eds) *The Agreements of the People, the Levellers and the Constitutional Crisis of the English Revolution*, (Palgrave, 2012), 197–8.

[44] See Woodhouse, *Puritanism*, 429–30, and also Gentles, 'Army', 140–2, discussing the evolving concerns of the Army during summer 1647, leading from the July *Heads of the Proposals* to the October *Case*.

[45] Written most probably by either Wildman or William Walwyn, or perhaps both. See Vernon, 'Debate', 197.

[46] See Woodhouse, *Puritanism*, 342 and Vernon and Baker, '*Agreement*', 50–3, suggesting that in doing so the *Agreement* took the form of a 'radical redeployment' of otherwise familiar common law notions of the 'ancient' constitution; the radical bit being the absence of a king.

est, which would emerge as a matter of defining contention at Putney, clearly owed something to contemporary writings of self-acclaimed 'True Levellers', Diggers, such as Gerard Winstanley whose writings were championed by Christopher Hill as expressions of percipient 'communist' idealism.[47] It was from Winstanley's pamphlet *Light Shining in Buckinghamshire* that Churchill took like inspiration, as well as a title. Winstanley's tract, the title of which was in turn derived from scripture, adopted the familiar 'Norman Yoke' thesis, arguing that land had been held in common up until 1066 when it had been wrested away by kings, nobles and their 'horseleech' lawyers.[48] Matters of liberty, property and godliness were inextricable. Winstanley's *Light Shining* took shared aim at the 'tyranny' of priests and 'parliament men' too, and 'inclosers'.[49] The contempt for law and more especially for 'horseleech' lawyers crossed puritan and independent lines. In Milton's opinion, the language of the law was 'no human speech at all'.[50] Lodowick Muggleton took consolation from the fact that all the lawyers were 'damned without mercy to all eternity'.[51] Shakespeare's Cade had said much the same.

The presentation of the *Agreement*, which proposed such 'very great alterations of the very government of the kingdom', on the first morning of the Council appeared to take Cromwell and the Grandees by surprise. Indeed so great were the likely 'consequences of such an alteration' that 'wise and godly men ought to consider' taking their time; otherwise, there will be 'utter confusion'.[52] The recommendation that everyone should slow down a bit would recur. When urged to be 'doing' rather than just talking, Cromwell was quick to caution that they must first 'understand one another before we come to act'.[53] The matter of 'engagements', made variously by Army

---

[47] In Hill, *Liberty*, 273–4.

[48] The New Testament source is 2 *Peter* 1:19. The Leveller *Agreement* evinced a similarly dim view of lawyers, 'vermin and caterpillars'. See Woodhouse, *Puritanism*, 366, and for commentary on the 'Norman yoke' thesis, at Introduction, 95–6. For further commentary see Hill, *Liberty*, 85–9.

[49] In April 1649, the Digger leader George Winstanley published a pamphlet justifying the digging up the 'waste' common at George Hill. It was entitled *The True Leveller's Standard Advanced*. For a discussion of the 'True Levellers' and the extent to which they preferred to distinguish themselves, see Hill, *Upside Down*, 113–14, 124, and more recently A. Hughes, 'Diggers, True Levellers and the Crisis of the English Revolution', in P. Baker and E. Vernon (eds) *The Agreements of the People, the Levellers and the Constitutional Crisis of the English Revolution*, (Palgrave, 2012), 218–25.

[50] In Hill, *Liberty*, 266.

[51] In Hill, *Liberty*, 267.

[52] Woodhouse, *Puritanism*, 7.

[53] Woodhouse, *Puritanism*, 44.

and Parliament, was remitted, at Cromwell's behest, to a 'committee'.[54] But only after the first day had been swallowed up with the 'business', leading Colonel Thomas Rainborough to suspect that it was indeed part of a grander plan to avoid talking about the deeper implications of the *Agreement*.[55] It was Rainborough, who emerged as the most eloquent of the radical officers, famously articulating the case for universal suffrage on the morning of the second day:

> For really I think that the poorest he that is in England hath a life to live, as the greatest he; and therefore truly, sir, I think it's clear that every man that is to live under a government ought first by his own consent to put himself under that government; and I do think that the poorest man in England is not at all bound in a strict sense to that government that he hath not had a voice to put himself under.[56]

The counter-argument of the 'Grandees' was presented most forcefully by Cromwell's son-in-law Henry Ireton.[57] The absent Lilburne would later condemn Ireton as 'angry and lordly', resembling nothing other than 'an absolute king'.[58] In fact, he far more closely resembled the nit-picking common

---

[54] The matter was apparently 'disputable'. See Woodhouse, *Puritanism*, 16–17, 26.

[55] See Woodhouse, *Puritanism*, 44–5, and also I. Gentles, 'The New Model Army and the Constitutional Crisis of the Late 1640s', in P. Baker and E. Vernon (eds) *The Agreements of the People, the Levellers and the Constitutional Crisis of the English Revolution*, (Palgrave, 2012), 148. Earlier in the debate the question of engagements prompted Ireton, who argued the 'Grandee' case, to treat the Council to a long speech on 'equivocation' and 'justice', emphasising the distinction between negative and positive aspects; a rather striking precursor to the same distinctions later and more famously raised by Bentham and Berlin. The importance of adhering to sworn 'covenants' was widely appreciated. Indeed adhering to the Solemn League and Covenant was commonly presented as the most credible justification for going to war in the first place. Rainborough, predictably, took a rather more prosaic view; observing that by going to war they had already broken a number of engagements, so why worry about breaking another. See Woodhouse, *Puritanism*, 27–9, 32–4 and again at 49–52. For a commentary on the matter of engagements in the mid-seventeenth-century intellectual and political mindset, see Vernon, 'Debate', 200–2.

[56] Woodhouse, *Puritanism*, 53.

[57] Ireton had forged a close relationship with Cromwell, both on and off the battlefield, having assumed prominent command at Naseby. He would later become Lord President of Munster, and earn a reputation for the consequence of his brutal siege of Limerick.

[58] In his *Legal Fundamental Liberties*, in Woodhouse, *Puritanism*, at 349. Lilburne was in prison at the time of the debates. See Vernon and Baker, '*Agreement*', 45 and 48, suggesting that his reputation as an influential figure amongst Army radicals might have been overplayed by previous historians, and preferring instead to emphasise the influence of Sexby and Wildman, and above all the republican parliamentarian Henry Marten.

lawyer that he had, until war broke out, been.[59] In his opinion 'engagements' could never be ignored, the 'poorest' were most certainly 'bound' to theirs, whilst each and every assumption written into the *Agreement*, particularly the more flaky historical ones, had to be minutely dissected. Wildman would later make complaint in regard to Ireton's obsession with 'particulars'.[60] He certainly preferred 'material points' to metaphysical whimsy, as his response to Rainborough evinced:

> Give me leave to tell you, that if you make this the rule I think you must fly for refuge to an absolute natural right, and you must deny all civil right, and I am sure it will come to that in the consequence . . . I think that no person hath a right to an interest or share in the disposing of the affairs of the kingdom, and in determining or choosing those that shall determine what laws we shall be ruled by here – no person hath a right to this that hath not a permanent fixed interest in this kingdom.[61]

There was nothing in the 'fundamental constitution' that vested in every man a right to 'share' in government.[62]

This was, of course, precisely the issue. For a common lawyer such as Ireton, the tenets of the 'fundamental' or 'ancient' constitution were unimpeachable. In Rainborough's opinion, they contravened 'natural right' and the 'Law of God', and for that reason, their 'tyranny' over the common man must be swept away. Horrified, Ireton cut to the chase: 'All the main thing that I speak for, is because I would have an eye to property . . . For here is the case of the most fundamental part of the constitution of the kingdom, which if you take away, you take away all by that'. To argue the 'right of nature' is to argue against 'property'. How can someone be trusted to have a say in government, 'have so real a regard to the peace of the kingdom', if they 'hath no permanent interest' in it? The *Agreement* looked to 'destroy' property.[63] As the discussion heated, Rainborough accused Ireton of dissimulation, of trying

---

[59] One of a generation of young common lawyers who militated towards the parliamentarian cause and who, in due course, distinguished themselves on the battlefield. Another was General Charles Fleetwood who commanded cavalry regiments at Naseby and then later at Dunbar in 1650; in both cases with considerable distinction.

[60] Woodhouse, *Puritanism*, 118.

[61] Woodhouse, *Puritanism*, 53–4, and also 85 for Ireton's further plea that they should above all seek 'practicable' solutions.

[62] Woodhouse, *Puritanism*, 54.

[63] The implication being that once they have power the un-propertied might look to elect representatives who would, by legal means, destroy the law of property; a view vigorously supported by other 'Grandees', such as Colonel Rich. See Woodhouse, *Puritanism*, 57–8, 62–3.

to 'make the world believe that we are for anarchy'.[64] Ireton was angry in his denial, contemptuous of the notion that God might be a closet Leveller: 'The Law of God doth not give me property, nor the Law of Nature, but property is of human constitution'.[65] Rainborough's response is renowned. He 'would fain know what' every 'soldier hath fought for all this while', the 'old law of England – and that which enslaves the people of England'?[66] An exasperated Sexby asked the same question: 'I wonder we were so much deceived'.[67] Ireton had the answer. They had fought so that men with 'fixed interest' would have the power to hold a tyrannical king to account.[68]

The exchange between Rainborough and Ireton was the centre-piece of the debate; both in terms of constitutional consequence and dramatic moment. There would, of course, be no resolution. It was all far too 'hot', as Cromwell averred.[69] Instead, there would be another committee. The debates 'fizzled out', as Cromwell had always intended that they should.[70] By the close of the third day, attention had drifted back the reign of King Alfred and the associated mythologies of the 'ancient' constitution. Parliament and the Army continued to bicker in the weeks that followed. A gathering of Leveller agitators and sympathetic soldiers at Corkbush Fields was broken up. A year and a half later, Cromwell moved with equal decision to suppress a more threatening mutiny of four regiments at Burford. Three ringleaders were shot. By then, of course, much had changed. The King had been decapitated, and England was a republic.

In the meantime, back in autumn 1647, Cromwell had found himself agonizing over a second question, simply put, but seemingly no less intractable: what did God want of His 'chosen people'? It was a question which, in Cromwell's perpetually agitated mind, begged another: what did God want of him? Reflecting on his stunning victory at Marston Moor in summer 1644 Cromwell had felt confident. God had made the royalists 'as stubble to our swords'.[71] He was even more confident a year later, after the battle of Naseby. It was quite clear that God had wanted the Roundheads to win. But it was not so clear what he expected them to do next. Milton, for whom

---

[64] Woodhouse, *Puritanism*, 59.

[65] Woodhouse, *Puritanism*, 69.

[66] Woodhouse, *Puritanism*, 61, 71.

[67] Woodhouse, *Puritanism*, 69 and again at 74.

[68] Woodhouse, *Puritanism*, 72.

[69] A view shared by a number of other participants, including Audley and Clarke. See Woodhouse, *Puritanism*, 59, and also 75.

[70] Morrill, *Revolution*, 326.

[71] In a letter to his brother-in-law Colonel Valentine Walton.

conscience was the 'best part of our liberty', was similarly concerned.[72] The extent to which God might approve the liberating of 'tender consciences' was certainly significant; not least in regard to the more prosaic matter of public office. But Cromwell's concerns ran deeper than the 'dross and dung' of office-holding.[73] It was ultimately the sense that God was disappointed which finally persuaded Cromwell to act in autumn 1647. Political dissension, he feared, was a consequence of 'carnal imagination' and a failure of 'faith'.[74]

It was this same anxiety which Sexby famously articulated at the very outset of the Putney debates: 'Providence hath been with us, and yet we have found little fruit of our endeavours'.[75] By late 1647 everyone was frustrated. Time and again during their deliberations, Colonel Goffe, known as 'Praying William' to his men, would suggest they all take pause and 'wait upon God'. He too feared that 'God hath not been with us as formerly'.[76] So did John Clarke, who opened the second day with a long and sober reflection on the consequence of following the 'candle of reason' rather than the 'Spirit of God'.[77] And they did pause, even taking a couple of days off in the middle of the Council to 'inquire' more closely 'what hath been in the mind of God'.[78] It did not seem to help that much. But at least they had tried, and they would keep trying. Much of the Whitehall debates which took place in December 1648 and January 1649 would be devoted to the same anticipation; most immediately contemplation of the extent to which God might approve freedom of conscience. On this occasion, the Council would even invite along the famed mystic Elizabeth Pool in the hope that she might have a closer sense of what God wanted of them. She certainly knew that God did not think much of the Levellers. He was not, she advised, a supporter of 'tyranny or injustice', or democracy or, she inferred, the killing of kings.[79] But Elizabeth did not otherwise get into specifics. It was perhaps as much as could be expected of an old woman living in a cottage near Abingdon; and of course, no one was supposed to know exactly what God wanted. But it was all the same very unsettling.

---

[72] In Woodhouse, *Puritanism*, Introduction at 43.

[73] As he curtly reminded fellow officers on the final morning at Putney and as he would repeatedly during the 1650s. The phrase, taken from *Philippians* 3:8, was popular amongst puritans including Richard Baxter. For Cromwell's use at Putney, see Woodhouse, *Puritanism*, 97.

[74] Woodhouse, *Puritanism*, 8.

[75] Woodhouse, *Puritanism*, 1.

[76] Woodhouse, *Puritanism*, 19, 100–1.

[77] Woodhouse, *Puritanism*, 38–9.

[78] Wildman, in Woodhouse, *Puritanism*, 107.

[79] In Woodhouse, *Puritanism*, 469–70.

The Devil abroad

Not the least because, as Goffe kept endlessly reminding those who had assembled at Putney, the Antichrist was everywhere present.[80] For a people 'living in the pages of the Bible', as Patrick Collinson so resonantly put it, the reality of the Devil was unarguable.[81] Of course, he seemed to be more obviously present at particular times and in particular places. He had, for example, been conspicuous in North Berwick in 1590 and 1591. His discovery there had persuaded the future James I to write his essay *Daemonology* in order to better inform properly concerned gentlemen.[82] Shakespeare, in turn, wrote his three witches into *Macbeth* in honour of his king's endeavours. The Antichrist had proceeded to pop up all over the place during the first two decades of the seventeenth century, most notably in Pendle in 1612 and Northampton, and then again in the Vale of Belvoir in 1619; in each case taking possession of certain unfortunate women who had, as a necessary consequence, been prosecuted and hanged. The discovery that the Antichrist was abroad across large swathes of East Anglia in 1646, though discomforting in the extreme, should not, therefore, have come as a total surprise. Indeed if God was in fact 'no longer with' His chosen people, as Goffe feared, the presence of the Devil was only to be expected. It could even be interpreted as a test, an opportunity to purge the commonwealth and reaffirm the faith. This is certainly the conclusion suggested by Peter Elmer in his recent study of witch-hunting in revolutionary England.[83] And there is a distinct sense of this at the very close of *Light Shining* too. So long as the revolution remains on hold, they are fated to live in a kind of 'hell' (239).

But discovering the Antichrist is hard work, requiring very particular skills. Shakespeare's witches might be easy enough to spot, what with all the incantations and dismembered amphibians. But the Devil and his familiars were more commonly dissembling. There were, of course, self-help manuals, such as *Daemonology*. The notorious witch-hunters John Stearne and Matthew Hopkins obligingly placed their peculiar experiences on record

---

[80] See Woodhouse, *Puritanism*, 39–42 for a lengthy lecture, at the opening of the second day, on the consequences of failing to detect the presence of the Antichrist in their deliberations.

[81] P. Collinson, *The Birthpangs of Protestant England: Religious and Cultural Change in the Sixteenth and Seventeenth Centuries*, (Macmillan, 1988), 10.

[82] James was passionately interested in witchcraft, his greatest concern, exhibited in his treatise, being the need to root out frauds. In his opinion the Devil deployed frauds precisely so as to provide cover for his genuine minions. His son Charles conversely displayed virtually no interest in the subject.

[83] P. Elmer, *Witchcraft, Witch-hunting, and Politics in Early Modern England*, (Oxford UP, 2016), 2–5, 36–7, 54–8.

too, in their respective best-sellers *A Confirmation and Discovery of Witchcraft* and *The Discovery of Witches*. Inside their covers could be found accounts of previous incidences of alleged witchcraft, observations in regard to the kinds of things that witches might do, and suggestions for their discovery, where the 'marks' of the devil might be discovered on the bodies of suspected witches, how they might be most effectively 'swum'. So too could be found descriptions of the various likely acts of *maleficium*, which could range from drying up the neighbour's cow to reducing her children to gibbering idiocy, sometimes by means of simple cursing or incanting their possession, other times by sticking pins into wax images.[84]

In principle, such acts might be committed by either men or women. In practice, however, it was assumed that the Devil preferred to consort with women. Trial records certainly suggest that the overwhelming majority of those prosecuted were female, and almost as often poor.[85] Social historians have long argued that the punishment of witches should be placed within a broader regime of localised, customary regulation of female behaviour, commonly noting a particular coincidence with local responses to alleged 'scolds' and women who kept disordered houses.[86] It was noted indeed by the late Elizabethan sceptic Reginald Scot who confirmed that the 'chief fault' of those who found themselves accused of witchcraft 'is that they are scolds'.[87] The 1634 play *The Lancashire Witches* opens with a scandalised visitor declaiming a house that is 'upside-down'; the only possible explanation being that they are 'all bewitched'.[88] Many clearly traumatised women confessed their guilt on precisely this basis, despairing of life and God, unable to keep their home or feed their children. It is no coincidence that witchcraft 'panics' tended to coincidence with infanticide 'scares'.[89] Many of the accused

---

[84] The matter of possession remained especially contentious, the rite of exorcism smacking of Catholicism to many. See K. Thomas, *Religion and the Decline of Magic*, (Penguin, 1991), 570–2, 579–86 and also 599–613.

[85] Thomas, *Magic*, 620–1.

[86] The forms of customary punishment ranging from ducking and bridling to more elaborate charivaris. See Fletcher, *Gender, Sex and Subordination in England 1500–1800*, (Yale UP, 1995), 25–7, and also D. Underdown, 'The Taming of the Scold: the Enforcement of Patriarchal Authority in Early Modern England', in A. Fletcher and J. Stevenson (eds) *Order and Disorder in Early Modern England*, (Cambridge UP, 1985), 126–32.

[87] In Fletcher, *Gender*, 25.

[88] In Underdown, 'Taming', 118. The play was written by Thomas Heywood and Richard Brome, and was clearly intended to exploit contemporary interest in further recent 'discoveries' in the area.

[89] The law of infanticide was strengthened by a statute of 1624 which held that concealment of birth would be taken as evidence of murder. See L. Jackson, 'Witches, Wives and

in Essex and elsewhere would attest to their satanic seduction in return for food or clothing, some relishing the fact that the sudden inexplicable death of a violent spouse might be somehow be attributed to devilish compact.[90]

An inherent, and very obvious, affinity can be seen in contemporary attitudes to female sexuality.[91] Women were born lewd, as the Bible proved, and so easily seduced. There was an especial concern in regard to cuckoldry and its possible consequence. It is for this same reason that historians again have noted a particular association between witchcraft and reproduction. The infamous witch-hunting manual *Malleus Maleficarum* suggested that wives frequently conspired to cheat husbands of their rightful progeny.[92] There was nothing more terrifying, particularly to men who had property, than the thought that the Devil was mucking about with their heritable estates. There were, inevitably, manuals on the subject of demonic midwifery too, as there were on pretty much every conceivable species of satanic activity. But reading about the Devil could only take a God-fearing gentleman so far. In practical terms, he still had to be rooted out.[93] The putatively demonic midwife occupied a curiously ambivalent position in the history of early modern witchcraft, for whilst she could indeed be the most dangerous of the Devil's minions, she could also as a consequence be the most valuable of double agents. Many midwives found employ, not just as local 'cunning women', dishing out herbal tinctures for this and that, but as expert 'searchers' or 'prickers'.[94]

The Devil could indeed be maddening in his dissemblance; but there were ways and means, and thankfully enough well-informed and zealous gentlemen who knew exactly where to look and what to prick. It was they who had written all the manuals. And, reassuringly, for the right price, most were available for hire. So troubled were the gentlemen of Manningtree near Chelmsford in spring 1644 that they sought the services of Matthew

---

Mothers: witchcraft persecution and women's confessions in seventeenth-century England', 4 *Women's History Review* 1995, 71.

[90] See here Jackson, 'Witches', 63–4, 73–5.

[91] See Fletcher, *Gender*, 25–6 and Underdown, 'Taming', 118–19, 127–9.

[92] As well as induce abortions, eat unwanted babies and castrate sleeping husbands. See Johansson, 'Herstory', 418–19 and Jackson, 'Witches', 76, and also Fletcher, *Gender*, 233–4, noting the assumption in contemporary literature that the reproductive role made women especially susceptible to satanic influences.

[93] The most famous examples, from the period, being Nicholas Culpeper's 1651 *A Directory for Midwives* and Nicholas Fontanus's *The Womans Doctour* published in the following year. For a discussion, see H. Smith, 'Gynecology and Ideology in Seventeenth Century England', in B. Carroll (ed) *Liberating Womens History: Theoretical and Critical Essays*, (Illinois UP, 1976), 97–114.

[94] See Thomas, *Magic*, 653–4, and Jackson, 'Witches', 68–9.

Hopkins, the notorious self-styled Witchfinder-General. Hopkins was not cheap, charging twenty shillings per town in order to 'maintain three horses and his company'. In Ipswich, they even levied a special tax to cover his fees. But few witch-finders had found more witches. With the assistance of his similarly skilled assistant John Stearne, he duly managed to discover and successfully prosecute twenty-three witches in Manningtree, and having done so immediately found himself invited over to Stowmarket and then Bury St Edmunds to provide the same service. All the purging was, of course, exhausting. Hopkins died in 1647, at which point Stearne went into well-heeled retirement.[95] By then approximately two hundred witches had been discovered across East Anglia, appropriately tortured and then hanged.[96]

There was again nothing particularly unusual in trying witches and hanging them. The destruction of the witch was the only sure way that the *maleficium* could be ended.[97] And as we have noted, there was plenty of precedent. And there was plenty of law too. Witchcraft Acts had been passed in 1542, 1563 and most recently in 1604. The first two evinced a rather greater concern with acts done than with anything more metaphysical. Conjuring spirits and consorting with the Devil was proscribed. But the primary purpose of the Acts was to deal with harm to individuals and property. The 1604 Act was different insofar as it recognised the doctrine of diabolical compact; something much more familiar in continental writings on the subject. The Act made it a felony to 'consult, covenant with, entertain, employ, feed, or reward any evil and wicked spirit to or for any intent or purpose'.[98] The idea of diabolical compact likewise coloured Coke's commentary on the subject in his *Institutes*, which confirmed that a witch was 'a person that hath conference with the Devil in consult with or to do some act'.[99] Coke, like his King, was fascinated by witches, fully convinced of their veracity and the threat they posed to the commonwealth.[100] But even after 1604 the law still

[95] Where, perhaps inevitably, he wrote his own advice manual and autobiographical testament, entitled *A Confirmation and Discovery of Witchcraft*.
[96] The use of torture was theoretically forbidden in England. But it is difficult to conceptualise 'swimming' witches as anything other. Hopkins moreover strongly recommended a variety of 'softer' strategies, including sleep-deprivation, starvation and 'walking' the witch, in essence round and round their cells for hour after hour. See Thomas, *Magic*, 617–20 and Jackson, 'Witches', 69.
[97] Thomas, *Magic*, 650.
[98] In Thomas, *Magic*, 526.
[99] *Institutes* iii, cap.6. Quoted in Thomas, *Magic*, 524.
[100] Like many contemporaries, Coke presumed the thinnest of lines between diabolical witches and diabolical Jesuits; a line that he wilfully blurred time and again in his prosecution of the Gunpowder plotters in 1605–6. For a commentary here see G. Wills, *Witches and Jesuits*, (Oxford UP, 1995), 22–7.

seemed reticent to get involved unless there was evidence of an act causing harm.[101] Three-quarters of the cases brought to trial in Essex in 1645 and 1646 involved alleged harms to person or property. One in five involved cattle. The sceptical common law mind could countenance dead cows and reduced dairy yield.[102] It was less comfortable with rumours of old women flying around on broomsticks and sucking at the teats of the neighbour's cat.

Even so the Chelmsford witch trials of 1645 were unarguably different, quantitatively and qualitatively.[103] For a start, proceedings were conducted by justices of the peace rather than assize judges and presided over by the devoutly puritan Earl of Warwick. The Earl had no legal standing or experience, but he happened to be one of the most powerful men in the county.[104] More importantly still he happened to be one of the most powerful men in the country, Lord High Admiral of the parliamentarian fleet and intimate of Cromwell.[105] Warwick's presence confirmed the interest of nation, faith and government. Never had so many witches been tried together. Across the region, a hundred and five communities presented witches for trial. Never had so many witnesses, in total ninety-two, come forward.[106] And then there was Hopkins and Stearne, and all the thrilling evidence, not just of weird old women casting spells over cows and chickens, but of diabolical compacts, satanic sexuality and demonic rites.[107] As Malcolm Gaskill has noted, the trying of witches lent itself to 'staging', whether in court or in the local playhouse; taking the like form, as 'intricately plotted human dramas' designed to entertain and to educate.[108] But here again, the Chelmsford trials represented something

---

[101] Thomas, *Magic*, 532–3.

[102] On the power of this residual scepticism, see Thomas, *Magic*, 546–8.

[103] The conclusion is reached by Thomas, in *Magic* at 537, and more recently Elmer, in *Witchcraft*, 69.

[104] Owning vast estates across Essex and Suffolk.

[105] His grandson and heir would later marry Cromwell's daughter Frances.

[106] For commentaries, see Thomas, *Magic*, 545.

[107] In his study of the case of Anne Bodenham, Malcolm Gaskill notes the peculiar fascination which came from 'fastening together' matters of 'high politics and low morals, sorcery, and sex'. See his 'Witchcraft, Politics and Memory in Seventeenth-Century England', 50 *Historical Journal* 2007, 302. The same is just as true of the Chelmsford trials. For a commentary on the peculiarity of sexual accusation in the Chelmsford trials, see Jackson, 'Witches', 72.

[108] Gaskill, 'Witchcraft', 306. The same perspective is ventured by Mariangela Tempura in 'Languished . . . and then died: Courtroom Drama and the Bodies of the Victims in Thomas Pott's *The Wonderful Disoverie of Witches*', in S. Fiorato and J. Drakakis (eds) *Performing the Renaissance Body: Essays on Drama, Law, and Representation*, (DeGruyter, 2016), particularly 63–6.

more, considerably. They were show trials staged and produced by the two most celebrated witch-finders of the age.

The dramatic potential invites a necessary irony. Hopkins and Stearne were not just producers. They were also enchanters, the success of their enterprise depending on their capacity to keep their audience spell-bound. Modern critics have liked to read a humanising impulse into some Jacobean witchcraft plays.[109] Hopkins and Stearne preferred to terrify. There would be no sympathy for the Devil or his minions. The Chelmsford witches had to be convicted, their diabolism incontrovertibly proved. It was never a question of justice. The moment mattered too much. England was still at war, the integrity of its 'chosen' people under the sharpest interrogation. It was not simply a matter of zeal, of course. There were other factors, not least governmental dislocation. Revolutionary England was a peculiarly febrile place, even in those areas such as Essex where military engagement had been slight. Local governance tended to be unstable, factionalism rife. Here again, Essex was no exception. Food could be scarce too, harvests unpredictable, local communities at such moments peculiarly prone to petty vengeances.[110] Dairy yield mattered. So did feral children and suspicious-looking cats.

But God mattered most. It was only too clear to every right-thinking Godly gentleman what was now occurring.[111] Having lost on the battlefields of Marston Moor and Naseby, the Antichrist had opened up a new front, seducing the women of the 'new Jerusalem', fornicating his way into their hearts and homes, breeding their bastards, poisoning their swine and laying waste to their farms. More particularly he was seducing the women of East Anglia, the very heartland of 'godly' England, the intended model of the kind of Jerusalem that might be built. The challenge was immediate. Marston Moor in 1644, Chelmsford in 1645, Putney in 1647; it was all part of the same revolution, the same crusade, the same providence.[112]

---

[109] See B. Neumeier, '(Disciplining) Monstrous Renaissance Bodies: Staging the Witch', in S. Fiorato and J. Drakakis (eds) *Performing the Renaissance Body: Essays on Drama, Law, and Representation*, (DeGruyter, 2016), 52–4.

[110] As Keith Thomas observes, in simple terms 'the witch and her victim were two persons who ought to have been friendly towards each other, but were not'. See *Magic*, 669 and also 698 concluding that witchcraft accusation was 'essentially a local phenomenon'. A similar conclusion is reached by Elmer in *Witchcraft*, at 16–17, 65.

[111] According to Elmer, Hopkins represented a 'revived providentialism', the famed witch-finder perceiving himself to be a kind of 'exorcistic healer'. See his *Witchcraft*, 87, 120–1, 125–7.

[112] See here Elmer, *Witchcraft*, 108–12, noting the particular fervour and militancy exhibited in puritan fast sermons, at Westminster and elsewhere, and also 115–16, 135–6, suggesting that what happened in East Anglia in the mid and late 1640s represented a localised version of a nation-wide struggle between godly and moderate factions.

Churchill's War

So much for England in the 1640s. Back to Britain in the 1970s. A political scene generally described in similarly dark tones, a succession of 'winters of discontent' as the Callaghan government struggled to deal with mounting economic crisis and consequential social unrest. And yet, as Michael Billington suggests, the theatrical scene at the same time was remarkably robust. It is a curious 'paradox'.[113] And 1976 might indeed be presented as something of a watershed 'moment' in this smaller history. The National Theatre re-opened on the South Bank in 1976, under the directorship of Peter Hall.[114] The Manchester Royal Exchange opened in the same year. So did the first RSC production of David Edgar's masterpiece, *Destiny*.[115] It can certainly be suggested, with the benefit of some hindsight, that a new 'wave' of radical theatre was seeding. A year earlier Hare had produced *Fanshen*, and a year before that there was Brenton's acclaimed *The Churchill Play*, the title of which permits, in our context at least, a slightly contrived irony. Common themes were emerging; an anxiety about authoritarian government, the seeming intractability of properly addressing social injustice and inequality, and perhaps more particularly still the plight of left-wing politics in post-war Britain. The arrival of Margaret Thatcher in 1979 would provide the necessary focus and stimulus for a more directly engaged political theatre.[116]

But the mood of simmering 'discontent', as Billington infers, was certainly tangible three years earlier, as Caryl Churchill put the finishing touches to her two 'revolutionary' plays. Looking back, it might be ventured that the discontent accounts for the original paradox; the energy derived from the anger. In her brief introductory essay to the published edition of *Vinegar Tom*, Churchill recollects their shared compositional context, overlapping 'both in time and ideas'. The animating questions, of 'religion, class, the position of women', were 'relevant to both plays'.[117] The particular influence of Christopher Hill's left-wing revisionism is patent. The year before, Hill

---

[113] Billington, *State*, 241–2.

[114] Though it should be noted that its first years were at times difficult. See Billington, *State*, 252–4, referring to its 'anguished opening', but also noting the significance that can now be read into the fact that the Theatre, and more particularly its first director Peter Hall, was able to quickly attract the support of younger radical playwrights such as Hare and Brenton.

[115] A play which, Billington asserts, exemplified a greater subtlety in its author's latent 'aggression' towards the political, and to an extent literary, establishment. See *State*, 247–9, further confirming that the play was a 'manifest success' and as such a key moment in the seeding of a distinctive new wave of radical theatre in Britain.

[116] See here Aston, *Stage*, 20.

[117] Churchill, 'Introduction' to *Vinegar Tom*, in *Plays 1*, 129.

had published *The World Turned Upside Down*, a study that did much to make 'history from below' so fashionable.[118] Churchill had also read A. L. Morton's *The World of the Ranters* published a couple of years earlier. But more especially, as Reinelt notes, Churchill was determined to engage the question of female 'identity' in 'turbulent historical moments'.[119] These questions, of gender and class, and religion, were as relevant in 1976 as they had been three centuries earlier.[120]

Light Shining in Buckinghamshire

Light Shining in Buckinghamshire emerged from Churchill's involvement in a workshop on the seventeenth-century revolution run by the Joint Stock Company in spring and summer 1976. It is, as Jean Howard has recently suggested, an 'astonishing and astonishingly different play'. Much of the final script was devised by the actors during workshop sessions; something which, according to Howard, makes the play 'daringly socialist' in its invention.[121] Much also is taken from original transcripts, most obviously from the Putney debates and associated radical tracts. As we have already noted the title is itself borrowed from a Digger pamphlet of the same name. *Light Shining* can thus be categorised as species of documentary or quasi-documentary historical drama, the writing of which asks much the same questions as the writing of any other kind of documentary drama. Critics surmise why certain texts are chosen, why certain events and certain characters are presented to the audience, and by implication why others are not.

Light Shining invites precisely this kind of critical interrogation. Scenes based on documentary accounts of real events, such as the Putney debates and the Digger occupation of George Hill are interspersed amongst a number which owes their existence to Churchill's imagination and the energies of the Joint Stock workshop. At the start of the published edition of the play,

---

[118] As well as inspiring left-leaning intellectual groupings such as the History Workshop and the Workers' Educational Association.

[119] See Reinelt, 'On feminist and sexual politics', 21, and also 'Churchill', 177–8, discussing the broader environment of socialist history and historiography.

[120] See here A. Solomon, 'Witches, Ranters and the Middle Classes', 12 *Theater* 1981, 54.

[121] Jean Howard comments on the 'radically democratic approach to theatre' for which Joint Stock was renowned. See her 'On owning and owing', in Aston and Diamond, *Churchill*, at 42–3. At a variant Sian Adiseshiah suggests that the workshop style betrayed a 'utopian desire'. See her 'Utopian Space in Caryl Churchill's History Plays: *Light Shining in Buckinghamshire* and *Vinegar Tom*', 16 *Utopian Studies* 2005, 3–4, 9–12. For further commentaries on the collaborate process and its consequence see E. Aston, 'On collaboration', and D. Rabellato, both in Aston and Diamond, *Churchill*, at 145–9 and 170–3, respectively. Churchill would move away from workshop theatre during the 1990s.

alongside the list of scenes, Churchill provided a list of 'documentary mate-rial'; to include various contemporary political tracts and passages from scripture, plus verses from a Walt Whitman poem. Her discretion lies in their choice and, of course, their positioning. The play pivots around the presentation of extracts from the Putney debates, which are placed at the very end of the first of the two Acts. Putney and its consequence dominate *Light Shining*. It is, as Reinelt ventures, a moment of Brechtian 'dramaturgy'.[122] Up until Putney, there was hope; after Putney disappointment, then despair.

Unsurprisingly, perhaps, Churchill reinvests the most renowned and resonant passages; including Sexby's opening in which he wonders 'the little fruit of our endeavours' and Cromwell's reaction to the presentation of the Leveller *Agreement* in which he expresses his concern regarding the 'very great alterations' which it demanded. But much the greater space is given over to the famous interchange between Ireton and Rainborough on the relation of property and proprietary rights. For Churchill, this exchange evidently represents the defining moment of the Putney debates; for which reason, at a remove, it represents a defining moment in the fashioning, and the failure, of English radicalism. Notably, Churchill ends the scene with 'both parties at a stand' and Cromwell suggesting they remit the matter of representative rights to a committee (217–18). The moment had gone.

The decision to focus on these more renowned passages is entirely understandable. It would be odd if they were omitted. But there is always a consequence to the exercise of editorial discretion. Churchill's account con-veys a peculiar coherence, not least because it prefers passages which engage more closely the question of constitutional reform. But as we have already noted for much of the time, the Council was distracted by a variety of other subjects, anxieties regarding various engagements, the seemingly irreducible question of what God might want, all the moments of petty bickering, all the indecision, the comings and goings of various regimental representatives conveying various messages and entreaties, all the broken conversation and interruptions, all the ellipses and fragmentary comments. Editorial discretion leans, for obvious reasons, towards clarity. But it might be ventured that the humanity lies elsewhere, in all these murkier moments of anxiety, confusion and indecision.

In the same way that Churchill's editorial discretion is constrained by the need for clarity, so too does history determine characterisation, at least to an extent. The population of the Putney scenes is necessarily familiar; Cromwell, Ireton, Rainborough, Sexby. So too the names of Winstanley and the two

---

[122] See Reinelt, 'Churchill', 175, and also Adiseshiah', 'Space', 10–14.

Ranters, Claxton and Cobbe, both of whom are based on real historical figures; in the former case Lawrence Clarkson, known as 'Captain of the Rant', in
the latter, Abiezer Coppe, author of the notorious tract *A Fiery Flying Roll*.[123]
Other characters, however, are invented; precisely it can be supposed so that
Churchill can give a voice to those whom historical record has silenced. There
are more of these, and needless to say many are female.[124] Ultimately in regard
to both its composition and its characterisation *Light Shining* is a composite,
part documentary, part written, part improvised. It could be no other.

The discretion is, of course, further shaped by perspective. The dominant
themes in *Light Shining* might be familiar; the relation of liberty, property and religion.[125] But Churchill's interpretation of 1647 is set by the
more immediate context of 1976. As we have already noted the landscape of
seventeenth-century history in the 1970s assumed a romantic hue. The idea
that the 'causes' of the English revolution might be socio-economic chimed
with the dominant mood in much historical scholarship, and it chimed with
the political mood too, at least amongst left-wing intellectuals. Radical sects,
most prominently the Levellers and Diggers, were celebrated for the integrity
and courage of their incipient socialist credentials. The Putney debates represented a defining moment in this history; bearing comparison perhaps with
the Philadelphian 'moment' of 1776. It is hardly surprising that Churchill
was inspired; the ideals were noble, the failure heroic, and the resonance
irresistible. Socialist history often assumes a Whiggish veneer, militating
naturally towards the romantic. *Light Shining* does.

At the same time though, Churchill's appreciation of history is rather
more subtle. Her subsequent comments regarding the inadequacy of the
'simple Cavaliers and Roundheads history taught at school' assume a readily
revisionist tone. Such history, she continued, 'hides the complexity of the
aims and conflicts of those to the left of Parliament', so that: 'We are told
of a step forward to today's democracy but not of a revolution that didn't
happen; we are told of Charles and Cromwell but not of the thousands of

---

[123] For the attribution, see Churchill, 'Introduction' to *Light Shining*, in *Plays 1*, at 184.
Coppe had formerly served as a Baptist chaplain in the New Model, but in 1647 he had
been visited by God during a four-day trance. His tract was published in December 1649.
By March he was, as a consequence, incarcerated in Newgate prison, whilst his *Fiery Roll*
was being burnt by the public hangman. Coppe recanted a year later and was released. He
then disappeared from history until after the Restoration when he re-emerged as a physi-
cian named 'Dr Higham'. Clarkson also reinvented himself as medical man, of a kind, as
we shall shortly see.

[124] The bringing together of real and fictional characters is definitively Brechtian, as a number
of critics have noted. See Howard, 'On owning and owing', 39.

[125] See here Luckhurst, 'On the challenge of revolution', 59.

men and women who tried to change their lives.' The latter observation, necessarily sceptical again, reinforces the particular aspiration to write history 'from below', to raise the voice of the silenced majority: 'Though nobody now expects Christ to make heaven on earth, their voices are surprisingly close to us'.[126] Here again, it is an aspiration which, to various degrees, might be termed both revisionist and romantic. It is also rather obviously poethical.

It is for this reason perhaps that the scenes drawn from Churchill's imagination are at least as interesting as those which are recast from original documentary sources. And the characters she imagines, much indeed like those she reinvests from history, are animated by the same shared and consuming necessity; to eat and to pray.[127] In some cases, it is the former which matters most. In one early scene, the vagrant Margaret Brotherton is brought before the justices for begging. Later she encounters another man who has 'tenpence'. It seems like riches. He offers one of his pennies if she will 'lie' with him (197–8). In another, a group of women break into a deserted house and steal blankets and a mirror. In still another, a desperate mother leaves her baby on the steps of a rich man's house in the hope that he will take it in (226–7). As we noted before there was nothing particularly original, in 1976, in suggesting that economic necessity drove political unrest in mid-seventeenth-century England. But what Churchill can do is use her dramatic licence to articulate the personal experience of dispossession and despair. And more particularly, of course, the female experience. *Light Shining* is not perhaps an 'overtly' feminist play in the same way as *Vinegar Tom*; but it is, all the same, a feminist play.[128]

It is faith which provides consolation, and hope. Star, the corn merchant, uses prayer meetings to recruit soldiers, tempting them with the prospect of a ready wage and the thought that they will be doing God's work. Star has read his 'true' Leveller tracts. He knows that his language and his laws have been corrupted. All the 'Norman words' (198): 'Even the laws of this country aren't written in English' (199). It is against the Normans that they are still fighting, and for God:

> You are fighting an invasion of your own soil. Parliament is Saxon. The
> Army is Saxon. Jesus Christ is Saxon. The Royalists are Norman and the

---

[126] Churchill, 'Introduction' to *Vinegar Tom*, in *Plays 1*, 183.

[127] A coincidence that finds a striking expression in a later scene where Hoskins invests spirituality in an apple which is then shared by the characters, in a gesture loaded with the symbolism of community. For a commentary see S. Pocock, 'God's in This Apple: Eating and Sprituality in Churchill's *Light Shining in Buckinghamshire*' 50 *Modern Drama* 2007, especially 69–74.

[128] See Reinelt, 'Churchill', 176.

Normans are Antichrist. We are fighting to be free men and to own our own land ... We're Christ's saints. It's an army that values godliness. There's no swearing. The men don't like swearing. They like reading their Bibles. They like singing hymns. They like talk. We don't discourage talk. (199)

Others do. Brotherton is silenced in court. It is not her place to speak; Churchill leaving an ellipsis where she might have done (194). Hopkins is thrown out of church when she challenges the preacher's Calvinist prejudices. God may be everywhere, but He is not always easy to understand, and neither is His scripture. It is Claxton who rescues Hopkins when she is chased out of the church and beaten. She too is 'travelling', not as a 'beggar' but as a lay preacher (203–4).

Claxton and Cobbe take the audience to the radical edges of millenarian mysticism. The play opens with Cobbe praying, as the Chorus sings from *Isaiah* 24:17–20. Later an actor reads extracts from Coppe's *Flying Fiery Roll*, which insinuated a parallel between the author's experience of divine visitation and that of the prophet Ezekiel. The claim to be acting as a consequence of divine instruction distinguished the 'True' Leveller, or so Coppe liked to think. Winstanley claimed the same. Whilst in 'a trance', he recorded in his 1649 tract *The New Law of Righteousness*, 'I heard these words, Worke together. Eat bread together; declare this all abroad'[129] He had gone to George Hill and done just that. The second Act opens with a reading from Winstanley's account of the settlement, *The True Levellers Standard Advanced*, and confirmation that Cromwell's troopers had duly arrived and razed it to the ground. Cobbe has received a similar instruction, albeit to a different destination. 'Go to London, to London, that great city, and tell them that I am coming', God had told him in a dream, and 'write, write, write' (206).[130] This was 'true' levelling as opposed to 'sword levelling'; praying, writing, digging (231). Claxton meanwhile has taken to wandering from village to village, rushing on to the 'infinite nothing that is called God' (221). Churchill concludes *Light Shining* with Claxton musing on his fate and that of the revolution. He has left England for Barbados but 'sometimes hears from the world I have forsaken'. It is still 'fraught with tidings of the same clamour, strife and contention'. 'There is an end of perfection. There may be a time'. But for now, the former 'Captain of the Rant' is left with the simple consolation of quiet reflection. His 'great desire is to see and say nothing' (241).

---

129 In Hughes, 'Diggers', 227.

130 Churchill extracts from the original text of *Fiery Flying Roll*. The closing injunction to 'write, write, write' is omitted from the play, but is quoted in Hughes, 'Diggers', 227.

It is tempting to assume Claxton has, at least, retained his faith. Faith matters because it is faith which permits hope, despite everything. *Light Shining* is a chronicle of 'failure', of debates lost and dreams dashed.[131] The Levellers are brutally suppressed, Winstanley and his Diggers chased off George Hill, the Ranters sent scurrying from parish to parish. Allusions are made to executions of Leveller agitators following incipient mutinies at Corkbush in November 1647 and then again at Bishopsgate and Burford in spring 1649 (222–3). Churchill provides a brief account of the funeral of Robert Lockyer, at which it was reported that four thousand attended, fixing green markers in their hats to show their support for Leveller principles (228).[132] History does not always permit a happy ending; though it does relish martyrs. In place of idealism and democracy comes 'an authoritarian parliament, the massacre of the Irish, the development of capitalism'.[133] It is for this reason that the apostasy of Star the corn merchant matters far more than the fate of Lockyer the martyred Leveller. The formerly militant Star leaves the play in conversation with the local vicar, trying to explain why his plans for enclosing and cultivating the common are different from the kind of enclosures favoured by 'the old squire'. Some of the rhetoric might have resonated with Winstanley's writings; the consequence would not. The vicar hardly cares. He just likes the idea of driving away the squatters (224–6). It is men like Star who will progress the agricultural revolution of the eighteenth century and lay the seeds for the industrial revolution of the nineteenth.

But all this does not preclude hope and charity; not entirely. Humanity endures. The penultimate scene is set in a tavern. They pray together, crack some jokes, and share food and remembrances. Their mood is mixed, angry and resentful. There will be 'justice' when 'every judge is hanged' (230). They remember all the fallen Leveller martyrs. But the anger is tempered. There is belief. 'Christ the chief of Levellers is at the door', Cobbe assures them (231). Hoskins confirms the same. He is 'coming in clouds of glory in a garment dyed red with blood' (233). Towards the end, they sing verses from *Ecclesiastes* 5: vii-ix, xii. The 'profit of the earth is for all'. It is a gesture of defiance. They know the moment has passed. A little later, Hoskins wonders if Christ 'did come and nobody noticed' (240). But there will be another moment. They

---

[131] See Aston, *Stage*, 19, aligning *Light Shining* with two other plays about the 'possibility' of revolution, *The Hospital*, based on the writings of Frantz Fanon, and *Mad Forest*, which was inspired by the revolution against the Romanian revolution in 1989.

[132] Lockyer was executed following the Bishopsgate mutiny, shot in the square before St Paul's Cathedral. Leveller papers proudly claimed that twice as many had joined his funeral procession as had that of King Charles a few weeks earlier.

[133] Churchill, 'Introduction', 183.

have to believe that. The 'spirit' of God is 'in us, and its getting stronger and stronger' (233). It is a matter of patience and faith. And it is a test. For one thing, they now know; before they can 'become perfect Christ', they must first find and then 'cast out' the 'Antichrist' (234).

Vinegar Tom

In a sense, the finding did not take long. He was after all everywhere present and a month later discovered on stage at the Humberside Theatre in Hull. It was here that Churchill's *Vinegar Tom* was first performed, in October 1976. As we have already noted, witchcraft plays frame a peculiar genre of their own in modern feminist theatre. Churchill records being first approached by Monstrous Regiment earlier in the spring of 1976 with the idea of writing a witchcraft play.[134] The moment was propitious. She had just agreed to write *Light Shining* for Joint Stock, and the idea of writing a companion piece which fleshed out its feminist implications was irresistible. As was the case with *Light Shining*, and as was her habit, Churchill researched extensively, drawing considerably from both contemporary and secondary historical sources.[135] And she made a critical intellectual choice. Leaving 'aside the interesting theory that witchcraft had existed as a survival of suppressed pre-Christian religions' she 'went instead for the theory that witchcraft existed in the minds of its persecutors', making an immediate parallel with other familiar historical 'scapegoats', such as 'Jews and blacks'. In doing so, Churchill aligned herself with a more obviously sceptical and feminist historicism.[136] She might, in anticipation of the later mysticism written into *The Skriker*, have conjured all kinds of spirits. But she did not. The witches who populate *Vinegar Tom* are not witches at all. They are simply women who have been cast to the 'edges of society', fated to live at a particular moment of historical instability. She 'wanted to write a play about witches with no witches in it; a play not about evil, hysteria and possession by the devil but about poverty, humiliation and prejudice, and how the women accused of witchcraft saw themselves'.[137] *Vinegar Tom* is a dramatic, distinctively feminist, expression of 'history from below'.

But it can also be read as a modern contribution to a much older dramatic tradition. Critics have liked to read an ironic and humanising

---

[134] For commentary here see Z. Ravari, '*Vinegar Tom*: Women's Oppression through Patriarchal-Capitalist Dominations', 2 *Review of European Studies* 2010, 154–5.

[135] On the extent of Churchill's research, for all her history plays, see Aston and Diamond, 'Churchill', 7.

[136] For an appreciation of the critical distinction between the two plays, see Aston, *Stage*, 29.

[137] Churchill, 'Introduction' to *Vinegar Tom*, in *Plays 1*, 129–30.

impulse into a number of contemporary witchcraft plays written in the first part of the seventeenth century, such as Middleton's *The Witch* and Dekker and Ford's *The Witch of Edmonton*.[138] And with the irony and the humanising, they suggest, comes a nascent feminism. The plays tend to be about the female experience for the simple and prosaic reason that most witches were women. The primary characters in Churchill's play are most definitely female.[139] *Vinegar Tom* moves around the cases of Joan and her daughter Alice, Alice's friend Susan, and Ellen a local 'cunning' woman. Each is accused of witchcraft. Of course, it becomes quickly apparent that there is nothing satanic going on in *Vinegar Tom*, not much that is even very terrifying. But there is a series of unhappy coincidences, of calves dying and milk not churning, of trees falling down and children stillborn. And there is an awful lot of careless 'gossiping' (143).

In this sense, the world of *Vinegar Tom* seems rather ordinary. But it is also, of course, extraordinary; for it is a world in which the 'charms' of a cunning woman are believed to prevent pregnancy, cure 'heartache' and impotence, lift existing spells and maybe even kill an unwanted lover (145, 148, 155). But more dangerously it is also a world in which rats and spiders are 'imps' and cows are believed to be enchanted by cats, where suspects are pricked for marks, and where innocent women are strung up because they are supposed to have compacted with the Devil (157, 172). It is a world in which there are witches because witches are needed, more than ever. In a world 'turned upside down' the fantastic can explain the otherwise inexplicable. When the accusers Margery and Jack visit Ellen the 'cunning' woman they are invited to look in a 'cloudy glass'. They 'see' Joan; or rather they see what they 'come to see' (158).

Whilst *Vinegar Tom* is primarily about women, male characters like Jack have a necessary function. There cannot be misogyny without men. Impotent and angry, Jack prefers to think that he is 'bewitched' by Alice, rather than being punished by God for his lust (152–3, 158–9). And there is, of course, Packer the 'famous finder of witches'. Packer may be a bit pricey, at 'twenty shillings a time', but like Hopkins and Stearne he has an enviable record, having had 'above thirty hanged in the country round' (164, 168). He shares the same sense of missionary zeal too, gesturing to the consequence of the larger commonwealth beyond the pages of *Vinegar Tom*. The fate of the 'kingdom' is at stake. If the diabolical 'infection' is not purged, England will be shortly 'overrun' with witches (167). It is Packer who 'pricks' Joan and Alice,

---

[138] Neumeier, 'Witch', 34–42, 52–4.
[139] See here Aidseshiah, 'Space', 20–4.

assisted by Goody the 'searcher' who 'holds' them fast (165). Goody could have pricked too.[140] But Churchill prefers a man, in her prefatory comments keen to emphasise that the 'pricking scene is one of humiliation rather than torture', and it is all the more humiliating for being undertaken by Packer, 'an efficient professional, not a sadistic maniac'.[141] 'Miss' Betty, who refuses to marry as she should, is treated in much the same way by the Doctor, 'tied to chair' and bled and blistered in the hope that it will cure her rebellion, or at least terrify her into obedience (149). Deploying a distinctively Foucauldian rhetoric, Churchill has the bodies of both 'invaded', and taken 'away'.[142]

Alice has of course been pricked before, in the very opening scene, by the Man. The manner of penetration might be slightly different, but the humiliation amounts to much the same. In some ways, the generic 'Man' assumes a similar role to Packer; the two oddly aligned by a shared antagonism. Both are invaders, and not just of Alice's body. Both bring a sense, however dim, of a larger commonwealth and a larger confusion. But whereas Packer pretends to bring order and reassurance, the Man gestures to the radicalism of London 'tavern' talk, to ideas of sexual and political liberation. Tempted by both Calvinism and Catholicism, but also by the kind of Ranter radicalism which finds expression in *Light Shining*, the Man is clearly finding life in a 'world turned upside down' thoroughly unsettling. The image of the burning 'witch' haunts him (136–7). In their different ways, both Packer and the Man might have stepped into the pages of *Light Shining*. It is not that far from *Vinegar Tom* to Putney. They would have stood on different sides of the church hall, and there would not have been much upon which they agreed. But there is a pleasing conceit in imagining their presence, lurking in the background, casting their various aspersions.

Back in the world of *Vinegar Tom*, however, their shared purpose is to inflict violence on Alice. The Man teases Alice with the thought that she has fornicated with the Devil. Alice has certainly come across devils before, all the various 'clergy and gentlemen' who, it might be surmised, have already pricked her (135). And part of her might believe in the Devil too. Interested in 'potions' and charms', fascinated by stories of witches 'flying' (136–7). But the other part does not. The opening scene reinforces two defining and complementary themes; scepticism and sexuality. Alice has not compacted with the Devil. She has just slept with a stranger. It might still be a 'sin', but it is not a satanic one. And neither is it new. She knows what a man feels like

---

[140] It was not uncommon for 'searchers' to serve as 'prickers' too, as we have already noted. See here Fletcher, *Gender*, 259–60.

[141] Churchill, *Plays 1*, 134.

[142] For the Foucauldian resonance, see Reinelt, 'Churchill', 178–9.

on top of her, she has 'been hurt by men' before, and she already has a child without a 'father' (135). Later Packer will condemn her for precisely this; evidence of a diabolic sexuality. The Man disappears from the play at the end of the scene, dismissing Alice as nothing more than a common 'whore' (137). But he has left his 'mark', and not just on Alice.

The abuse of Alice is the first in a sequence of violations which will be visited upon the women of *Vinegar Tom*. Along with sex comes marriage; and here the violations are familiar indeed. In *Vinegar Tom*, there is the matter of Miss Betty's anxieties regarding her prospective marriage. The anticipation of violence is just as terrifying as its infliction; for along with marriage comes, inevitably, the wife-beating. Joan was beaten by her husband, and there are the same intimations in the troubled marriage of Margery and Jack (141). Susan views the fact that she has not been beaten, yet, as some kind of miracle. Neither is it the only pain which sex and marriage imports. With three babies already and three miscarriages Susan dreads the prospect of childbirth. As a consequence, she gets a 'potion' from Ellen the 'cunning' women in the hope that it might make her abort (147, 155–6).[143] Witchcraft manuals warned gentlemen about women such as Susan and Ellen and their connivances. It is why they had to be watched so closely; monitored not just for what they did and where they went, but also for what they said.

The relation of violence and voice is common in Churchill's writings, importing a necessarily testamentary dimension, and with it a whole range of further ambiguities.[144] It finds expression in *Light Shining* when Hopkins justifies her decision to depart her church with the simple declamation: 'It's a man wrote the bible' (236). The ambiguity is evident in Margaret Brotherton's despairing confession 'I'm wicked, all women are wicked', shortly after which she ventures that critical step which could so easily lead to the hangman's noose. She has sinned, she confesses, because 'the devil's got me' (236–7). Margaret was safer when she said nothing. Self-incriminatory testaments, as we have already noted, were far from uncommon in contemporary accounts. Margaret escapes; because she is in a different play. Susan, who makes the same confession in *Vinegar Tom*, does not. She blames herself for her abortion and Alice for encouraging her: 'I'm wicked. You're wicked' (162). Shortly afterwards, a hysterical Susan denounces Alice, relating how she 'did uncleanness' with the Devil and sought to learn her 'wicked magic' from the 'cunning' woman Ellen (167). The evidence is damning, literally.

---

[143] For a commentary on Susan as 'failed mother', see Ravari, 'Dominations', 157.
[144] See here Ravari, 'Dominations', 155–6.

And it also damns Susan. It is not just that she killed her baby, but that she 'cursed' it (167). Susan is accepting: 'I was a witch and never knew it. I killed my babies' (174). Joan is accepting too. 'I been a witch these ten years', she informs Packer, before she fantasises a series of past diabolical triumphs (173). There is defiance here, as there is in Alice's anger: 'I am not a witch. But I wish I was. If I could live I'd be a witch now after what they've done' (175). Alice leaves the play as she arrived; tormented by the irreconcilable temptations of scepticism and Satanism.

Women implicated themselves, and they implicated other women. As Joan and Ellen are hanged, Margery prays her thanks to God, and to Packer, 'for saving us' (174). It is possible to read into Margery the anxieties of an incipient capitalist, for whom financial stability in an increasingly unstable environment consumes any countervailing sense of humanity.[145] Goody the 'searcher' spotted a job opportunity too, in the same difficult market. Humanity is variable, context presses. People say and do all kinds of things. Language can be liberating, but it can also be dangerous. London 'tavern' talk is dangerous, so too Leveller manifestos and Ranter tracts on free love. *Light Shining* is again full of this kind of talk. But casual asides are just as dangerous; as Margaret Brotherton nearly discovered. Miss Betty wants to jump off a tree and 'fly' away from a marriage she dreads (140). She escapes the noose because she is 'Miss' Betty, and because the Doctor thinks he can make her 'better' (169). Joan is not so lucky. A casual curse is enough to send her to the gallows. She damns Margery's 'butter to hell' (145). Alice is brought down in the same way, chattering away as she sticks pins in a 'mud man'. It is just a bit of fun, she tells a horrified Susan, 'just words' (163). But it is again enough to hang her and Susan.

The ambivalence of language finds its sharpest, most gruesomely ironic, expression in the penultimate scene, orchestrated by Kramer and Sprenger, the authors of the infamous *Malleus*. Most women are witches because they are 'credulous' and have 'slippery tongues', and they like sex too much (177). They fornicate their way and gossip each other to the gallows. The presence of Kramer and Sprenger is necessarily disruptive, reinforcing another critical theme in the play; the disruption of time and place. In the original production of the play, Churchill had them performed as an Edwardian music hall act. The songs which recur throughout the play serve much the same purpose; a 'kind of Brechtian cabaret', as Janelle Reinelt suggests, which by 'catapulting the historical references in the drama into the present' serve to 'enable

---

[145] Though it is also possible to read into Margery the mindset of the puritan 'automaton'. For the alternatives see Solomon, 'Witches', 51–2, and also Ravari, 'Dominations', 161.

spectators to see both change and continuities'.[146] Here again, the violence is both temporal and testamentary. According to Sue Todd, who played Susan in the original production, the purpose of the songs was to disrupt, to emphasise that the material was 'combative' and 'anguished' and that it defied temporality.[147] Churchill closes the play with two songs, between which she places Kramer and Sprenger's performance. Both are intended to drive home the historical parallels.

The first is the 'Lament for the Witches'.

> Where have the witches gone?
> Who are the witches now?
> Here we are . . .
> Look in the mirror tonight.
> Would they have hanged you then?
> Ask how they are stopping you now.
> Where have the witches gone? (175–6)

One way they are 'stopping you now' is the same way women have always been stopped:

> The witches hanging the sky
> Haunt the courts where lawyers lie. (175)

The second song 'Evil Women' is no less bitter and just as resonant.[148] It concludes:

> Evil women
> Is that what you want?
> Is that what you want to see?
> On the movie screen
> Of your own wet dream
> Evil women
> Evil women
> Women. (179)

The insinuation is patent. The 'evil' woman is a sexualised construct, and a violent construct, and it is constructed by men; priests, lawyers, farmers, wife-beaters, theatre-goers. It was in 1645 and it is still.

---

[146] Reinelt, 'On feminist and sexual politics', 23.
[147] Margaret Todd, quoted in Reinelt, 'On feminist and sexual politics', at 23.
[148] Solomon, 'Witches', 53.

Legacy

Some things stay the same, and some things change; most things do both. There is, of course, a necessary irony in the fact that Churchill's two 'revolutionary' plays should themselves assume the shape of historical documents. But half a century is a long enough time. England has changed since 1976, the 'history' of the seventeenth century has changed, and Churchill has changed. The 'causes' of the English revolution have never been more hotly contested, nor the consequences. Certainly, the inexorable march of revisionism has made more 'romantic' histories of the period seem antiquated, and whilst the religious dimension of the English revolution has never been more fashionable, the socio-economic has rarely been so studiously neglected. It was fear of God, not fear of famine, which made the English revolution; or so we now prefer to believe. God was present in *Light Shining* of course. But He struggled to impose himself on all the proto-socialist romanticism. And it was the Antichrist who stole the show in *Vinegar Tom*. This is not to make the facile suggestion that Churchill's history was somehow mistaken or misjudged. It is simply to suggest that it was of a time.

History has moved on, and so has Churchill, who moved away from 'workshop' drama during the 1990s. The writing might be different now, but here again, some things have stayed the same. The political imperative has certainly remained, and the feminism. And some things have grown; not least Churchill's reputation. Max Stafford-Clarke has teasingly referred to the canonisation of 'Saint Caryl'. The American actor and writer Wallace Shawn has likened himself to being inducted into a devotional cult.[149] In rather more sober terms, Mark Ravenhill has recently suggested that no British playwright is currently 'regarded with more affection and respect by her peers'.[150] The evident risk, as Dan Rabellato has recently suggested, is that Churchill's work might almost transcend the possibility of critical appraisal.[151] It should not, of course. And it does not. There is plenty of Churchill criticism.

It is interesting to trace the respective, and very differing, critical fates of her two 'revolutionary' plays. Dramatic fashion changes too. This is most evident perhaps in the case of *Light Shining*. In a sense, it has lost little of its prescience. In the opinion of Mary Luckhurst, its 'contemporary relevance' is 'striking'.[152] Michael Billington similarly attests to the 'brilliance' of a

---

[149] Observing 'we members have a special handshake'. In Rabellato, 'On Churchill's influences', 165.

[150] See Rabellato, 'On Churchill's influences', 163.

[151] In Rabellato, 'On Churchill's influences', 163–4.

[152] M. Luckhurst, 'On the challenge of revolution', in Aston and Diamond, *Churchill*, 62.

play that continues to be 'both historically informative and suffused with contemporary relevance'.[153] The original conceit that the compromised state of left-wing politics in 1970s England might be attributed to the failure of revolution three centuries earlier was still credible.[154] Billington was certainly persuaded. In its moment, *Light Shining* was definitive, one of the 'best plays of the decade', 'like all good history plays' finding 'in the past a metaphor for the present'.[155] At the same time though he also noted its apparent demise; 'never revived, never discussed'.[156] And he was right. The relative neglect of *Light Shining* was remarkable. The moment had seemed to pass, much as it had seemed at the end of the play indeed. The reality of the Thatcherite government during the 1980s brought new challenges. The modern Labour party mutated dramatically during the 1990s. The pending Blairite revolution seemed to matter more than the nearly-forgotten Leveller. It is only very recently, most obviously with the 2015 production at the Lyttelton Theatre, that the neglect has been redressed. Billington was one of many admirers a version of the play which assumed 'epic' proportions. At the same time though he also noted that it was, in a sense, a different play. Back in 1976, Churchill cast six actors. The 2015 production found employment for sixty-two.[157]

The fate of *Vinegar Tom*, which conversely does not even merit a mention in Billington's magisterial account, has been different. It has been repeatedly revived, not just in various London and provincial theatres but in countless school and youth productions up and down the country. It is a frequent visitor to many GCSE and A-Level syllabuses too, and not a few University curricula. The first generation of critics might have moved on, but their successors continue to encounter *Vinegar Tom* for the first time. And it has certainly lost little of its larger thematic consonance. The persecution of witches might have ceased, symbolically closed with the repeal of the 1604 Act in 1736. But the persecution of women did not. Lynching would continue well into the eighteenth century. Incidences of rape, sexual assault and domestic violence continue to this day; and they are not occasional. This historical par-

---

[153] Billington, *State*, 269.

[154] Acknowledged by Churchill in her 'Introduction' to *Vinegar Tom*, in *Plays 1*, at 183.

[155] Billington, *State*, 269.

[156] Billington, *State*, 271.

[157] Interestingly whilst expressing his approval of the production Billington maintained that the play, in his opinion, worked best when 'presented with a minimalist austerity that matches Churchill's text'. See M. Billington, 'Light Shining in Buckinghamshire review – Caryl Churchill's portrait of a historic moment for England', available at <https://www.theguardian.com/stage/2015/apr/24/light-shining-in-buckinghamshire-review-caryl-churchill> (last accessed 26th June 2020).

allel is just as credible today as it was in 1976. And the dramatic consequence is undeniable too. It is not just that *Vinegar Tom* stimulated a sub-genre of modern witchcraft plays, each written to the same larger purpose, but in the very fact of its writing, the play presented a historiographical challenge.[158] The gendered nature of witchcraft history remains conspicuous; not simply that it is a history of gendered persecution, but that it has, like most history, been written by men.[159] This does not make it bad history. But it does again remind us that all history is prejudiced, dramatic or otherwise.

Light Shining and *Vinegar Tom* are then different in their particular histories. They are different in other ways too. The documentary element is more evident in *Light Shining*. It could even be termed a 'state of the nation' play. Conversely, *Vinegar Tom* is very obviously animated by a feminist impulse which assumes a more incidental presence in *Light Shining*. But there is still more that is the same. Churchill only rarely gives interviews. But on one occasion, when asked that most difficult of questions, what does she write about, she replied 'power, powerlessness, exploitation, people's longings, obsessions, dreams'.[160] In simpler terms, she writes about the relation of the political and personal. *Light Shining* and *Vinegar Tom* are both about this, and when read together more so still. Half a century on it might still be argued that there are no better examples of how this conjunction plays out than in the two plays which Churchill set in the 'upside down' England of the mid-seventeenth century.

---

[158] See here Rabellato, 'On Churchill's influences', 173–4, commenting in particular on its evident influence in Daniels's *Byrthrite*

[159] See here Ditz, 'History', 23–5.

[160] In Rabellato, 'On Churchill's influences', 168.

4

Uneasy Heads

Howard Brenton's *55 Days* was first performed at the Hampstead Theatre in October 2012.[1] Its subject-matter is the events which led up to the execution of Charles I on 30th January 1649. The fifty-five days referent establishes dramatic, and in a sense, historical margins. Fifty-five days earlier the Army, under the instruction of Cromwell's son-in-law Henry Ireton, had purged Parliament, removing those Presbyterian MPs who had rejected an Army proposal to put the King on trial.[2] It has become known as Pride's Purge, so named after the Colonel who commanded the troops who barred entry to the Commons. These margins are not, of course, stable; historical margins rarely are. The events which led up to the execution of the King can be traced long before 6th December 1648, and their consequences were to be felt long after the 30th January. But the historical focus serves its purpose; concentrating our attention on the days and weeks which led up to one of the most dramatic moments in English history.

We have, of course, already glanced at this moment, the broader context at least, in the previous chapter. The 'great seventeenth century time', as Charles Dickens liked to term it, full of gay cavaliers wearing improbably

---

[1] Directed by Howard Davies, whose work attracted particular critical approval; 'excellent' according to Michael Billington in the *Guardian*. See <https://www.theguardian.com/stage/2012/oct/25/55-days-review> (last accessed 26th June 2020).

[2] The proposal was contained in a document entitled the *Remonstrance of the Army*. It was largely drafted by Ireton. Forty-one MPs were detained by the Army on 6th December, being first held in a cell at Westminster and then removed to a couple of local taverns. The rest were merely told to go home. The most famous of the detainees was the preacher William Prynne, a long-standing critic of Army radicalism. It was, according to one recent commentator, a 'very English coup'. The definitive account remains D. Underdown, *Pride's Purge: Politics in the Puritan Revolution*, (Oxford UP, 1985), 143–72. See also G. Robertson, *The Tyrannicide Brief*, (Vintage, 2006), 118, and also T. Royle, *Civil War: The Wars of the Three Kingdoms 1638–1660*, (Little Brown, 2004), 474–8, 484–5, and A. Fraser, *Cromwell: Our Chief of Men*, (Mandarin, 1989), 270–1.

feathered hats, and dour-faced looking roundheads wandering the country smashing church-windows. The especial place of the civil wars in our historical consciousness is unarguable. As Blair Worden has recently suggested, much of English intellectual history over the last four centuries can be written in terms of a defining dispositional dichotomy; between those who, to borrow from Sellars and Yeatman's glorious pastiche, *1066 and All That*, might be termed 'Wrong but Wromantic' and those who were 'Right but Repulsive'.[3] Cavaliers and Roundheads. We might wonder where Brenton fits in this disposition. That theatre's 'history man', as Michael Billington terms him, should turn his attention to the moment is no surprise; the 'chief chronicler of the nation's past' possessed of a peculiar 'genius for turning the history of ideas into powerful drama'.[4] The 'tragedy' of King Charles I has transfixed plenty of poets before, and will likely continue to do so for the centuries to come.

What kind of 'history man' is, of course, another matter, for writing history is never simply a matter of chronicling things that happened. Critics have tended to prefer a revisionist Brenton, someone who 'deconstructs history', who is attracted to moments of 'rupture'.[5] And there are of course few more such dramatic moments than late morning on 30th January 1649. And yet, whilst there is much about the events of that moment which seems sudden, not least the idea of bringing the King to trial, there is also and always a longer story. Radical writing, as David Edgar has suggested, is no less radical for being written as part of a 'grand narrative' There is here a further context. *55 Days* is a sequel. Two years earlier, in July 2010, Brenton's *Ann Boleyn* was first performed at Shakespeare's Globe Theatre. It and *55 Days* are two parts of a larger dramatic chronicle, investigating the consequences of the English reformation. Much of *Ann Boleyn* actually moves around the antics of a slightly comic King James I. A monarch who has struggled to excite later historians in quite the same way as his fated son. Interesting for constitutional lawyers though. The origins of modern judicial review are often traced back to his dispute with Lord Chief Justice Sir Edward Coke, in cases such those of

---

[3] B. Worden, *Roundhead Reputations: The English Civil Wars and the Passions of Posterity*, (Penguin, 2001), 4–6.

[4] See <http://www.theartsdesk.com/theatre/55-days-hampstead-theatre> (last accessed 26th June 2020); <http://www.timeout.com/london/theatre/55-days> (last accessed 26th June 2020); <http://www.theguardian.com/stage/2012/oct/25/55-days-review> (last accessed 26th June 2020).

[5] M. Zelenak, 'The Politics of History: Howard Brenton's Adaptations', 18 *Theatre* 1986, 55. A similar conclusion is ventured by Michael Patterson in his *Strategies of Political Theatre*, (Cambridge UP, 2003), at 100.

Prohibitions and *Commendams*.[6] No thrilling military engagements though, and he died, rather boringly, in his bed.

The strategy is of course intrinsically Whiggish, making the 'moment' of 30th January 1649 the product of a much longer imagining; much longer than fifty-five days. The English civil war, as Brenton appreciates, was 'a long time stirred'.[7] England decapitated its king because it had never properly reconciled itself to the consequences of what an earlier Cromwell, Thomas rather than Oliver, had chosen to do.[8] Reformation to civil war, and then on to the 'great and glorious' revolution of 1689. A very big history; which Brenton has to engage, like it or not. The civil wars, in this narrative, become wars of liberation, the execution of the King the moment when the essential principles of English constitutionalism were set down, the sovereignty of Parliament, the independence of the judiciary, the rule of law.[9] The purpose of this chapter is then to revisit a familiar moment in a very familiar history. And comprehend its writing. In a sense Brenton's play can be read, and indeed performed, as another piece of documentary drama; the documents, upon which Brenton draws, simply being that little bit older. But the provenance matters. Not just because it alters the authorial exercise, but because it changes the way in which the audience reads and watches. In the first part of this chapter, we are going to revisit the broader intellectual context; ground we covered, in a slightly different context, in the previous chapter. In the second we will take a closer look at the dramatic heart of *Fifty-Five Days*, an encounter between the two protagonists of the play, Charles and Oliver Cromwell. In the third, we will reflect on Brenton and the writing of history.

---

[6] See here G. Burgess, *The Politics of the Ancient Constitution: an Introduction to English Political Thought 1603–1642*, (Macmillan, 1992), 21–27, 72–8, and also *Absolute Monarchy*, 102–6, 156–9, 184–208.

[7] A point noted by Brenton in '55 Days'.

[8] The two were very distantly related, Oliver being descended from Thomas's sister, Katherine. Christopher Hill speculates that Oliver's reputation as an iconoclast may owe something to a broader popular confusion regarding the two Cromwells. See his *Englishman*, 262. For the revisionist argument see Wedgwood, *King*, 12.

[9] Albert Kiralfy famously concluded that it was the 'common law' which 'forged the axe which beheaded Charles I'. See his *Potter's Introduction to English Law and its Institutions*, (Sweet and Maxwell, 1958), 43. For accounts of these disputes see Robertson, *Brief*, 23–6, 148–9, suggesting the extent to which the final charge which was laid against Charles in January 1649 owed much to the arguments ventured by Coke against prerogative jurisdiction, and also 355–6 citing the similar conclusion of the great Whig historian G. M. Trevelyan in his *England under the Stuarts*, published in 1915: 'Never perhaps in any century have such rapid advances been made towards freedom'.

His Work

The grander constitutional visions so firmly embedded within Whig historiography repeatedly assume centre-stage in Brenton's chronicle; quite literally in Act 1 Scene 8 which revisits the Whitehall debates of 13th and 14th December 1648. As we have just intimated, this is familiar ground. The Whitehall debates represented, in a sense, a sequel to the Putney debates just over a year earlier. The tone of the debate had shifted slightly; a little less about property and constitution, and a little more about godliness, or the seeming lack of it. But it had not shifted that much. A proposal for greater religious toleration, included in a recently revised Leveller *Agreement of the People*, could never be detached from broader questions of government, of liberty of conscience, and the relation of 'the restrictive power and the compulsive power'.[10] And it is towards these that Brenton directs his audience's attention. The more esoteric theological questions are divested. Instead, Brenton takes the opportunity to establish political parameters; between the conservative Army officers and their more radical Leveller antagonists. Not all radicals thought the same, of course. Colonel Pride adopts a grimly prosaic attitude to the question of what to do with the King; 'Drag' him 'from his castle, and beat him to death' (45). A more considered radicalism finds a voice in John Lilburne, the author of the *Agreement*. It has been suggested that Lilburne is the real 'hero' of Brenton's play, perhaps indeed articulating the voice of his creator; a perception which led one reviewer to suppose that whilst the play was undoubtedly 'gripping' its author was evidently 'too much on the rebel's side'.[11] Perhaps; but then striking political balances has never really been Brenton's thing.

Lilburne's principal antagonist is Cromwell's son-in-law Henry Ireton, a common lawyer by training who had served as a parliamentarian general during the war. Ireton has little patience with Lilburne and his 'ragbag of followers' (49). In one sense, Lilburne and Ireton have much in common; both claim to be arguing the case for an English constitution. It is the interpretation of this constitution which divides. Ireton presumes to be arguing for the 'ancient' constitution, where power is balanced between Parliament and King.[12] Cromwell will appeal to the same kind of 'settlement' in his later,

---

[10] Woodhouse, *Puritanism*, 151.

[11] <http://www.timeout.com/london/theatre/55-days> (last accessed 26th June 2020).

[12] For a commentary on the contemporary 'politics' of the 'ancient' constitution, and more especially the place of 'balance', see Burgess, *Constitution*, 3–4, and also D. Smith *Constitutional Royalism and the Search for Settlement 1640–1649*, (Cambridge UP, 1994), 19–20, 62–4, 189, emphasising the extent to which moderate 'constitutional royalists' could be found subscribing to much the same idea of an 'ancient constitution'.

imagined, conversation with Charles; though, ever the pragmatist, he is not so inclined to couch his appeal in the same species of jurisprudential mysticism. If Charles agrees to be a 'constitutional monarch', Cromwell avers, he can at least save his neck. Charles however, by then relishing the idea of martyrdom, dismisses the idea with the pertinent question 'what newfangled thing is that?' (88)

The idea of restraining Parliament is similarly uncertain, as Ireton senses. There must be such 'restraints' because 'Rights must be protected' (45). When pressed on what he means by 'restraints', Ireton seeks recourse to the language of 'Checks and balances', implying that a purge might be justified on these terms (46). As a consequence, it is Ireton whom the Presbyterian William Prynne holds responsible for the 'rape' of Parliament on 6th December (18). Lilburne likewise holds Ireton responsible for the evolving events of late 1648, rejecting his interpretation of constitutional propriety. 'No man', he advises when asked whether the army should support a purge, 'should obey an order he thinks unjust' (15). Parliament is inviolable. There should be 'no other power in the land but Parliament'. Mindful no doubt of Ireton's famous injunction at Putney, that 'no person hath a right to' partake of government 'that hath not a fixed interest in this kingdom' Lilburne suggests that Ireton's idea of 'rights' is limited to the 'rights of landowners' (45).[13] Ultimately, however, as Cromwell intercedes, it is about 'stability'. The constitution exists not to facilitate democracy or equality, but to ensure the stability of the nation; for which reason the 'extremists' must be 'cast out' (48).[14]

The same arguments in regard to constitutional propriety and its interpretation animate the prospective trial of the King; 'that great work', as Cromwell was fond of calling it.[15] At the Whitehall debate, Harrison supposes that the King might be brought 'to justice, under the law'. Not everyone is convinced. And when evidence is uncovered of Charles's negotiations

---

[13]   As we noted in the previous chapter, the question of property loomed large at Putney, and was the subject of a renowned, and fierce, argument between Ireton and the radicals led by Colonel Rainborough, in whose opinion property law was the 'most tyrannical law under heaven'. Ireton repeatedly confirmed that he 'would have an eye to property', for 'The law of God doth not give me property, nor the law of Nature, but property is of human constitution'. The Leveller argument, to the contrary, was that property was given by God to be held in 'common'. See Woodhouse, *Puritanism*, 54, 57–61 and 69.

[14]   Such a perspective resonates with the supposition, advanced by the likes of Glenn Burgess, that the ancient constitution was really 'a model of legalism rather than constitutionalism'. See Burgess, *Absolute Monarchy*, 146–7, and also Smith, *Royalism*, 178–9, reaching much the same conclusion.

[15]   Robertson, *Brief*, 151.

with Ormonde, it still remains uncertain as to whether a king can commit 'treason against himself'. It is, as Ireton concedes, 'the conundrum of our time' (51). Harrison has a simple solution to such concerns. If the common law does not accommodate such a charge, then they should simply 'make a new law' (46).[16] Ireton is similarly adamant that there must be the pretence at least of 'a legal process', even if he is rather less keen on the idea that they might, if necessary, just invent a new law, and when he is found 'guilty', as must be the case, he can then be forced to 'come to an agreement'; a supposition that informed the *Remonstrance* which Ireton had drawn up a few weeks earlier (46–7).[17] Inevitably, after the customary squabbling, everyone defers to Cromwell, who silently nods his agreement.[18] And so the King will be tried before a court established at Westminster. It is 'decided', no matter how strongly the radicals protest (48). Lilburne remains opposed to the trial throughout the second Act precisely because it is premised on the authority of a 'purged Parliament' (77).[19] But it is not Lilburne's opinion that matters; it is Cromwell's.

These constitutional questions assume, quite literally, centre-stage during the second Act of the play; as, for the same reason, do the two leading lawyers, John Cooke, who served as chief prosecutor at the King's trial, and the Lord President of the Court, John Bradshaw.[20] The second Act opens with Cromwell and Bradshaw inviting Cooke to serve as Solicitor-General. Cromwell admires Cooke, as the man who defended Lilburne; though, with

---

[16] An attitude which leads Wedgwood to suppose that he is something of a 'fanatic'. See *King*, 26.

[17] For the idea that Ireton was the most urgent advocate of a public trial, see Robertson, *Brief*, 134. It was Ireton who found and then persuaded both Bradshaw and Cooke to assume the leading legal roles in proceedings.

[18] The same debate, regarding what to do about the King, had generated a similar amount of heat at Putney the year before; so much heat indeed that the note-taking had to be stopped. It is this note-taking which has, of course, in the form of the Clarke MSS, proved to be such a rich resource for later historians.

[19] On Lilburne's consistent objection to the trial see Wedgwood, *King*, 72–4. Aside from Lord Grey, other significant 'parliamentarian' opponents included Prynne and Algernon Sidney, whose exchange with Cromwell on the subject is renowned. 'First', Sidney observed, 'the King can be tried by no court; secondly, no man can be tried by this court'. To which Cromwell is recorded as having replied 'I tell you, we will cut off his head with the Crown upon it'. In Robertson, *Brief*, 139.

[20] Cooke has generally enjoyed a rather disparaging reputation down the centuries; perhaps because the history of the King's trial has been more commonly written by historians hostile to the regicide. Wedgwood was clearly discomforted by his 'ferocious zeal'. See her *King*, 114. For an alternative view see Robertson, *Brief*, commending at 1 the 'the bravest of all barristers'.

typical bluntness, he further admits that pretty much every other lawyer has run away.[21] The most striking aspect of this scene, however, is the intense religiosity, the sense of calling which each share. When, in the following scene, Fairfax expresses his disdain for men of such 'low' birth, Cromwell responds simply; they 'are doing His work upon Earth' (63). It is enough. England, fallen and 'ripped to bits', must be remade 'for ever' (64–5). They are not just trying a king; they are securing the redemption of a 'chosen' people. And it was for this reason that the 'tryal' of the king, as Milton later confirmed, had to be 'faire and op'n', in full view of the broader Christian world.[22]

It was not, however, easy. The decision to stage a public trial imports an obvious risk; that the scene is likely to be stolen by the best actor.[23] And it quickly becomes apparent that the best actor in Westminster Hall in early January 1649 is the accused, 'Charles Stuart, King of England' (68). Indeed, Brenton has subsequently confirmed that what attracted him to the idea of writing a play about the events of late 1648 and early 1649 was an initial reading of the trial transcripts and more particularly the 'eerily graceful lines' which were ascribed to the King.[24] As Colonel Harrison admits, having witnessed the King's performance on the first day of his trial, 'The public have never heard his voice before. Now they find that he speaks like an angel' (71). Ireton reaches the same conclusion: 'We have been ambushed. The King's sense of law is better than we thought. And his sense of expression' (72). And it is not simply a matter of poetry; there is theatricality too. Brenton incorporates a number of happenings familiar from these transcripts, including the dramatic moment when Charles tapped Cooke's shoulder with his cane as the

---

[21] Cooke was appointed following the last minute defection of the Attorney-General Anthony Steele, who pleaded ill-health. The nomination and attendance of those appointed as Commissioners was similarly affected. The vast majority of the 135 nominated Commissioners were drawn from the massed ranks of common law MPs. Roughly half attended the trial. Sixty-eight attended the first day of the trial, and the average daily attendance was around 60. In the end 59 signed the death-warrant. Amongst the most notable of the serial absenters was Fairfax, Cromwell's close friend Oliver St John, and Philip Skippon, a leading Parliamentary general who commanded the London militia. For commentaries here see Royle, *War*, 491–2, Wedgwood, *King*, 95–6, 108, and Robertson, *Brief*, 9–12, 144–5.

[22] See *Political Writings*, 33, and also Wedgwood, *King*, 93.

[23] And the best dressed actor. Charles had chosen his apparel carefully, clothed in black, the Order of the Star of the Garter prominent on his cloak and the bejewelled St George hanging from his neck on the order's blue ribbon.

[24] '*55 Days*: Will Mortimer interviews Howard Brenton', <https://www.hampsteadtheatre. com/news/2012/10/55-days-will-mortimer-interviews-howard-brenton/> (last accessed 26th June 2020).

charges were being read out. The top of the cane fell off and, when no one else rushed to pick it up, Charles was obliged to do so himself.[25] It is, despite the apparent indignity, another moment that Charles steals; everyone 'gasps' and the King on returning to his chair 'looks about with disdain'. 'I did not know the man was a play actor', Cromwell observes with a begrudging admiration; to which Ireton mutters in return 'We closed the theatres, we will close him' (68). The prose will, in the end, overcome the poetry. Ireton suggests that they abandon a public trial and continue 'in secret' (71). It is the lawyers, Cooke and Bradshaw, who protest: 'Justice must be seen to be done' (71).[26]

The charges duly read, Charles's primary strategy, as the same transcripts confirm, was to question the jurisdiction of the Court.[27] 'I would know by what power I am called here', he immediately responds, waving away Cooke's attempt to interject, 'let me know by what lawful authority I am seated here' (69). Rather than simply asserting their jurisdiction and moving on, Bradshaw and Cooke allow themselves to get distracted, and increasingly frustrated. They needed the King to plead to the charge. If he did not, then his guilt would be presumed, *pro confesso*; as the common law determined in cases of alleged treason. And if this was the case, the grander plans to parade a string of witnesses all evidencing the King's guilt would be thwarted.[28] But Charles refused. Once again, it seemed, the King had outmanoeuvred his prosecutors. Bradshaw's response is to assert that the accused has been 'brought here in the name of the people of England, of whom you are elected King, to answer them'. The argument, which resonated with nascent ideas of contractarian sovereignty, would have been familiar to readers of Milton and had been recommended by Cromwell at Putney, 'the King is King by contract'.[29] But it would still have seemed somewhat novel, and to many common lawyers both inside and outside Westminster Hall rather discomforting too; not least because of the uncertain consequences which might flow from any notional breach of trust.[30] Charles is contemptuous:

---

[25] For commentaries on this event see Royle, *War*, 494, Wedgwood, *King*, 127–8, and Robertson, *Brief*, 17, 154–5.

[26] An opinion they had both strongly argued during the various debates in late autumn 1648. See Robertson, *Brief*, 146–7

[27] In his recent account of the trial, Geoffrey Robertson refers to this as the 'King's gambit'. See his *Brief*, 6 and 155–8.

[28] In the end the witnesses, thirty-three in total, were called anyway. See Robertson, *Brief*, 171–3, and 188–90 noting that the principle of *pro confesso* would not be abrogated until 1827.

[29] See J. Somerville, 'Oliver Cromwell and English Political Thought', in J. Morrill, *Oliver Cromwell and the English Revolution*, (Longman, 1990), 237.

[30] See here Robertson, *Brief*, 125 and also 136 suggesting that the original idea, articulated in

'Elected? England was never an elective kingdom. It is an hereditary kingdom and has been for a thousand years' (70). Bradshaw would cling to the same argument throughout the trial, citing it in his final judgement.[31] And Charles would dismiss it with the same disdain, consistently demanding to be shown any 'legal warranty by the Word of God, the Scriptures, or the constitution of the Kingdom'. By now even Cromwell is troubled, and no longer prepared to leave matters to a providential throw of the 'dice', decides it is time to put a stop to matters, and the first trial scene is brought to a close (66, 70).[32]

Whilst Hugh Peter commends 'the more glorious beginning of the work', the Army leaders and the lawyers hurriedly convene to assess the damage and try to chart a new course.[33] But, as Cooke admits, 'We sail in uncharted waters' (73). Bradshaw agrees. Whilst tyrants have been removed by force before, and he cites Richard III as the prime example, 'never' before has an English king been removed by 'law' (73). Whilst Harrison and Ireton continue to argue the case for just making a 'new' law, Cooke is adamant that they must continue to 'act within the established common law' (73). As contemporary accounts confirm, here Cooke argued hard the distinction between the office and the person of the king; such that the person of a king might always be held accountable for tyrannical acts, regardless of whether his office might or might not be held inviolable.[34] Otherwise, as Speaker Lenthall confirms, the 'execution will be seen to be unlawful' and all credibility lost (73). It is Cromwell who concludes that they should simply carry on, advising the King that if he continues to refuse to plead, and thereby acknowledge the jurisdiction of the court, a plea will be entered for him. That way they should still be able to get it all done in time for an execution by the end of the week. Cooke demurs at the presumption. But there is no question, at least not in Cromwell's mind: 'We will get there in the end. Find him guilty, within the law' (75).[35]

---

the draft charge, that the King was somehow guilty for breaching his 'trust', was the 'sort of argument that might pass muster in a tavern, but not in a criminal court'.

[31] See here Robertson, *Brief*, 184–5.

[32] As Wedgwood concludes, it very quickly became apparent that the 'progress of the trial was little short of disastrous'. See *King*, 146, and for a similar conclusion, Hoyle, *War*, 494–6.

[33] There is no record of what happened at this session, for which reason Brenton can only surmise. For further conjectures, see Royle, *War*, 495–6 and Robertson, *Brief*, 160.

[34] See Robertson, *Brief*, 15–16, suggesting that Cooke was reaching towards the modern doctrine of 'command responsibility'.

[35] Although Brenton has Cooke demur at the presumption of guilt, Robertson notes subsequent testimony which suggests otherwise; that the Solicitor-General had assured a young George Starkey that 'The King must die, and monarchy die with him'. The testimony was produced at Cooke's later trial in 1660. See Robertson, *Brief*, 176, 312, 319–20.

As the court reassembles the same question dominates. 'A king', the King declares, 'cannot be tried by any superior jurisdiction on earth' (79). Neither can he be tried by his peers, as is the right of any Englishman; quite simply because the King has no 'peers'.[36] Bradshaw again struggles to assert himself, earning ridicule when he suggests that the King might be 'charged as a high delinquent' (79). Charles gets all the laughs, and when he again challenges the assertion that the Commons might be considered a 'court of judicature', there are cries of 'Justice! The King!' heard in the gallery. Another 'crack' in the case, as Ireton mutters to Cromwell (79–80). Proceedings are once again brought to a hurried close and the King is hustled away. Further discussions follow, at which it becomes apparent that Cromwell is losing patience, with the lawyers in particular. Bradshaw confesses that Charles is indeed right. The Commons is not a court of 'judicature'. 'What', an exasperated Cromwell responds, 'in the bowels of Christ, is that!' If the Commons is not now a court of law, it can be made one 'By Act of Parliament. In the morning' (81). Bradshaw and Cooke immediately consult on the possibility of a Chancery ordinance. Cromwell, however, is not inclined to waste any more time on 'quaint' legal devices. It is the 'future ground of England' that concerns him, the idea of making 'Parliament the most powerful thing in the land' (81). What matters is fulfilling the 'Lord God Almighty's purpose', not ferreting out common law precedents (82).[37]

The final trial scene, which takes place immediately after the imagined conversation between Charles and Cromwell, is shorter. The court reconvenes and Cooke reads out the opinion of the court, that 'the charge is true, as clear as crystal and as the sun that shines at noon', that Charles has been found 'guilty of a wicked design to introduce a tyrannical government, with himself at the head, in defiance of Parliament and its authority' (90). In response, Charles, as has been predicted, again challenges the jurisdiction of the court. On this occasion, however, he is silenced. Led by Cromwell, who senses an initial reluctance, the commissioners step forward in turn and

---

[36] This particular defence was recommended by Sir Orlando Bridgman, who served as one of Charles's principle legal advisers during the trial. Bridgman would subsequently return to centre-stage at the Restoration when he presided over the trial of the remaining regicides. See Wedgwood, *King*, 32, and Robertson, *Brief*, 123, 129.

[37] It was, as the radical preacher Hugh Peter confirmed outside Westminster, God's 'work' and it was 'glorious'. See Wedgwood, *King*, 134, and also Robertson, *Brief*, 71–2, contemplating the extent to which there was a broader discontent with the devices of the common law in early seventeenth-century England. Cromwell had read law at Cambridge, and yet his dismissal of legal devices is characteristic. For a commentary on this seeming ambiguity, see J. Morrill, 'The making of Oliver Cromwell' in Morrill, *Cromwell*, 23–4.

confirm Cooke's opinion. It is, Cromwell mutters, a 'cruel necessity' (91).[38] It is left to Cooke to confirm the sentence, that 'Charles Stuart shall be put to death, by severing his head from his body' (92).[39]

Uneasy Heads

The trial scenes reinforce a critical dramatic insight; that the larger questions of constitutional and religious settlement are calibrated by particularity, by particular human actors saying particular things and making particular choices at particular moments in history. Thirty years ago, Brenton identified himself with a species of 'new Jacobean' playwright in part because he was writing about the human experience of 'power and suffering'.[40] The same aspiration underpins *55 Days*. It is, after all, a drama, populated by particular characters. And they all suffer in different ways, sometimes majestically, sometimes more prosaically. Brenton's 'great' Fairfax is a broken man, so laid low by the 'burden' of office that he now resembles 'a walkin' skeleton' (13). The very first scene of *55 Days* reinforces the same juxtaposition; three 'bloody freezing' parliamentarian soldiers huddled over a fire contemplating what it means to be part of 'God's army, fighting for a new Jerusalem'(7–8). A few lines later, a young trooper wonders if the army really can purge a Parliament it has 'sworn to protect'. His older, more pragmatic companion in arms replies simply 'It's called politics boy' (12). The same essential tensions recur time and again in *55 Days*, between the poetry and the prose, the cavalier and the roundhead.

Ultimately however *55 Days* is about Charles and Cromwell, their very different perceptions and experiences of magistracy, and the conversation which Brenton, with the facility of dramatic license, fashions between them. This latter invention caused some critical consternation.[41] There were later

---

[38] The attribution of this particular phrase remains uncertain. It was first recorded by Alexander Pope, and was originally supposed to have been muttered by Cromwell on visiting the corpse of the King in the very early hours of the morning after his execution. There is no credible evidence that Cromwell did visit the corpse, still less make any comment. There again there is no hard evidence that he did not. See Robertson, *Brief*, 201, and Fraser, *Cromwell*, 293–4.

[39] The sentence was actually read out by Bradshaw, as President of the Court. He sought extensive recourse to Bracton, but also emphasised once again the rather more novel idea that the Crown was held in 'trust', as a 'contract and a bargain between the King and his people', and that this contract had been breached. See here Wedgwood, *King*, 159–61.

[40] Brenton, 'Red Theatre', 198.

[41] There again Quentin Letts in the *Daily Mail* recommended the play nevertheless for being 'balanced, serious' and 'interesting'. See <http://www.dailymail.co.uk/tvshowbiz/article-2223339/55–Days-theatre-review> (last accessed 26th June 2020).

rumours, chiefly propagated after the Restoration by royalist polemicists such as Clement Walker, that the King had indeed been approached, sometime around the 28th of January, with the offer of a conditional reprieve. But the reports did not suppose that Cromwell had carried the offer in person, nor indeed is there any credible evidence that anyone else carried such an offer.[42] Charles and Cromwell did meet in person, perhaps most notably in July 1647 at Childerley, shortly after Cornet Joyce had famously seized the King on behalf of the Army at Holdenby House. Cromwell was part of a deputation led by Fairfax and was recorded as having behaved 'with good manner' to the King.[43] Interestingly Brenton has Charles ask, on arriving for the first day of his trial, 'Which one is Master Cromwell?' (67); a tactic which presumes that Cromwell had made little or no impression at Childerley. It is certainly true that they never met as Brenton has them meet, in close and earnest conversation. The meeting, which is set at the Cotton house, where the King was held during his trial, allows Brenton to crystallise and contrast two very different men and two very different perceptions of magistracy.[44] Most importantly, however, it impresses what is perhaps Brenton's defining insinuation; that the vision cannot be distinguished from the prejudices of the visionary.

Brenton creates his Charles and his Cromwell and creates them human, for which reason they are supposed to be confused and conflicted and frustrated; 'one fighting for a future he struggled to imagine, the other for a past that was a fantasy'.[45] It is reasonable to suppose that, in the matter of their respective politics at least, Brenton feels a rather greater affinity with Cromwell than with Charles. As a dramatist however there is, rather obviously, something about Charles to which Brenton is drawn; the king who could indeed conjure such 'eerily graceful lines', 'slippery' maybe, but also a consummate actor.[46] Charles first appears in the play to a chorus of Richmond's admiring

[42] See here Wedgwood, *King*, 169 and 190, evidently sceptical of the idea.

[43] A. Fraser, *Cromwell: Our Chief of Men*, (Methuen, 1985), 196, J. Bowle, *Charles I*, (Weidenfeld and Nicolson, 1975), 293–4, and Royle, *Civil War*, 400–1.

[44] Charles resided at the Cotton House during his trial, and was transported daily to Westminster by barge. It was convenient. Sir Robert Cotton, who had died in 1631, was famous as a great collector and early member of the Society of Antiquarians. His vast collection, including the famed Cotton Library, was later donated to the British Library.

[45] Brenton, '55 Days'.

[46] For Brenton's observations see '*55 Days*: Will Mortimer interviews Howard Brenton', available at <https://www.hampsteadtheatre.com/news/2012/10/55-days-will-mortimer-interviews-howard-brenton/> (last accessed 26th June 2020). The perception of Charles as 'slippery' resonates with Wedgwood's supposition that he was 'a brave man, but he was also secretive and devious'. See her *King*, at 11.

'Oh played, played Your Majesty' (22). Charles has just won a game of bowls. But it is the playing which has impressed, and Brenton has chosen his words carefully. Later in the same conversation, Charles reassures Richmond that, despite the assurances he has given the Presbyterians regarding the abolition of bishops, he has no intention of keeping his word (23–4). Later still it becomes apparent that Charles is negotiating with the Duke of Ormonde for the raising of a new Royalist army in Ireland; evidence in Ireton's opinion that the King is a 'liar'. Cromwell prefers a different language and a different judgement. The evidence simply confirms that Charles is a 'political man', doing what kings do (51). And, as we have already noted, Charles consistently steals the trial scenes during the second Act. Time and again he bests the lawyers Bradshaw and Cooke, leading to a series of hurried adjournments. It is interesting that when he and Cromwell finally meet, at the Cotton house, Charles is seated 'reading law books' (84). But it is not, of course, his knowledge of jurisprudence which really matters. It is his ability to act.

Brenton thus fashions his Charles as an actor-king in much the same way that Shakespeare fashioned his Henry V or Richard II. Such a fashioning was certainly appreciated by reviewers. In the original production, Charles was played by Mark Gatiss, in the admiring opinion of one critic as a 'lanky, vicious fop with perfect comic timing'.[47] From a slightly different angle, Michael Billington appreciated the capacity of Gatiss to induce the 'sympathy' of the audience, whilst reinforcing 'the Shakespearian point about the essential solitude of kingship'.[48] Charles Spencer in the *Telegraph* ventured a different, but no less perceptive, parallel; with the dramatic Charles brought to poetic life in Andrew Marvell's *Horatian Ode Upon Cromwell's Return from Ireland*.[49] Marvell's poem, which was written in 1650, though not published in 1681, placed the events of 30th January at its pivot-point; thus making a poem which seemed to be about Cromwell, at least as much about the King he had killed. There is much else about Brenton's Charles which is familiar, aside from the foppishness and the slipperiness. There is, for a start, the defining delusion of Stuart monarchism, that the King has been anointed by 'divine right', that he is 'so much more' than a mere 'man in the eye of God' (39). Such a supposition had found famous expression in a succession of treatises penned by Charles's father, King James I. Monarchy, as readers of James's *The Trew Law of Free Monarchies* would have discovered, 'is the trew

---

[47] See <http://www.timeout.com/london/theatre/55-days> (last accessed 26th June 2020).

[48] See <https://www.theguardian.com/stage/2012/oct/25/55-days-review> (last accessed 26th June 2020).

[49] See <https://www.telegraph.co.uk/culture/theatre/theatre-reviews/9633745/55-days-Hampstead-Theatre-review.html> (last accessed 26th June 2020).

patterne of divinitie', for 'Kings are called Gods' because 'they sit upon God his throne in the earth'.[50]

The extent to which Charles is wedded to this perception of kingship is evident during his conversation with Cromwell at the Cotton house. Cromwell's proposition that there might be a constitutional 'settlement' in which the King would become 'the figurehead of the nation' is countered by a simple referent to the 'oil' (88). To Cromwell, it is just a 'dribble of sticky stuff'. But to Charles, it is everything, evidence of his quasi-divine authority, and, in words which resonate very obviously with those articulated by Shakespeare's Richard II at the moment of his deposition, Charles confirms his opinion that 'It is the power. It is on me. Not all the water in the sea can wash it away' (88).[51] It is for this reason that Charles cannot countenance the idea of being a 'constitutional monarch'. Monarchs are not defined by constitutions. They are chosen and invested by God.

The idea that the English civil wars were primarily 'wars of religion' has become a centre-piece of modern historical scholarship; and Brenton clearly approves.[52] What has aligned the various 'parliamentarian' factions, as an early exchange between Prynne and Harrison confirms, is a shared distaste for 'bishops'. Charles, as Harrison confirms, is 'damn well near a papist' (18–19). As ever with Charles, it is as much a matter of perception, of what he seems to be 'near'. But perception, in late 1648, was everything. And Charles does nothing to suggest otherwise. Historians have long speculated that Charles may well have relished his martyrdom, in the end at least; an impression which is reinforced by the refusal of Brenton's Charles to accept Cromwell's proposed 'settlement' at their meeting. When Cromwell suggests that they 'are all on a dark path', Charles replies 'Not I. I am in the light of Heaven, I am God's anointed and all is clear to me' (89). During his final months, Charles apparently became obsessed with George Herbert's *Devotions*. John Donne's coronation sermon was eerily prescient: "The last thing Christ bequeathed to thee was his blood, refuse not to go to him but the same way too, if His Glory require that sacrifice'.[53] This was certainly the

---

[50] J. Somerville (ed) *King James VI and I: Political Writings*, (Cambridge UP, 1994), 64. For commentaries on James's idea of kingship, see J. Somerville, *Politics and Ideology in England 1603–1640*, (Longman, 1986), 9–12, 23–36, and Burgess, *Constitution*, 143–56.

[51] In Act 3 Scene 2 of *Richard II*, the doomed Richard, at ll.54–55, observes to Bolingbroke that 'Not all the water in the rough rude sea/Can wash the balm off from an anointed king'.

[52] For a compelling and influential statement on the religious dynamics of the civil wars, see J. Morrill, *The Nature of the English Revolution*, (Longman, 1993), 33–68.

[53] J. Donne, *Selected Prose*, (Penguin, 1987), 291. For a commentary on this prescience, see Wedgwood, *King*, 14–15.

kind of king and the kind of martyrdom encountered by those who, in their hundreds and thousands, purchased copies of the *Eikon Basilike*, otherwise known as the 'King's Book', which appeared on the streets of London within days of the regicide; the sentiment of a man who, as he touched the edge of the axe which would cut of his head, retained the presence of mind to declare, famously, that he was passing from a 'corruptible to an incorruptible Crown, where no disturbance can be'.[54] It is also the role which, in the end, Brenton assigns to his Charles Stuart.

It might be supposed that the attempt to humanise the distinctly un-romantic Cromwell would be more challenging. Even his admirers have, down the ages, struggled with this particular brief.[55] As the acerbic Richard Baxter observed shortly after Cromwell's death, 'no man was better or worse spoken of than he'.[56] Two centuries later, Thomas Carlyle would try to reha-bilitate a heroic, if hardly loveable, Cromwell.[57] Samuel Rawson Gardiner would try to soften the Carlylean Cromwell at the very end of the nineteenth century, applauding the 'greatest because the most typical Englishman of all time'.[58] Gardiner's Cromwell was a little more human; but not a lot more. 'Is he a man at all?' Brenton's Charles wonders in resonant terms when he first hears that Cromwell would like to meet, 'Or just a force' (54). An echo, perhaps, of Marvell's famous depiction, in his *Ode*, of Cromwell as a providential 'force'. Brenton does not make his Cromwell any more love-able. But he does try to make him more human, a man who likes a drink indeed, who is haunted by indecision and uncertainty, prone to 'episodes of depression', but also a man who understands politics, a 'knocker-together of heads'.[59] And a man who can in one breath evince the strongest possible faith in the providential indications of the Lord Almighty, but in the next exhibit utter scorn when Charles confirms his belief that he is, by consequences of his anointment, answerable only to God: 'You believe God gave you power over all the rest of us because of a dribble of sticky stuff on your head?' Be 'damned'. It is 'magic stuff, superstition' (88).

It is this prosaic Cromwell that England in late 1648 so desperately

---

[54] See Wedgwood, *King*, 192, and Robertson, *Brief*, 200.

[55] See for example Antonia Fraser, *Cromwell*, 700–714, striving to reconcile the 'darker' evi-dently more 'manic' Cromwell with a man who could on occasion display not just consider-able personal 'charm' but a remarkable 'tenderness' for those under his charge.

[56] In Fraser, *Cromwell*, 699.

[57] On the creation of so 'many Cromwells', see Hill, *Englishman*, 257–60. On the difficulties of writing about Cromwell the man, as opposed to Cromwell the hero or indeed anti-hero, see Morrill, 'Cromwell and his contemporaries', in Morrill, *Cromwell*, 259–81.

[58] In Hill, *Englishman*, 259.

[59] Brenton, '55 Days'.

needs, the knocker-together of heads.[60] As the play opens, pretty much everyone, on the Parliamentarian side at least, sees Cromwell as the only hope. But 'God's Englishman' is up in Knottingley, enjoying a bit too much Yorkshire 'ale', musing on the nature of 'hatred' and 'listening for the voice of providence' (21, 27–30).[61] In the end, it is the voice of Fairfax who persuades him that it is time to return to London and get back to some 'politicking' (31). And yet still Cromwell dithers, forever waiting on the Lord, and events. Much of the first Act is spent just waiting, and much of the second too. Be 'blithe', an anxious Ireton is advised, as the trial of the King commences and things quickly start to go awry, 'Dice are thrown, we all tumble, to come up face or not' (66). Cromwell does pause to contemplate the England that he is trying to build. Having reflected on the text, from *Numbers 13:18*, 'And what the land is that they dwell in', he muses 'Yes, what is the land we dwell in? What is it to be? Kingdom? Republic, like in Roman times? Democracy, like some lunatics in the Army dream of, all things held in common?' (83) But there are only the questions, and the texts, and the endless 'waiting' upon the Lord.

Such characterisation can trigger rather different critical perceptions. It leads Michael Billington to conclude that Brenton's Cromwell is a 'thundering great hypocrite'; a perception that echoes Richard Baxter's famous observation that the Lord Protector was only too ready to justify any 'fault in a case of necessity'.[62] The reviewer in *Time Out* conversely detected a man who, if not exactly likeable, was still possessed of 'charisma and conscience'.[63] The confusion is entirely understandable. Perceptions of the 'historical' Cromwell continue to conflict, so it is hardly surprising if perceptions of the 'dramatic' do much the same. And it is of course precisely this confusion, the sense of inner torment, which makes Brenton's Cromwell so intriguing and so compelling. Towards the end of the first Act, as the prospect of the King's trial looms, Cromwell conceives the idea of meeting his adversary, in the hope that he can get behind the actor and engage the man:

---

[60] The 'frantic enthusiast' perhaps, as David Hume famously termed him. See Hill, *Englishman*, 258.

[61] Historians have contemplated the extent to which Cromwell was deliberately staying his hand, waiting in the north to see how events in London unfolded, or perhaps how God chose to direct them. See Hoyle, *War*, 487.

[62] A man who, the disapproving Baxter confirmed, 'thought secrecy a virtue, and dissimulation no vice'. See Fraser, *Cromwell*, 702–3. For Billington's observation see his review of *55 Days*, available at <http://www.theguardian.com/stage/2012/oct/25/55-days-review> (last accessed 26th June 2020).

[63] See <http://www.timeout.com/london/theatre/55-days> (last accessed 26th June 2020).

Within the Royal shell. The hard carapace of ceremony, his claim to a divine right to rule. What man is in there? If I could crack the shell, reach him. Put my hand in his, pull him to me, our faces close. Then we could speak, low, as human beings, both fallen, both redeemed by the Saviour's blood. And despite all the killing and the horror of these past years, we would settle this. With a prayer. A glass of wine. Even a smile. (51)

It is perhaps the closest Cromwell comes to a philosophy of magistracy; the hope that anything might be resolved by the promise of redemption and the facility of a good chat. When later he and Charles meet, Cromwell opens by hoping that they might 'come to understand each other' (85). It is not a hope that resonates much with Charles.

The Ordinary and the Extraordinary

Brenton is certainly reconciled to the reality of dramatic confliction; indeed, as a 'new' or perhaps now rather older Jacobean, it might be reasonably supposed that he embraces it. Asked more broadly about his 'job', dramatising historical 'moments', Brenton acknowledged the consequential complexities which attend to the necessary alignment of the 'personal' and the 'political'; complexities which so often trigger those moments of comic as well as tragic rupture, moments which seem to defy reason. In regard to the writing of 55 Days, Brenton identified the particular and 'extraordinary moment of hysteria that broke out' when Cromwell and his fellow regicides, faced with signing the death-warrant, descended into a collective fit of giggling and began flicking ink at one another. It might be supposed that the uneasiest head at this particular moment in history was that of the doomed King. The ink-flicking scene suggests otherwise. A number of regicides would later claim that they were bullied into signing the warrant by Cromwell.[64] If so, the apparent levity would indeed have masked a broader collective unease.

The ink-flicking scene serves the same purpose as the famous mirror-shattering scene in Act 4 Scene 1 of Shakespeare's *Richard II* or the moment when Lear finally breaks down on the 'blasted heath' or when Henry V wanders through camp on the night before Agincourt. It impresses the simple fact that politics, no matter how high, is ultimately a human experience. It might be something done by heroes. But more commonly it is something done by men who are dithery or 'slippery', or both, who may cherish certain principles or beliefs, but who are most likely to settle for just knocking heads together, getting stuff done as best they can, who find themselves far more

---

[64] Historians evince varying degrees of scepticism in regard to later regicide protestations. See Royle, *War*, 496–7.

often reacting to events than trying to shape them. Shakespeare knew this, and so does Brenton. In an exchange in Act 2 Scene 5, Lilburne tries to dissuade Cooke from continuing to serve as chief prosecutor. 'You sadden me', he says, 'I thought you dreamt with us of a better world'. Cooke's response is simple: 'Dreams achieve nothing. We must wake and do as best we can' (77). Another slightly earlier scene is similarly suggestive. Cromwell and Ireton discuss the implications of the Leveller *Agreement*, more particularly the case for a 'new constitution' founded on the 'sovereignty of parliament' and a principle of 'universal suffrage'; an 'excellent thing' Cromwell agrees, as he peruses the document, before screwing it up and tossing it on the floor. It would 'ruin us all' (35–6).

It is the human dimension which makes the exercise of magistracy and power so uncertain and on occasion so tragic, and which also makes the drama of history so constantly fascinating. There are no heroes in *55 Days*; just two leading men, human, flawed, uneasy, thrown together by the most extraordinary of circumstances. The most striking feature of the final scene in Brenton's play is again how simple it is. Marvell's *Ode* reached its highest point as Charles laid down his 'comely head'. *55 Days* closes with Charles fiddling with his hair, and then chatting to his executioner about the best height for the block.[65] Rarely has the decapitation of a king seemed so very ordinary. John Milton would have nodded his approval. It was Milton who, famously, recommended that writers should 'cast down' their imaginations when they came to write of history and God. Not easy, though. Brenton may want to follow the injunction, but it is precisely the same imagination which he must conjure in order to fill his theatre. As critics have noted, whilst his politics might be undeniably round-headed, there is more than a little of the literary cavalier in Howard Brenton, the hopeful, perhaps even the 'incurable romantic'.[66] It is the romantic who wants to write history as a history of men and women, and who therefore appreciates that the interests of a progressive politics is sometimes written in poetry as well as prose. Moreover, it is precisely the same imagination which must be conjured if Brenton is to achieve his larger aspiration, to make history speak to the present. In an early interview, a much younger

---

[65] It has been surmised that Charles was anxious to ensure that there was no botched execution, as had happened most notoriously in the case of Mary Queen of Scots, when the first blow of the axe had failed to sever the head. The hair was to be properly tucked away so that the executioner had a clear view of the neck.

[66] The phrase 'incurable romantic' is put into the mouth of a character in Brenton's *Diving for Pearls*, and one which Duncan Wu surmises to be possibly testamentary. See his *Dramatists*, 81, 88–90.

Brenton ventured two reasons why history matters. First because 'of the old truth – that if you don't understand the past, you'll never understand the present, let alone the future', and second because it is 'continually destroyed and lost'.[67]

Both aspirations resonate in regard to *55 Days*, written not just to celebrate the birth of English radicalism, but to transform our 'vague impressions' of the English revolution into something altogether closer and more informed, to make the revolution and its consequences 'part of our national consciousness'.[68] One reviewer of *55 Days*, though generally admiring, thought it to be 'hard work', like 'attending two double-history lessons at school'.[69] Perhaps, but such a conclusion does not diminish the importance of the endeavour, or the significance of the writer. It is what a dramatic historian, a writer of 'history plays for now', is supposed to do.[70] Once again, as we have already noted, whilst *55 Days* purports to be about the eight weeks minus a day which preceded the execution of Charles I, it is about far more than just this. In terms of historical reach, it is about a hundred and fifty years of post-reformation history, and then another four centuries which followed; for whilst Brenton is writing about something that happened in the middle of the seventeenth century, he is also writing about the state of England today, its politics and its constitution.

Discussing his earlier political affiliations, Brenton placed himself with a 'great radical tradition' of British theatre; left-leaning, oppositional, republican to a degree, and accepting of the historical fact that there is always likely to be 'blood in the Revolution's cradle'.[71] The revolution to which Brenton was alluding more particularly was, in fact, the French, the events of which he had revisited in his adaption of Buchner's *Danton's Death*. But there is a broader resonance. Contemplating the consequences of the French revolution tends to make writers think rather more about the English. It did Carlyle, and Edmund Burke before him. A different, but no less pertinent, resonance can be heard in the celebrated rejoinder of the Chinese premier

---

[67] Brenton, 'Interview', 136.

[68] Brenton, '55 Days'.

[69] See <https://www.telegraph.co.uk/culture/theatre/theatre-reviews/9633745/55-days-Hampstead-Theatre-review.html> (last accessed 26th June 2020).

[70] Brenton, 'Interview', 138.

[71] See comments made in an interview published in 1987, 'The Red Theatre Under the Bed', 3 *New Theatre Quarterly* 1987, 196, 200. He had said much the same eight years earlier, declaring that all his 'plays are written unreservedly in the cause of socialism'. See 'Interview', in 3 *Performing Arts* 1979, 135. See also S. Bennett, 'At the End of the Great Radical Tradition? Recent Plays by Howard Brenton', 33 *Modern Drama* 1990, 409 and 416, and D. Wu, *Six Contemporary Dramatists*, (St Martins, 1995), 86.

Zhou Enlai when asked about the implications of the French revolution. It was, he replied, too early to tell.[72] The same, it might be argued, could be said of the English. It can certainly be said of the revolution which the audience is invited to contemplate in *55 Days*. 30th January 1649 might have been a pivotal moment of 'rupture'. But it was the product of a much longer imagining, as we have already noted; and it still is, written and rewritten from one generation of historians to another.

And much the same is true of the constitution which it was supposed, in the grander Whig narrative, to have forged. Christopher Hill, as thoroughly Whiggish as he was socialist and radical, would later declare that January 1649 was the moment when the future constitutional shape of England, as a country 'ruled by Parliaments and not by absolute kings', was 'ensured'.[73] Other later historians can still be found arguing much the same. David Smith, for example, has recently suggested that the restoration 'settlement' designed by 'constitutional royalists' such as Clarendon owed much to the associated myths of 'ancient' constitutionalism so vigorously recommended by conservative parliamentarians such as Ireton; as well by evasive 'trimmers' such as Andrew Marvell.[74] And it was this 'settlement' which would be confirmed in 1688; finding expression in those two statutes so revered in Whig historiography, the Bill of Rights and the Act of Settlement. Except of course that it was not to be quite so simple, for the reason which David Hume articulated in his *History of England*, published in 1754, and which found later, famous, articulation in de Tocqueville's *Democracy in America*.[75] The English 'constitution' defies discernment. There might indeed be certain 'fundamental' statutes, many of which were written in the decades following the revolutions of the seventeenth century, and there would be plenty of defining constitutional cases to come, and any number of authoritative treatises, some written by Whig historians and jurists, some written by Tories. But there would be no such thing as a 'written' constitution; which is, of course, precisely as Ireton and Cromwell would have had it.

But it is not what Lilburne wanted. This is not to suppose that the Whiggishly radical Brenton would have aligned himself with the Tory Hume, at least not politically. But he might have shared a measure of Hume's scepticism, along with a similar measure of Lilburne's. He would certainly

---

[72] It has been subsequently suggested that Zhou might have misunderstood the question, and assumed that he was being asked about the rather more recent riots in Paris in May 1968. Zhou's comments were made in 1972 during President Nixon's famous visit to China.

[73] Hill, *Englishman*, 253.

[74] Smith, *Royalism*, 297–304, 310–13, 319–20.

[75] See here Burgess, *Absolute Monarchy*, 131–2.

have disputed the presumptions of progress and 'finality' which came to define the intellectual predilections of 'grand' Whiggery. And which, it might be added, continue to underpin the complacency which can be discerned in so much contemporary political and constitutional discourse; the supposition that a liberal constitution might work itself 'pure', that there is an internal rationality which constantly refines legal and governmental process.[76] Modern liberal jurisprudence commonly evinces a similarly Whiggish faith in certain 'principles' of liberal legalism, the rule of law, the separation of powers, and in the more particular context of the British constitution, the sovereignty of parliament.[77] Here again, Lilburne would have had no issue with the aspiration. It is the complacency against which he would have argued, and the dissimulation.

And exactly the same can be presumed of Brenton; so fiercely castigated, at the turn of the present century, for refusing to join 'the bandwagon of pro-Blair adulators' who fawned over the constitutional 'reform' project which encompassed, with varying degrees of celebration, the Human Rights Act, assorted devolution statutes, and then a little later the Constitutional Reform Act of 2005.[78] The insinuation that New Labour might be little more than a reinvested species of 'grand' Whiggery is intriguing; not least because it suggests a reason why so many of the more radically-inclined, such as Brenton, were so quickly disappointed. Constitutional reform tends to be insular. Social justice requires more than the occasional statute, no matter how 'fundamental' it might pretend to be. Most importantly, perhaps it requires committed political and intellectual debate. Brenton's generation of playwrights defined themselves in terms of this commitment, as in a rather different tone did the generation of 'in-yer-face' writers which followed in the 1990s.[79] The apparent return to a more reflective species of political theatre during the previous decade and a half, characterised by its particular interest in testament and history, might seem to intimate a lessening of energy, if not commitment. But what it denotes, in fact, is a strategic reversion. In their

---

[76] On the idea of the liberal constitution working itself 'pure', see most famously Ronald Dworkin, *Law's Empire*, (Belknap Press, 1986). On the internal, or immanent, rationality of liberal legalism, see E. Weinrib, 'Legal Formalism: On the Immanent Rationality of Law', 97 *Yale Law Journal* 1988, 949.

[77] For a recent example, see here T. Bingham, *The Rule of Law*, (Allen Lane, 2010).

[78] See Reinelt, 'Affinities', 310, and also Edgar, *State of Play*, 22–6, contemplating the often fraught, invariably complicated relationship which existed between New Labour and radical theatre during the first decade of the twenty-first century.

[79] For an interesting commentary on the place of 'new brutalism' within modern radical theatre, see D. Edgar, 'Unsteady States: Theories of Contemporary New Writing', 15 *Contemporary Theatre Review* 2005, 300–2.

return to a distinct species of historical realism, plays such as 55 Days signify, not a lessening of energy, but a return to a kind of theatre that is a little less 'in-yer-face' and a little more 'in-yer-mind', or maybe 'in-yer-past'.[80]

An immediate and obvious parallel can be made with the reinvestment over the same period of a distinctive genre of documentary or 'verbatim' theatre; so much of which, in seeking to interrogate the particular consequences of '9/11', has assumed a jurisprudential tone. Here 55 Days might be read as a piece of 'verbatim' historical drama; deploying a variety of testamentary materials in order to contemplate the various responses, political, intellectual, jurisprudential, to the consequences, immediate and longer-term, of a defining moment of 'rupture' in English history. In such a reading 30th January 1649 serves precisely the same purpose as 11th September 2001. It matters a bit more than other days, not simply because of what happened at that moment, or indeed what followed in the months and years to come, but because it makes us think rather more not just of then, but of now. In this way, history matters to political theatre; for the same reason indeed that it matters to a properly critical jurisprudence.[81] As the prominent critical legal scholar Allan Hutchinson argued so eloquently back in 1988:

> We are never not in a story. History and human action only take on meaning and intelligibility within their narrative context and dramatic settings ... There is no truth nor knowledge outside the dramatic context and idiom of history. All conversations occur within history.[82]

55 Days pivots around a conversation, one that is no less real for being imagined. The conversation between Charles and Cromwell may not have happened in January 1649; at least not how Brenton writes it. But it happens each and every time an audience watches a performance of 55 Days, as it does each and every time a reader reads it. It is a conversation between two very different visions of England, its governance and its constitution. And it is a conversation which is as resonant today as it would have been four and a half centuries ago.

---

[80] For interesting overviews of the state of 'realist', political and 'postmodern' theatre at the turn of the new century, see V. Gottlieb, 'Theatre Today – the new realism', 13 *Contemporary Theatre Review* 2003, 5–14, and J. Reinelt, 'Politics, Playwriting, Postmodernism: An Interview with David Edgar', 14 *Contemporary Theatre Review* 2004, 42–53.

[81] As David Edgar has recently argued, part of the 'literal conversation' which constantly and insistently questions how 'our contradictory affinities, histories and identities relate to each other'. See Edgar, *State of Play*, 34.

[82] A. Hutchinson, *Dwelling on the Threshold: Critical Essays on Modern Legal Thought*, (Carswell, 1988), 13.

5

The Haunting of King Charles III

Mike Bartlett's *King Charles III* was first performed at the Almeida Theatre in London in April 2014, after which it transferred to the Wyndham before going on tour across the UK throughout 2015 and into 2016. As the extent of its run suggests, it was an immediate critical and commercial success; a 'snowball success' according to the *Evening Standard*.[1] According to *Time Out*, Bartlett's play was 'brilliantly audacious', in sum 'theatrical dynamite'.[2] 'Bold, brilliant and unstoppably entertaining, an intelligent, empathetic, moving look at the power and limitations of the modern monarchy', in sum, the reviewer in *The Times* gushed, 'theatre doesn't get much better than this'.[3] The *Daily Telegraph* was just as impressed. 'Outstanding and provocative', its reviewer concluded, 'the most spectacular, gripping and wickedly entertaining piece of lese-majeste that British theatre has ever seen'.[4] *King Charles III* tells the story of what might happen in the weeks which follow the death of Queen Elizabeth II. More particularly, it anticipates what might happen within the respective walls of Westminster and Buckingham Palace if her eldest son decides to pursue a slightly different way of ruling. There are other locations and different environments. There is a comic subplot located

---

[1] See <https://www.standard.co.uk/go/london/theatre/writing-the-wrongs-mike-bartlett-on-his-plays-king-charles-iii-bull-and-game-9869931.html> (last accessed 26th June 2020).

[2] As well as being, on 'one massively enjoyable level', also 'gloriously, victoriously vulgar'. See <www.timeout.com/london/theatre/king-charles-iii> (last accessed 26th June 2020).

[3] See <www.thetimes.co.uk/tto/arts/stage/article4060056.ece> (last accessed 26th June 2020).

[4] Lese-majeste is an offence against the dignity of the sovereign, more familiar in Roman and medieval continental jurisprudence. It cannot, however, be consigned to history, not entirely. Lese-majeste remains on the statute books in various countries around the world, perhaps rather incongruously in the likes of Norway and Denmark, as well as Jordan and most conspicuously Thailand, where it has long been deployed as means for suppressing dissent. Only recently, two Thai students were prosecuted and convicted of the offence following their performance in a satirical University production. They are presently serving two and a half years in prison. It is easy to take dramatic freedom of expression for granted.

in London club-land. But *King Charles III* is principally about the highest of high-politics; for which reason critics have tended to place it, understandably, within the genre of 'state-of-the-nation plays'.[5] Such plays, as we have already noted, like to ask larger questions. In the case of *King Charles III* it is about 'the monarchy's future role in a country without a defined constitution'.[6]

Prospective though it might be, *King Charles III* is a history play, of a kind. It is commonly assumed and quite understandably that history looks backwards. But the fact that it lies in the past does not preclude its presence or indeed its place in the future. Indeed it might be said that history acquires its greatest urgency when we contemplate its prophecy. It lends a sense of certainty to a necessarily uncertain prospect; even if it is a certainty which we create for ourselves, and which is just as much the product of our own narrative prejudices. Historians and historiographers commonly deploy the term 'virtual' in order to categorise histories of what might have been, liking to wonder the consequences of Wellington losing at Waterloo, or more troublingly still a Britain enveloped into a Thousand Year Reich. Here, of course, the 'virtual' history can be said to lie partly in the past and partly in the future. The same exercise, and the same term, can, however, be applied to histories which concentrate still further on what might be likely to happen in a future which is immediate, or even intermediate. Such histories, for reasons which are self-evident, tend to assume a more overtly imaginative form. To the extent that they aspire to credibility, they do so by appealing to comparable events or moments in the past. The imagination is thus constrained by the history, to whatever degree the particular historian prefers.

Some virtual histories are, however, still more imaginary in their conception. *King Charles III* is such a history by virtue of its subject-matter and its medium. It is a virtual history in the immediate sense that it is prospective. But it is also virtual in the sense that it is presented in dramatic form. The consequence is a peculiarly poetic kind of virtuality. There is a necessary paradox here. Whilst acknowledging the inevitably poetic nature of his enterprise, Bartlett has repeatedly affirmed that his play should be 'defiantly unironic', neither a 'parody nor a pastiche', and it would not be stuffed with 'fairytale characters'. Given its aspiration, to encourage serious reflection on the nature of monarchy in modern Britain, it was vital that *King Charles III* should look

---

5 See <https://www.standard.co.uk/go/london/theatre/writing-the-wrongs-mike-bartlett-on-his-plays-king-charles-iii-bull-and-game-9869931.html> (last accessed 26th June 2020) and also <www.timeout.com/london/theatre/king-charles-iii> (last accessed 26th June 2020).

6 Michael Billington in <https://www.theguardian.com/stage/2014/sep/12/king-charles-iii-review-shakespeare-mike-bartlett-wyndhams-tim-pigott-smith> (last accessed 26th June 2020).

and sound 'believable'.[7] And there is, Bartlett argues, no better place in which to nurture this kind of reflection than in the 'theatre'; an injunction which of course echoes David Hare's renowned observation, that theatre is the 'best court of judgement' we have.[8]

It might also be assumed that just as history lies in the past, so do ghosts; or at least, so the cultural expression presumes. They come from the past, 'back to haunt us', as the saying goes; to unsettle the present, and perhaps the future too. There are lots of ghosts in Bartlett's *Charles III*. Some are more obviously ghostly than others, for the simple reason of their dramatic presence. Thus the recently dead Queen makes a 'floating' appearance early in the play, whilst the ghost of Princess Diana flits in and out at various moments, a 'Beshrouded lady, walking through the walls', chiding her troubled husband for rejecting her, and then riddling him with the idea that he might prove to be the 'greatest King we ever had', before her spectre 'drifts away, like mist at dawn' (32). A little later she appears to William and makes the same prophecy, with one crucial difference. Having tempted Charles to make his critical mistake, she can now be sure that her son will 'be the greatest King we ever had' (71). We will speculate on the ghostly Diana's theatrical origins shortly.

Other spectres can be raised from the distant, and not so distant, past of English history. As Bartlett's Charles agonises over the press regulation bill, to which he does not want to give his assent, the conniving leader of the opposition, Mr Stevens alludes to how William IV 'resolved a not/ Entirely different situation' in regard to the 'great' Reform Act of 1832. The allusion is evasive, spoken, as an irritated Charles observes, 'in circles' (61). It might simply refer to William's decision to give his assent *in absentia*; or it might be a tacit encouragement to dismiss the government and invite Stevens to form a minority administration; or it might be an invitation to dissolve Parliament and go 'Back to the people', a suggestion Stevens revisits rather later in the play (85). Then again, none of these strategies resolved anything much in 1831.[9] Two more ghosts, wilful antagonists, make a spectacular entrance in Act 3 Scene 6; when Charles does indeed decide to dissolve Parliament, in-person 'regally dressed, and with sceptre' (76). The first King Charles famously breached the same etiquette in January 1642, entering the

---

[7] See <www.theguardian.com/stage/2014/sep/20/king-charles-iii-mike-bartlett> (last accessed 26th June 2020).

[8] See <www.varsity.co.uk/culture/8945> (last accessed 26th June 2020).

[9] William dismissed Lord Grey's Whig administration in 1831 and asked Wellington to see if he could form an alternative Tory government. He could not and Grey returned a few months later. Charles later reflects to himself that he knows 'well the precedent' (62). But it gives him little comfort.

Commons Chamber with the intention of arresting five Members on charges of treason. They had of course 'flown', and Charles, not for the first time, looked a fool. Sat at the back of the Chamber that day was the Member for Huntingdon, Oliver Cromwell. Twelve years later he would do much the same, his patience with the Rump Parliament having finally run out. As Bartlett's Charles harangues his Parliament for its 'juvenile and selfish squall' Cromwell's voice echoes down the ages (76). 'Some of you are whoremasters, some drunkards, and some corrupt and unjust men and scandalous to the profession of the Gospel', Cromwell announced on the morning of 20th April 1653, as his soldiers bundled the remaining Members out of the Chamber.[10]

And then there are the spectres of all the kings who, down the ages, have been variously despatched. Some managed to depart with a modicum of grace. Having assigned his deed of abdication Edward VIII slipped off into a life of genteel retirement and petty controversy.[11] For most, however, the end was more grisly. And prospectively entertaining, for there is nothing which theatre-goers down the ages have seemed to relish more than a spot of dramatic and murderous regicide. Elizabethan theatre-goers were certainly no exception. *The Troublesome Reign and Lamentable Death of Edward II* was the subject of Christopher Marlowe's more renowned history play, whilst the *Tragedy of King Richard II* likewise attracted Shakespeare's critical eye. We will return to the latter shortly. Many of the ghosts that haunt the pages of *King Charles III* assume a distinctly Shakespearean visage. We will raise them first. And having done so, we will then revisit a different era in order to summon what appears, at first glance at least, to be a rather different kind of spirit. Though published a century and a half ago, the essays on monarchy found in Walter Bagehot's *The English Constitution* have retained their considerable influence. The ghost of Walter Bagehot haunts *King Charles III* every bit as much as the various Shakespearean ghosts that Bartlett conjures. And it proves to be just as evasive and elusive, and restless.

Shakespearean Spectres

Shakespeare's spectral presence was immediately spotted by critics. The play should be read as a 'dense tissue of Shakespearean references' according to

---

[10] T. Royle, *Civil War: the Wars of Three Kingdoms, 1638–1660,* (Abacus, 2005), 637–8.
[11] The least petty of the controversies was undoubtedly an ill-judged visit to Hitler at Obersalzberg, during which the now styled Duke of Windsor managed to get himself photographed making a Nazi salute. Thereafter the Duke, his lifestyle funded by a calculated strategy of tax-dodging, illegal currency trading, and sponging off a diminishing group of friends, spent the rest of his days between his residence in Paris and various fashionable European resorts.

Michael Billington in the *Guardian*.[12] A different critic went so far as to suggest that playing spot-the-Shakespeare was itself a 'side joy' of Bartlett's play.[13] Of course, the Shakespearean spectre might be said to exist as much in the mind of the audience. But it is not summoned by chance. Shakespeare was there from the very start. Having been especially struck by a particular production of *Richard II*, Bartlett 'realized that the best way to tell the story was to make Charles a Shakespearean tragic hero'. The 'idea that he's waited all his life to do a job that he would have for only a short while felt really Shakespearean'.[14] It may, Bartlett observed with necessary modesty, never 'be as good as Shakespeare', but his *King Charles III* would look and sound as Shakespearean as he could make it.[15] It would 'need five acts, quite possibly a comic subplot, but most worryingly, the majority of it would have to be in verse'.[16] And it seemed to work; according to Sarah Lyall, writing in the *New York Times*, Bartlett thus manages to 'transform his protagonists from cardboard figures of ridicule into full-blown characters of tragedy and pathos'.[17]

The Shakespearean canon is, of course, full of puzzled princes and usurped kings, some simply bemused by the responsibilities of magistracy, others consumed by what Billington terms the 'baffled rage' of familial disloyalty.[18] Students of Shakespeare's final play *The Tempest*, for example, will immediately spot affinities between Bartlett's Charles, a 'Thoughtful Prince' who struggles with the more prosaic responsibilities of kingship, and Prospero who likewise preferred to remain ensconced in his library 'rapt in his studies'. As Prince William observes of his father, in tones of evident disappointment, 'He stays inside, just reading books, and bills/ It isn't what I hoped' (45). Camilla expresses the same frustration:

> You sit there at your desk and work and read
> Which means we cancel trips that should be made

---

[12] See <https://www.theguardian.com/stage/2014/sep/12/king-charles-iii-review-shakespeare-mike-bartlett-wyndhams-tim-pigott-smith> (last accessed 26th June 2020).

[13] See <www.sfgate.com/entertainment/article/Review-Broadway-s-King-Charles-iii> (last accessed 2nd November 2015).

[14] See <https://www.nytimes.com/2015/11/10/theater/mike-bartlett-turns-to-shakespeare-to-voice-his-king-charles-iii.html> (last accessed 26th June 2020).

[15] See <www.varsity.co.uk/culture/8945> (last accessed 26th June 2020).

[16] More precisely it is written in iambic pentameters. <www.theguardian.com/stage/2014/sep/20/king-charles-iii-mike-bartlett> (last accessed 26th June 2020).

[17] See <https://www.nytimes.com/2015/11/10/theater/mike-bartlett-turns-to-shakespeare-to-voice-his-king-charles-iii.html> (last accessed 26th June 2020).

[18] See <https://www.theguardian.com/stage/2014/sep/12/king-charles-iii-review-shakespeare-mike-bartlett-wyndhams-tim-pigott-smith> (last accessed 26th June 2020).

And let down crowds who have looked forward to
Your presence there. (58)

It is not, she adds, 'what the people want' (59). We will revisit the relation of
kingship and kingly-thinking, and the consequence of not giving the people
'what they want', in due course. First, however, we must raise some particular
Shakespearean spectres.

Macbeth

Bartlett, by his own admission, is particularly keen to raise 'tragic' spectres. No
Shakespearean king expresses a more 'baffled rage' of course than Lear, and
it is certainly possible to detect a resonance in the anguished final moments
of Bartlett's play, as Charles staggers and 'collapses' on the 'step' before his
newly crowned son (122). The rage articulated by Lear on his 'blasted heath'
may not be as evident. But the pain is. And there are various strategically
placed textual referents too. When for example William refuses to comment
on news of his father's decision not to sign the contentious press regulation
bill, an exasperated Kate responds with the familiar 'nothing comes of nothing said'; the response which Cordelia receives when she confesses herself
unable to match the cloying rhetoric of her sisters (47). *Lear* is not, of course,
the only Shakespearean tragedy which moves around the cataclysmic fall of a
'baffled' and enraged 'tragic hero'. *Hamlet* too is full of bafflement and rage,
and ghostly spectres.

And so very obviously is *Macbeth*.[19] William's usurpation of his father
is of course rather different and his character altogether colder than that of
Macbeth. But he too is a ditherer, perhaps 'too full o'th'milk of human kindness', a man who must be persuaded to 'catch the nearest way' (1.5.17–18).[20]
But it is the parallel that Bartlett insinuates between Kate and Lady Macbeth
that is so irresistible. It is for the audience to decide whether Kate's query as
to whether Charles is already king, at the outset of the play, expresses a 'sweet'
ignorance, as Camilla supposes, or masks a deeper calculation (13). Kate
certainly expects to be 'future' Queen 'Some day', and she does not 'intend
to be a silent partner in that regal match' (66, 68). Like Lady Macbeth, she
perceives a shared 'enterprise' (1.7.48). Later in the play, she reflects at length
on her place, and her strategy:

---

[19] Critics further noted that the director of *King Charles III*, Rupert Goold, had previously
attracted considerable acclaim for his direction of Patrick Stewart in a much admired production of *Macbeth*. See <www.timeout.com/london/theatre/king-charles-iii> (last accessed
26th June 2020) and <www.sfgate.com/entertainment/article/Review-Broadway-s-King-
Charles-iii> (last accessed 2nd November 2015).

[20] All internal references are taken from W. Shakespeare, *Macbeth*, (Routledge, 1964).

> It is bewildering that even now
> These little rooms of power are stocked full
> With white, and southern, likely Oxbridge men . . .
> And so despite emancipation we must look
> Towards the harder sex to find the power.
> But I know nothing, just a plastic doll
> Designed I am told to stand embodying
> A male created bland and standard wife,
> Whose only job is prettying the Prince, and then
> If possible, get pregnant with the royal
> And noble bump, to there produce an heir. (91–2)

Like Lady Macbeth, Kate too must in time 'unsex' herself (1.5.41). But for now, she must wait and be patient, and play her part. She will 'Observe, and plan, and learn the way to rule', so that when the time comes, she is ready, not 'simply' to 'help my husband in his crown/ But wear one of my own' (92). Most immediately, she must cajole her 'distract and pensive-like' William into contemplating constitutional murder (44). So must Lady Macbeth 'pour my spirits in thine ear,/ And chastise with the valour of my tongue/ All that impedes thee from the golden round' (1.5.26–8). She chides her husband with the prospect of living 'a coward in thine own esteem' (1.7.43). Kate persuades William of his greater responsibility, to 'our children, and their children hence' (68). When William dithers, it is Kate who urges him to:

> Say the thing that must be said.
> The fact that both of us command support.
> That does near thrice outweigh the aged King
> And if we wanted might begin to itch
> In waiting for the throne. (69)

And it is Kate who organises the critical meeting with the Prime Minister in Act 4 Scene 3, in which it is agreed that William should become king. 'Parliament is impotent', Kate urges, 'And just become a meeting house of men' (95). It is for William to take the initiative. He must 'Become the man I know you are and act' (69). Lady Macbeth assumes a more taunting tone, but to the same end: 'When thou durst do it, then you were a man;/ And, to be more than what you were, you would/ Be so much more the man' (1.7.49–51). 'You set me up', William observes at the conclusion of the meeting. But he plays along all the same. He has come to know and fear a face that so quickly turns from 'soft' to 'doom and fury' (44). Kate is not to be resisted, at least not by him. And she might anyway be right, as he acknowledges rather awkwardly at the end of his press conference in Act 4: 'For all of this was actually her idea/ Turns out she is cleverer than all of us!' (101)

So the decision is made. There can be no more dithering. Consequences press. 'Then if it's done, it's done at once', William declares, in language which is very obviously intended to resonate with Macbeth's similar resolution at the outset of Act 1 Scene 7, ''twere well/ It were done quickly' (96; 1.7.1–2). Similar textual referents recur, from the 'Tempestuous waking sleeps' that are prophesied for all, to the ghostly shrieks which can be heard in Diana's room, to the riddles which her spectre visits upon the troubled Charles (61–3). The echo here, of course, is with the incantations of the three witches who 'trade and traffic' with Macbeth, and turn his mind to 'affairs of death' (3.5.4–5). And the parallel is just as obvious. Kate is the new Diana. Just as Kate endeavours to persuade her 'nervous future King' into taking action, Diana whispers into Charles's ear that he might, if he can summon the courage, be the 'greatest King'. Both in the end succeed, Diana in making Charles pursue his course of 'madness', Kate in becoming Queen Catherine (63). It might almost be surmised that they are conspirators; two witches in the place of three. It is they who destroy Charles. At the very bitter end, as Kate ascends to the throne, the spirit of Diana is raised a final time. As a devastated Charles stands speechless awaiting his son's coronation, Mr Stevens sidles past, assuring the man whose demise he did so much to engineer, that he will despite all 'Remain my king of hearts' (117).

Richard II

The extent to which Shakespeare's earlier *Richard II* might be considered a proto-tragedy remains a matter of critical conjecture. Chronology and editorial discretion has placed it amongst the 'histories'. Shakespeare entitled it *The Tragedy of King Richard II*. Either way, whilst it might indeed be rather shorter on dramatic visitations, its spectral presence in the text of *King Charles III* is undeniable. Indeed, as we have already noted, Bartlett was inspired by a performance of Shakespeare's *Richard II*. Most importantly, from the perspective of the constitutional historian at least, the deposition scene in Act 4 of *Richard II* represents Shakespeare's most considered reflection on the nature of kingship.[21] It presents two aspects, a tragic and a jurisprudential,

---

[21] The extent to which Richard formally abdicated, and indeed the extent to which Shakespeare properly records any such abdication, remains a matter of critical conjecture. In Holinshed, Shakespeare's primary source, Richard signed an instrument which released his liegemen from their formal oath of obedience and in which he renounced his titles and possessions. Froissart and Hall suggest a formal writ of abdication, and include the scene in which Richard actually hands the crown to Bolingbroke.

and both are the consequence of human fallibility. The tragic is, of course, cathartic. Vanity ushers the fall of Richard, as it does that of Prospero, Lear and Macbeth. Where Prospero spends too long in his library studying his books, and Macbeth too long in the forest listening to incanting witches, Richard spends too long in his chamber studying himself, dressing in the 'fashions' of 'proud Italy' (2.1.21).[22] Famously in Act 4 'plume-plucked' Richard dramatically 'dashes' a 'flatt'ring glass' to the ground (4.1.108, 279). Shakespeare would have expected his audience to be familiar with the various essays written in the later Elizabethan 'mirror for magistrates' genre.[23] And the insinuation is apparent. Richard has realised the extent of his self-delusion; just too late.

The glass is the first of three particular metaphors which Shakespeare uses in order to flesh out the human as well as the institutional dimension of king-ship. A second is oil and water; invoking not only the rituals of coronation, but also those of 'lament' (4.1.302). 'Not all the water in the rough rude sea', Richard reassures Aumerle, the Bishop of Carlisle, and himself, 'Can wash the balm off from an anointed king' (3.2.54–5). The same metaphor recurs in what can be read as Charles's deposition scene, as he threatens to 'wash' his 'hands' of own son (112). Richard is, of course, wrong, as he comes to realise: 'With my own tear I wash away my balm' (4.1.207).[24] And Charles will come to the same realisation too. In the meantime, however, he clings to the same delusion. He too is 'Anointed not by man, but God. I don't/ Negotiate, but issue my commands', for which reason he can 'wait/ A very long time, I have my books to read' (105). Books will not, however, save Charles, any more than they saved Prospero. A little later, Charles pointedly refers to himself as a book 'stuck on the shelf/ For years ignored and waiting'. But there is no time to wait, as William responds: 'You think too much on books and history' (107). Unrest has 'spread', and so the time has come for action; or at least so Kate has decided. Richard takes the crown off his head. William takes the tank off the terrace. The pending coronation service has been adjusted too. There will now be two thrones; but only one king. The spectre of a different King William will be raised, the third, with Queen Kate taking the place of

---

[22] All internal references are from W. Shakespeare, *Richard II*, (Routledge, 1966).

[23] The definitive edition of the duly entitled collection of essays on the subject, *The Mirror for Magistrates*, appeared in 1587. The genre was of course popular across much of Renaissance Europe. One of the most renowned examples of its type was Erasmus's *The Education of a Christian Prince*. Figurative mirrors recur throughout the Shakespearean canon, from 'thy mother's glass' invoked in Sonnet 3 to Hamlet's mirror 'held up to nature' at 3.2.23.

[24] A little later in Act 4 the metaphor recurs, a Richard accuses his deposers who 'with Pilate, wash your hands' (4.1.239).

his Queen, Mary Stuart. William is already acclaimed, his very presence in the Mall having silenced the 'mob'; a neatly turned Ricardian referent, invoking memories of the teenage Richard riding out to quell the Peasants Revolt in 1381 (109).[25] Charles must abdicate. That way he might, in a romantic sense, indeed become the 'greatest king', acclaimed for his selfless sacrifice (112–13). If not, he will be deposed. And 'So there, it's done', a broken Charles realises finally, 'the King is at an end' (116).

He falls as Richard falls, removed from office, his humanity laid bare, his 'glory made base' (4.1.251). It is a 'tragic, and a hard/ And bitter end' for Charles, as it is for Richard (117). Richard, of course, senses his 'end' before the deposition scene. On hearing news of Bolingbroke's victory, he muses on 'the death of kings:/ How some have been depos'd, some slain in war/ Some haunted by the ghosts they have deposed' (3.2.156–8). He anticipates the exchange of 'my large kingdom for a little grave' (3.3.153). Charles likens his prospect to that of an 'old/ Forgotten gardener, who potters around'; an allegory which in the closer context of *Richard II* inheres an obvious resonance (116).[26] Above all, both feel abandoned and alone, in Richard's case, perhaps most obviously in his final scene in Act 5. Charles, conversely, feels 'alone' from the very start (11). There is an especial poignancy in his confession that there is a 'constant fear/ That one might somehow lose one's son' (15). By the end of the play, the sensation is overwhelming. Consumed by the 'betrayal' of his own sons, in the end, both William and Harry, his worst 'fear' realised, he 'collapses' on stage (108, 122). He 'cannot live alone' (115, 116). Emotional devastation is the common destination, for Charles as it is for Richard and as it is of course for Lear. It is 'tough love', William supposes (115). But it is more than that, as their earlier conversation has already revealed. William is destroying his father in cold-blooded revenge for the misery he inflicted on his 'mum', Diana (111). At this point, it is possible to discern any number of referents from classical as well as Shakespearean and of course Jacobean, tragedy.

The suggestion, confirmed by Michael Billington in his review, that *King Charles III* 'offers a meditation on the violable solitude of monarchy', engages the second necessarily related aspect of kingship, and third magisterial metaphor which Shakespeare presents in *Richard II*; the peculiar constitutional

---

[25] Conversely in *Richard II* it is Bolingbroke who better appreciates the importance of 'courtship to the common people' (1.4.24).

[26] Shakespeare frequently used garden allegories of course. Act 3 Scene 4 of *Richard II*, in which the gardener muses on the unruly 'state' of 'our sea-walled garden', is only one of many such instances. Others include, perhaps most obviously *Hamlet* and *The Winter's Tale*.

fiction of the king's 'two bodies'. The fiction might pretend that the office is divinely ordained, but the person is all too human, the fall from monarch to gardener confirmed by the merest slip of the pen. It is only as he begins to sense the approach of his 'day of doom' that Richard comes to appreciate what the fiction means, that 'the hollow crown/ Rounds the mortal temples of a king' (3.2.160–1, 189). In his final scene, incarcerated in Pomfret Castle, Richard further reflects on the critical fiction, and what it demands of a prince:

> Thus play I in one person many people,
> And none contented. Sometimes I am king,
> Then treasons make me wish myself a beggar,
> And so I am . . .
> Then I am king'd again, and by and by
> Think I am unking'd by Bolingbroke,
> And straight am nothing. (5.5.32–4, 36–8)

The distinction between the public office and the private person is noted at the very outset of *King Charles III* when Kate queries 'constitutionally speaking' whether her father-in-law is now king. He 'rules today', Camilla confirms 'Tradition holds that on the death of kings/ Or queens, the next is monarch straight away'. And so 'Your father ruled the moment Granny passed' (13). William appreciates the same in their later conversation in the 'deposition' scene in Act 5. He is not speaking to his father, but to 'the King' (106). Charles, however, struggles to comprehend the same. 'You cannot make distinction between the two', he responds; or at least he cannot (108). Only at the very end is there a sense that he might finally have gained the same insight which at last came to Richard. Deploying the same reflective metaphor, he gazes at the crown which he is about to put on William's head, observing 'And from the side, bejewelled, it looks so rich/ But turn it thus, and this is what you see/ Nothing' (122). Shakespeare's 'unking'd' Richard makes the very same gesture, so that he too will 'nothing have' (4.1.216).

Hal

The same balance and the same delicate tensions are explored in the ensuing two parts of *Henry IV*, which chronicle the 'revolution of the times' which come to blight the troubled reign of Richard's usurper Bolingbroke (3.1.46).[27] And the theme of filial disloyalty is here again pivotal. Bolingbroke's son Hal is the supreme 'self-fashioning' Shakespearean prince, using and then

---

[27] All internal references are from W. Shakespeare, *King Henry IV Part 2*, (Routledge, 1967).

despatching successive parents with a brutal alacrity. Billington notes the immediate resonance between Hal's cold dismissal of Falstaff at the end of the second part, 'I know thee not old man', and William's usurpation of his father (5.5.47).[28] But Hal's emotional, or rather emotion-less, despatch of his father in the Jerusalem Chamber is no less brutal. In fact, the ghost of Hal assumes a bifurcated form in Bartlett's play. There is certainly an element of the older, colder Hal in William. But there is also an evident parallel between the younger Hal and Prince Harry. It is not just the fact that they share, by the nicest of conveniences, the same name. They also share the same liking for a 'classic night out' (19). These scenes, set in various London clubs, are an unsettling mix of the comic and vulgar and, written in what Bartlett terms 'tavern-prose', are clearly meant to resonate with the Eastcheap scenes that Shakespeare wove into his *Henry IV* plays.[29] It is possible to chortle at Harry's witless escapades, his thrill at going to Sainsbury's incognito and buying a Scotch egg, whilst feeling thoroughly discomforted by misjudged metaphors that allude to his looking as though he 'got raped by Primark' (20, 41). Much the same discomforting mix of the comedic and boorish is witnessed in Hal's evening sojourns at the Boar's Head, still more so perhaps in his juvenile venture at Gad's Hill in the first part of *Henry IV*

Bartlett's Harry does not go quite as far as Hal. He does not commit robbery and find himself committed for 'striking about' the Lord Chief Justice; as Hal does (1.2.55–6). But the procuring of a girl so that Harry can find out what it is like to 'knob a prole' is little more cheering (20). The girl in question, Jess, turns out to be rather more than Harry's friends had bargained for, immediately casting aspersions about the Prince's legitimacy before leading him so far astray that he falls in love and decides to 'free' himself from his family, to get a 'job' even, 'and house, and car and maybe wife' (22, 89). Jess is moreover an art student currently 'exploring Islam's relation to pornography'; a subject hardly likely to reassure the Palace's press adviser who is quick to remind his prince just how 'unstable' present matters are (41–2). But Harry is smitten, and thick, and fails to comprehend. It is just possible to feel a little sorry for Harry, the confessed 'ginger joke' destined to play the role of the family fool (64). Fortunately, Harry is also malleable and has been bred to conform. He has, moreover, in the tradition of so many Shakespearean brothers sworn an 'oath' to support William in times of 'crisis' (65). He will play his part, and so, in the end, comes round.

[28] See <https://www.theguardian.com/stage/2014/sep/12/king-charles-iii-review-shakespea re-mike-bartlett-wyndhams-tim-pigott-smith> (last accessed 26th June 2020).

[29] See <https://www.nytimes.com/2015/11/10/theater/mike-bartlett-turns-to-shakespeare-to-voice-his-king-charles-iii.html> (last accessed 26th June 2020).

Jess meanwhile is to be cast aside, with the same callousness that Prince Hal despatched his Falstaff. She has become an equal embarrassment, 'too big a risk', with a finely tuned irony brought down by an intrusive press (119). During an earlier relationship, Jess has indulged in a spot of sexting, for which reason she is now threatened with a different kind of exposure; 'Made weekly fodder for the *Daily Mail*' (117). She appeals to Harry's better nature, and his 'heart'. But Harry's brief flirtation with normality is over. He must revert to the role for which he has been so long trained, to be 'amus-ing/ Mostly, clownish and unthreatening' (119). The spectre of Hal never threatens in the same way as those raised in *Macbeth* or *Richard II*. Harry's ventures into Soho, like Hal's in Eastcheap, are designed to provide an element of light relief. But they also provide a thematic parallel, something which darkens the shade. As we shall now see, this process of shading is a critical aspect of modern monarchy. It is the bearable lightness of princes such as Harry which distracts our attention from the murkier realities of modern governance.

Constitutional Ghosts

If he is inclined to leave his audience to discern their own Shakespearean spectres, Bartlett assumes a more directive role in regard to raising one par-ticular ghost familiar to students of constitutional law. As his protagonist struggles to come to terms with the responsibilities of sovereignty, he turns, perhaps inevitably, to the great Victorian authority on the subject Walter Bagehot. More particularly Charles seeks succour in Bagehot's *The English Constitution*:

> And so.
> Here's Walter Bagehot, eighteen sixty-seven,
> Explaining changes to balance of
> The Crown and State. I read it as a child.
> One line stands out: Bagehot explains that now
> The monarch's mostly ceremonial
> And only can expect, from hereon in:
> The right to be consulted (which I've not)
> The right to encourage (which is all I do),
> And most importantly the right to warn. (103)

The recourse to Bagehot is hardly surprising, and Charles turns to it again a few lines later in conversation with his son. William, he insists, must read Bagehot. 'It's a thing of quiet beauty'; too quiet, for William at least, who has clearly never heard of Bagehot, and too 'ancient'. Too much 'history' dulls the senses (106–7). It certainly seems to have dulled his father's. The insistence is of course rooted in monarchical folklore. It is said that each putative monarch since Queen Victoria has been invited to study Bagehot as a kind of primer on what they should and should not do. Bartlett's Charles infers as much. He read it as a child. But if Bagehot is an obvious recourse, he is also an ambivalent one, for his commentary on monarchy, and its performance, is famously evasive. On the surface, being a monarch might seem to be surprisingly simple. But in practice, it is the finest, and most sensitive, of arts. Two essays in Bagehot's *Constitution* directly address the subject of monarchy. But it is further addressed indirectly time and again. And in these essays, as Charles again infers, Bagehot did two things. First, he stressed just how fine is the performance and the practice of monarchy. Second, he described what, in the matter of government, a monarch could and could not do; or more precisely what they could appear to do or not do. But before we take a closer look at Bagehot's commentary on kingship, we should pause to contemplate a little further the context within which he wrote his *Constitution*. For here again, there is a resonance.

The immediate context was set by the debates surrounding the second Reform Act. Bagehot liked to present himself as a progressive conservative liberal.[30] The idea of democratic reform, however, horrified him; as the introduction to the second 1872 edition of the *Constitution* confirmed. Bagehot was, in short, far more the old-fashioned Whig than the new-fashioned Liberal. He feared change, constitutional change especially. In regard to monarchy though there was a further and more particular context. Queen Victoria had retreated into a state of retirement which was beginning to look more than temporary. It was even rumoured that she might abdicate. Bagehot did not relish either prospect, but at least there was some constitutional precedent for abdication. There was nothing for retirement. The reason for Victoria's reclusion was, of course, the death in 1861 of her beloved Prince Albert. For a short while, her subjects had understood. Mourning was becoming. But then it had become tiresome. When *The Times* ran an April Fool's headline which suggested that the Queen was about to 'break her protracted seclusion', against all advice Victoria decided to publish a sober contradiction, alongside a doctor's note. 'The Queen', the letter confirmed, 'heartily appreciates the desire of her subjects to see her'. But, it continued, there 'are other and higher duties than those of mere representation which

---

[30] He stood repeatedly, and without any tangible success, as a Liberal candidate at successive elections during the late 1860s and early 1870s. And he counted himself a personal friend and confidante of the Chancellor of the Exchequer and later Prime Minister William Ewart Gladstone.

are now thrown upon the Queen, alone and unassisted'.[31] But she was wrong. There were no higher duties.

There is then a shared symmetry about the moments within which Shakespeare and Bagehot wrote. Both were bothered by their Queens. Shakespeare was worried about what might happen when his Queen died. Bagehot was worried about what was going to happen if she continued to live but declined to reign. She might as well be dead. And whilst there was constitutional precedent, abdication offered little by way of reassurance. Visions of Prince Bertie swaggering down the nave of Westminster Abbey to receive the coronation sacrament sent a collective shudder down the backs of all right-thinking mid-Victorian gentlemen; in much the same way as the prospect of James VI of Scotland coming south with his retinue of grasping Scottish chums did little to calm the nerves of right-thinking late Elizabethan gentlemen, especially those perhaps who had taken the trouble to wrestle with their putative king's rambling treatises on the 'trew law' of monarchy. In the end, the reality of King Edward VII proved to be a pleasant surprise; perhaps because expectations were so low. The reality of James I did not.

Will Charles III prove to be a bit more like Edward, or a bit more like James? If it is possible to discern a bit of John of Gaunt in Charles's muse on the 'wise and ancient bond between the Crown' which roots the constitution of 'this pleasant isle', it is just as easy, and that bit more troubling, to discern a bit of James Stuart in the sentiment which follows. For the 'last five hundred years' it is true 'That politicians and democracy/ Have led the way in policy'. But that is an 'option added on,/ Like satnav on a car, it does not come/ As standard' (58). James felt much the same. And there is something else which, in due course, it appears that they share; the same sense of divine appointment. As James informed his Parliament in 1610, the 'State of Monarchy is the supremest thing on earth: for kings are not only God's lieutenants upon earth and sit on God's throne, but even by God himself are called Gods'.[32] The beleaguered Charles, as we have already noted, clings to the same delusion, that sustained James and which will destroy Richard: 'Anointed not by man, but God, I don't/ Negotiate but issue my commands' (105).

Bagehot's essays on monarchy, as we observed before, emphasised two things; both of which can be likewise discerned in Shakespeare's reflections on kingship. There is the matter of appearance and the matter of doing. The distinction was of course written through the *Constitution* which famously distinguished the 'dignified' aspects of the constitution from the 'efficient'.

---

[31] L. Strachey, *Queen Victoria*, (Penguin, 1971), 184.

[32] King James, *Political Writings*, (Cambridge UP, 1994), 181.

The principal role of monarchy was to add lustre to the former; to furnish a 'visible symbol of unity to those still so imperfectly educated as to need a symbol'.[33] In a renowned passage, written with a customarily ironic eye, Bagehot observed:

> The use of the Queen, in a dignified capacity, is incalculable. Without her in England, the present English government would fail and pass away. Most people when they read that the Queen walked on the slopes at Windsor – that the Prince of Wales went to the Derby – have imagined that too much thought and prominence were given to little things. But they have been in error; and it is nice to trace how the actions of a retired widow and an unemployed youth become of such importance.[34]

It was the falling and the passing away that Bagehot feared. The same sentiment and the same irony recur throughout the chapters on monarchy. Englishmen and women are 'governed by the weaknesses of their imagination' rather than by the exercise of their reason, they prefer to 'defer' to the 'theatrical show of society', to the 'certain pomp of great men', and most especially to 'a certain spectacle of beautiful women'.[35] And it is the primary responsibility of monarchy to ensure that they continue to be so distracted, and enraptured; otherwise, they might all start to think about matters such as equality and democracy and suffrage.

Monarchy, Bagehot confirms in resonantly Shakespearean tones, is a 'stage' upon which the princes and princesses 'walk their parts'.[36] And Bartlett's Charles fully appreciates these performative responsibilities, as the very first lines of the play confirm:

> My wondrous Charles you looked composed throughout
> You did her proud, for as she would have liked
> You never showed your pain, but stood instead
> A virtuous man of dignity and grace.
> Immovable, inscrutable as stone. (11)

'It is', Charles responds, 'simply what I had to do' (11). Later in the same scene, he compliments his grandchildren for having 'understood' what to do too: 'They watched and listened, and like all of us/ They kept their real emotions to themselves' (15). Dignity to Charles means, above all else, reservation, and sacrifice, and mingling. Charles does not much relish the idea of

[33] W. Bagehot, *The English Constitution*, (Cambridge UP, 2001), 41.
[34] Bagehot, *Constitution*, 34.
[35] Bagehot, *Constitution*, 30, 41
[36] Bagehot, *Constitution*, 31.

mixing with his subjects, the 'baying mob' (18). Prince William is not much more enamoured of the idea. But he appreciates the need. Representation is everything. Following the funeral, accordingly, he knows they must now 'mingle with the crowds/ A single round should be sufficient' (14). And it is a bit more than simple representation too. Monarchy must also enchant. Half a century earlier, Dorothy Wordsworth had recorded a visit to Windsor, where she espied King George III walking along the terrace with his family. 'I fancied myself', she recalled, 'treading upon Fairy-Ground and that the gay company around me was brought there by Enchantment'.[37]

Monarchy must spread a little fairy-dust. As Bagehot appreciated, it must present itself as a 'charmed spectacle'. Charles bemoans the prospect of a monarchy that is nothing more than a 'pretty plastic picture with no meaning' (116). But that is precisely what modern monarchy is supposed to be, as Bagehot confirmed, the play of 'nice and pretty events'.[38] No one spread fairy-dust better than Princess Diana. The hope now is that Princess Kate will be able to do the same. It is her 'gift', as Charles confirms, it is what 'you've brought us./A sense of fashion, better hair as well' (12). There is, of course, a risk in becoming, as Camilla acerbically puts it, 'the King/ And Queen of column inches'; a risk which the life, and more particularly the death, of Diana, only too obviously laid bare (114). But it is a risk that must simply be managed. It is, as Kate retaliates, 'The greatest influence that we possess' (114). Spectacle is everything, an insight she evinces from the start:

> So coronation day itself is just
> The ancient costumes worn, and lines to learn,
> A slice of theatre, that's played for fun? (13)

And again later, having cajoled her husband into agreeing to usurp the crown, she confirms the 'way' in which it must be secured:

> We're told the world's a play of surfaces
> Where meaning's made through only what is shown
> You must then focus 'pon the public eye
> You dress your best. And so, of course, shall I. (97)

The second aspect of monarchy which Bagehot identified is that of doing; or not doing. Famously he observed that the monarch has 'the right to be consulted, the right to encourage and the right to warn', adding that a 'king of great sagacity would want no others'.[39] It is the line which, as Charles

---

[37] In A. Byatt, *Unruly Times: Wordsworth and Coleridge in their Time*, (Vintage, 1997), 107.
[38] Bagehot, *Constitution*, 37.
[39] Bagehot, *Constitution*, 60.

confirms to son, 'stands out'. But its opacity destroys him. Bagehot has cited a constitutional convention, and conventions are fashioned precisely to defy precision. It is all a matter of inference and practice, of 'history and precedence', as the Prime Minister later confirms to Parliament (75). Bagehot admits as much. It is the appreciation of 'history' which proves the 'sagacious' monarch.[40] Charles, however, is driven to despair and critical error. From the very outset, he struggles to place himself and his office; quite literally indeed. After the funeral service, the Prime Minister suggests that they should leave the Abbey 'side' by side, for 'public reassurance'. But Charles, at the last minute, changes his mind and decides that he 'should remain aloft/ From politics and walk with royals alone' (18). It is again a matter of representation. But the inference is misjudged. Charles wants the 'stage' to himself (19). It is the kind of mistake that Shakespeare's Richard would have made. It is just as easy to imagine Richard articulating Charles's ironic observation, on hearing that his son has fetched a glass of water for the Prime Minister: 'A future king waits butler-like upon/ The people! That awaits us all perhaps' (48). How merry the irony, and how sour, is a matter for directorial discretion. Constitutional conventions are sustained by performance and pretence, and the sharpest appreciation of place. And it is all too easy to get wrong.

In regard to consultation, Charles feels denied. In a prosaic sense there appears to be plenty of consultation, so much so that the prospective King feels almost overwhelmed in the days which have followed his mother's death: 'I'm trapped by meetings, all these people ask/ Me questions, talking, fussing, what to do' (16). Being King is rather less fun than being 'Thoughtful Prince' (16). But where Prospero did too little, Charles aspires to do too much, as becomes apparent in his very first audience with Mr Evans, the Prime Minister. Such meetings, between monarch and Prime Minister, are once again embedded in constitutional convention. It is at this meeting that Charles intimates his opposition to the proposed bill to regulate the press. If this was an undergraduate public law seminar, much of the conversation might be expected to move around possible infringements of Convention rights to free expression, something which would very evolve into a discussion regarding the limits of privacy, and then as a consequence end with a customary consideration of how to strike a reasonable balance between two apparently conflicting 'rights'. The conversation between Charles and Mr Evans engages a tangential aspect of rights-theory, as they seek respective recourse to matters of 'principle' and public opinion (26).

---

[40] Bagehot, *Constitution*, 60–1.

Here, however, the more immediate question is that of prerogative and its reach. Charles thinks that he is merely exercising his right to 'warn'. It is 'only what I do' (103). Evans sees it differently. It is interference, and he is puzzled as to the reason. He wonders why Charles should assume such a principled position, given his personal experience of press intrusion. Charles responds by reaffirming the distinction between his private inclination, as 'a man, a father, a husband', and his public responsibility as king to 'protect/ This country's unique force and way of life'. It is, he adds, a matter of representation too; a responsibility to 'demonstrate/ The way a just society should work' (27). At this point, Evans assumes that he can simply observe the niceties, take into 'account' Charles's opinion, and move on (28). But he cannot. When Charles presses his point, Evans is forced to reply that he would not anyway change his opinion. The bill is passed, it 'matters not' (28). The limits of prerogative, and convention, are laid bare. In the conversation with the leader of the opposition, Mr Stevens, which immediately follows, Charles reflects on his disappointment and frustration:

> I always hoped as Crown I'd have some small
> But crucial influence upon the State
> I'd given all my working life to serve. (31)

It is Stevens who strategically places the seeds of destruction in his monarch's mind. Charles can do more than merely warn. He can exercise his constitutional 'choice' not to sign the bill'. It is 'the power you possess' (31). When Charles expresses his doubts, Stevens pushes on by presenting an alternative constitutional principle, of 'checks and balances'. That is, of course, the essence of British constitutionalism, its strength and indeed its weaknesses. There is always another principle, and it is never entirely clear which matters most at any given time. Bagehot's near contemporary Albert Venn Dicey famously supposed that the principle of parliamentary sovereignty was the 'keystone' of the constitution. The case could not be made today, at least not with the same confidence. Bagehot also esteemed parliamentary 'supremacy'. Conversely, he did not think much of the 'supposed' theory of constitutional 'checks and balances'. He appreciated the functional importance of 'balance', in much the same way as Kate, who understands 'that it is/ A balance in a contradiction/ 'Tween those elected and those born to rule/ That is unique and does protect and make us all' (68). It was the checking function that bothered Bagehot rather more. Charles however, mistaking discretion for 'choice', is intrigued. The thought stays with him. The following day he makes the fateful decision to send Evans a note confirming his refusal to sign the bill.

Matters, predictably, come to a head at their next audience. The Prime

Minister seeks to balm his monarch's 'conscience', promising that they might in due course 'talk some more' regarding Charles's larger concerns regarding the responsibilities of office (49–50). But for now, he must sign the bill. Charles refuses, in terms which will be especially familiar to students of *Hamlet*:

> For if my name is given through routine
> And not because it represents my view
> Then soon I'll have no name, and nameless I
> Have not myself, and having not myself,
> Possess not mouth nor tongue nor brain, instead
> I am an empty vessel, waiting for
> Instruction, soulless and uncorporate (50)

But that, as Evans replies simply, is his 'role' (51). It is what his mother did, time and again, even as she faced 'far greater revolution', signing away empires, approving laws which radically altered the sexual, cultural and political morality of the nation. She 'hated' it all. But still, she 'always signed' (51). Charles is however resolute, bolstered by the advice of his lawyers, and the riddles of his dead wife, and by his own interpretation of Bagehot and the reach of their respective 'prerogatives' (52). The bill cannot pass without his assent. Evans disagrees. The bill 'will be law within a month' whether or not the King assents (53). Thereafter the matter becomes a battle of personal and political will. Charles decides to exercise his 'ancient' right to dissolve Parliament. It represents another critical misjudgement of his prerogative and its reach, for such powers are once again described by convention. Charles has not read his Bagehot closely enough. The final chapter of the *Constitution* treated readers to a rather breathless 'history'; too breathless to find time to recount Charles I's fateful bid to arrest the five Members, but not so breathless that Bagehot could not confirm the 'folly' of peremptory dissolutions.[41] If Charles had spent a little longer reading this final chapter, he might have known what to expect if he chose to ignore the lessons of English constitutional history. In the end, the matter is resolved by a palace putsch, and the constitutional crisis is abated.

The Shape of Things to Come

Some ghosts simply flit about. Others like to gesture towards the future. Prophetic ghosts tend to be more unsettling. Bagehot's contemporary Charles Dickens summoned one of the most famous, and disturbing, of prophetic

---

[41] Bagehot, *Constitution*, 177–8.

ghosts; the spirit of Christmas 'still to come'.[42] The final of the spectres which haunt Scrooge's dreams the night before Christmas, one of the most terrifying in English literature, says nothing, merely gesturing towards the particular horror of a death un-mourned. Plenty of Shakespeare's ghosts assumed a more prophetic aspect too, and generally of the darker, more foreboding kind. The ghosts which visit Richard III the night before Bosworth do little to calm the nerves. Neither does the ghost of Hamlet's father. And neither, of course, does the ghosts which haunt Macbeth's imagination. Shakespeare's ghosts tend to serve a quasi-judicial and providential as well as prophetic purpose; confirming what will, as a matter of divine retribution, befall the perpetrators of heinous acts. In raising these spectres, Shakespeare intended to both warn and reassure his audience. God will ensure that vengeance is visited upon the wicked.

Bartlett's purpose is different, not least because his audience is different. These days we do not expect God to visit much on anyone. Kingship is more prosaic, as William appreciates. 'This is a job', he coldly informs his father as he moves his deposition, 'You should have got it right, and you did not' (112). And the future is more speculative too; though it is not entirely unsure. The reach of history directs the future. Bartlett's ghosts merely serve to point the way. The ghost of Diana, like the third spectre in Dickens's *Christmas Carol*, suggests what might happen unless future behaviour is adjusted. The months after her death in 1998 stimulated considerable debate in regard to the future of the British monarchy. In the narrower terms of constitutional law, it should not have. But it did because, as Bagehot appreciated, the monarchy does not exist in narrower terms. Its function is far larger and far more precarious. It is there to provide theatre, and to cheer us all up a bit. Diana did that for a while, for which reason her sudden departure, though undoubtedly dramatic, was also thoroughly unsettling. With Diana gone, the rest of the royal family just seemed variously boring and boorish. So long as Queen Elizabeth II remained on the throne, commentators agreed, the monarchy would survive. But what would happen the day after Elizabeth died? It is the premise of Bartlett's play.

Two decades have passed since Diana's death, and it might be argued that not much has changed. Queen Elizabeth remains on the throne, and her eldest son remains in waiting, as he has for seventy years. And the same uncertainties as to how he might envisage his responsibilities as king linger; which is again the premise of Bartlett's play. There are suspicions that he

---

[42] It is interesting that Bartlett's Charles, when he first thinks he has seen a ghost, reaches much the same conclusion as Scrooge. It is a consequences of 'nerves', and the solution is to take some sleeping tablets (32).

might indeed assume a more interventionist position. But they are only suspicions, founded on little more than an apparent liking for writing letters to ministers about various matters that interest him, commonly architectural or environmental.[43] At what point such correspondence begins to press at the necessarily fluid margins of constitutional convention remains a matter of conjecture. It is just as likely that Charles appreciates the place of monarchy in much the same terms as those articulated by his son William who, musing on Kate's cajoling, reflects on his grandmother's advice:

> She told me that temptation lies as royal
> To act, and speak, and lead, and always move,
> When actually the greatest influence
> That we can wield is through our standing still
> Not rash, and never changing, a great Crown
> Is made by dint of always being there,
> I'll keep my silence. And let life unfold. (70)

The appreciation is subtle and classically Bagehot, the natural complement to representation, of seeming to do whilst 'standing still'. It suggests two critical features of modern monarchy; and there is no reason to suppose that the prospective Charles III will fail to appreciate either. First 'standing still' should not be mistaken for inactivity. Doing nothing can take an awful lot of doing. Second, the seeming is vital. In the meantime, however, the strategy suits Bartlett's William. It legitimates dithering, and cultivated dithering, it might be suggested, has become the essence of modern monarchy. The institution can survive any number of 'idle' monarchs, as Bagehot again appreciated. They will probably 'do little good', but more importantly do 'as little harm'. The risk is found in the 'acting and meddling fool'.[44] This William seems to appreciate. In the place of 'Romantic gestures', he will provide 'Stability and certainty, above all else' and the surety of not doing much. And thus, the 'brand' will be 'renewed' (112–13).

Academic opinion prefers to paint an assuring picture too. Provided it respects the propriety of the various conventions which hedge its constitutional

---

[43] The extent of his ministerial correspondence became apparent following a successful campaign pursued by the *Guardian* under the terms of the Freedom of Information Act. The so-called 'black spider' letters, so named as a consequence of the Prince's handwriting, revealed a wide-range of interests, some of which addressed matters of higher politics, such as the funding of the armed services, but most of which touched on matters of more personal concern, including badger-culling, the European directive on herbal medicine, the plight of the Patagonian Toothfish and the importance of maintaining expedition huts in the Antarctic.

[44] Bagehot, *Constitution*, 66.

place, the British monarchy will remain secure simply because it 'alone can represent the whole nation in an emotionally satisfying way'.[45] For good or bad, it is probably true. It cannot be said that contrary arguments, in favour of a republic, enjoy any great traction in contemporary public culture. Pressure is born of necessity, and there does not appear to be much of a need. The test is again classic Bagehot; what is most 'useful'.[46] In his *Constitution*, Bagehot famously observed that a 'republic', had anyway already 'insinuated itself beneath the folds of a monarchy'.[47] The situation has not changed. Britain is already a republic, in everything but name, for which reason the abolition of monarchy would be little more than representational. Of course, there are arguments from principle. And there is dramatic license.

It is this licence which allows Bartlett to conjure the consequences of a monarch who misunderstands the nature of convention and misconceives the reach of prerogative. When Charles declines to sign the press regula-tion bill the 'people' are reported to be 'enraged./ They march at day, and then at night they camp/ Outside the Palace, shout against the King' and their 'numbers grow' (78). Charles certainly fears for his 'preservation' (83). The Chief of Staff is altogether more relaxed; merely the 'unemployed and students' making a bit of 'noise' (82). Their attention will be soon distracted. Constitutional crisis will not hold the 'public's eye' for long. It will 'drift to this instead/ A photo of a girl in bed' (79). In this suitably perverse manner, Jess will save the monarchy. Bagehot would have relished the irony, however grim. Back in 1872, when he wrote the Introduction to the second edition of his *English Constitution*, Bagehot, like so many of his contemporaries, feared that revolution was, quite literally, a stone's throw away. But the dif-ference between a riot and a revolution is considerable. Occasional riots have become part of political life in modern Britain. Revolutions have not. All the same, sensing his monarch's mood, the Chief is persuaded that rolling a tank onto the terrace might be a good idea. It is possible to smile at the Swiftian absurdity of the gesture, a Lilliputian 'show of strength' intended to 'send a message out' (83). There is, however, a darker inference. As he departs, the Chief assures his sovereign that, should the need arise, the army is at his 'command'; and not that of Parliament's 'changing whims' (86). Except of course it is not. The situation changes and Charles loses his tank along with his crown.

If it is difficult to imagine the institution of a republic in the near future, either by accident or by design, it is more possible to imagine an unfolding

---

[45] V. Bogdanor, *The Monarchy and the Constitution*, (Oxford UP, 1995), 301.
[46] Bagehot, *Constitution*, 170.
[47] Bagehot, *Constitution*, 44.

which sees Charles cede the succession to his eldest son. And it is certainly possible to imagine a rewriting of constitutional convention in the event of any prospective monarch choosing to do what Bartlett's Charles does. This latter supposition can be inferred from Mr Stevens's counsel in Act 3 Scene 3. The consequence of refusing to sign the mooted press regulation bill cannot be over-stated. Henceforth:

> Not only this particular law but all
> The legislation still to come, will not
> Appear before the monarch's eye or pen. (60)

In such a circumstance, the government will force through an 'enabling' or 'constitutional' statute; of the kind which resembles previous Parliamentary Acts, or the 2005 Constitutional Reform Act. Such a statute, should one be deemed necessary in the future, could be readily compassed within our constitutional jurisprudence. There again it is probably not jurisprudence that really matters; nor academic opinion. It is notable that when he finds his king to be immovable, Bartlett's Prime Minister turns not to the Supreme Court, nor to the dusty halls of academia, but to public opinion. It is not a matter of constitutional nicety, but of defending 'Democracy itself' (53). And Charles does precisely the same, appealing not to the precedents discovered by his lawyers, but to public 'trust' and the demands of 'conscience' (54). Even the deployment of a tank on the terrace is intended to make a 'show' (83). In the end, Charles is usurped not in Parliament or even at Westminster Abbey, but in the television studio in which he was supposed to be going to address his subjects. Having arrived unannounced, William walks in front of his father just as he is about to speak and takes the podium. Though his father has acted from 'conscience' such is the degree of public 'disquiet' that he must 'try to mediate/ Between the King and the House of Commons' (101). In short, he steals the scene and the crown. Performance is everything.

'A kingdom for a stage. Princes to play' as the Chorus advises at the start of *Henry V*, and 'spectators' to ogle as Bagehot reiterates in such similar tones at the start of his *Constitution*.[48] It is why Bartlett's Charles, like Shakespeare's Richard, must be 'unking'd' in 'common view' rather than simply sent into quiet retirement (4.1.155, 220). Reception and perception is everything. Bartlett has repeatedly maintained that theatre must speak the real concerns of real people. It 'has to appeal to people who do jobs and have lives'.[49] It is again the defining aspiration of drama which chooses to address the 'state of

---

[48] Bagehot, *Constitution*, 31.

[49] See <www.theguardian.com/culture/2009/nov/08/mike-bartlett-royal-court-cock> (last accessed 26th June 2020).

the nation'. The purpose of *King Charles III* is not simply to laugh at the man who would be king, still less at the institution itself. It is rather to 'engage', to make the audience contemplate the inherent tensions which a modern monarchy conceives, and which Bartlett himself acknowledges; between the 'head' which suggests that monarchy is 'dangerous', and the 'heart' which finds 'a comfort in long-standing institutions'. *King Charles III* is written, accordingly, in a distinctively Wordsworthian spirit. In the 1798 Preface to *The Lyrical Ballads* Wordsworth claimed that his principle aspiration was to 'speak a plainer and more emphatic language', the 'language really used by men'.[50] It is a noble ambition, and a difficult one to realise. But it is not just noble. It is also necessarily dangerous, as Bagehot suggested, even subversive. No matter what other mistakes might be committed, by monarch or minister, the 'mystery' of monarchy must be preserved. 'We must' never 'let in daylight upon magic'.[51] But this, of course, is precisely what Bartlett does. 'If you take enough layers away what have you got left, underneath, know what I mean?' asks one of William's putative subjects (73) It is not that the question has an answer. The issue is whether William, or Charles, can forestall its asking, or at least an asking that is too urgent. It is why ultimately the future of the British monarchy will depend less on perceived breaches of constitutional convention than on the quality of Kate's hair.

---

[50] W. Wordsworth, *Complete Poetical Works*, (Oxford UP, 1936), 734
[51] Bagehot, *Constitution*, 50

6

Feasts of Filth

Few modern plays have created a greater furore than Sarah Kane's *Blasted*, first performed at the Royal Court Theatre in London in January 1995.[1] The violence was pervasive, the structure seemingly incoherent, the purpose elusive. Critics were almost uniformly hostile. It was, according to one, a 'disgusting feast of filth', whilst another concluded that 'it's not a theatre critic that is required, it's a psychiatrist'. Jack Tinker, in the *Daily Mail*, declared himself 'utterly and entirely disgusted' by a play that 'appears to know no bounds of decency'.[2] A few were more circumspect. David Greig, writing in the *Guardian*, suspected that once the 'hysteria dies down' it might be recognised as something of a masterpiece. John Peter, in the *Sunday Times*, concluded that however disturbing the experience, 'We need these moral

---

[1] All the more remarkable perhaps given that barely a thousand people saw the first production. For an overview of this furore, see E. Aston, 'Reviewing the Fabric of *Blasted*', in L. De Vos and G. Saunders (eds), *Sarah Kane in Context*, (Manchester UP, 2010), 13–27, and also A. Singer, 'Don't want to be this: the elusive Sarah Kane', 48 *Drama Review* 2004, 145–6. According to Aleks Sierz the 'controversy it excited made Kane's play a significant cultural moment' in modern British theatre. See his *In-Yer-Face: British Drama Today*, (Faber and Faber, 2001), 36, and also 93 reiterating that *Blasted* remained undoubtedly the 'most notorious play of the decade'.

[2] The director of the Royal Court Theatre, where *Blasted* was premiered, referred to a critical 'witch-hunt'. See Sierz, *In-Yer-Face*, 95 and also 108. Kane clearly felt the hostility personally. She was, it should be noted, only 23 years old at the time of writing *Blasted*. It is no coincidence that the sadistic torturer in her later *Cleansed* is called Tinker. The reason for the nature of the hostility was readily appreciated by Kane. Attending one of the press nights, she noted that aside from three women, 'everyone else was a middle-aged, white, middle-class man – most of them had plaid jackets on! It was literally at that point that I realized that the character in my play was a 'middle-aged, male journalist, who not only rapes his girlfriend but is then raped and mutilated himself. And suddenly it occurred to me that they weren't going to like it'. See G. Saunders, *About Kane: the playwright and the work*, (Faber, 2009), xxii, 2, 52. Elaine Aston ventures the thought, necessarily ironic, that the 'shell-shocked reviewers' betrayed the same 'vulnerability and fragility of Cate' the rape victim in *Blasted*, 'whose body feints and fits under pressure'. See Aston, 'Fabric', 17.

ordeals. Theatre is only alive if it is kicking'.[3] But most were just appalled. And not much more enamoured of later Kane plays such as *Phaedra's Love* and *Cleansed*. Criticism has tended to soften over time.[4] Indeed, the greater danger today, a decade after her tragic early death, is that of critical hagiography, with Kane lauded as one of the most original of a new breed of dynamic 'in-yer-face' dramatists who rose to prominence during the 1990s.[5] One of the characteristics of this new genre of drama was a peculiarly intense embrace of sex and violence.[6] Violence certainly emerged as a defining feature of Kane's writing.[7] And when Kane sought to intensify the violence of her plays she turned repeatedly to rape.[8] The purpose of this chapter is to explore Kane's presentation of rape within the context of the ongoing debate regarding sexual violence and its attendant 'myths'. As we shall see this presentation creates as many tensions as it does affinities. The first part of the chapter will revisit rape, and more particularly, the enduring force of 'rape myths'. The

---

[3] In G. Saunders, *Love Me or Kill Me: Sarah Kane and the Theatre of Extremes*, (Manchester UP, 2002), 37, and Sierz, *In-Yer-Face*, 96.

[4] The most famous recantation is that of Michael Billington, who later wrote 'I deplored the tone with which I reviewed it, which was one of lofty derision. I can now see that it was a serious play, driven by moral ferocity'. In Saunders, *Love Me*, 9.

[5] The quintessential in-yer-face writer of the decade' according to Aleks Sierz, who was not alone in worrying that the manner of Kane's death, by suicide, might generate a 'Saint Sarah' cult. Kenyon likewise expressed misgivings that some people impelled by a sense of 'depressive empathy' might be 'attracted to her work for the wrong reasons'. See Sierz, *In-Yer-Face*, 90 and 239, Saunders, *About Kane*, 124 and *Love Me*, 144, and on the same subject, 'Just a Word on a Page and there is the Drama: Sarah Kane's Theatrical Legacy', 13 *Contemporary Theatre Review* 2003, 98–9, and also H. Ball, 'Room Service: En Suite on the *Blasted* Frontline', 15 *Contemporary Theatre Review* 2005, 321.

[6] See D. Edgar, 'Unsteady States: Theories of Contemporary New Writing' 15 *Contemporary Theatre Review* 2005, 300–1.

[7] As Sierz noted, anyone who turned up to see *Blasted* was treated to scenes of 'anal rape, masturbation, micturition, defecation, fellatio, frottage, cannibalism and eye-gouging', all in the space of less than two hours. See his *In-Yer-Face*, 100. Kane wrote just five plays during her lifetime, leading a number of commentators to bemoan a sense of incompleteness and potential unrealised. Kenyon, however, has suggested her 'body of work was absolutely complete', and that Kane may not have been able to progress much further. See *About Kane*, xxii.

[8] Not that Kane was alone in this. Sierz notes the frequency with which 'in-yer-face' dramatists sought recourse to rape in their writings. See his *In-Yer-Face*, 3–4. At the same time, as Kim Solga recently suggested, the subject of rape remains largely 'missing' from Kane 'scholarship'. See her '*Blasted*'s Hysteria: Rape, Realism, and the Thresholds of the Visible', 50 *Modern Drama* 2007, 347. Graham Saunders notes the peculiarly prophetic observation of Tom Morris, writing just as *Blasted* was being first put on at the Royal Court. Speaking to the genre as a whole, Morris observed that 'Watching the cruellest of these plays in a small studio theatre is like watching a simulated rape in your own living room'. In Saunders, *Love Me*, at 5. As we shall see Kane wrote simulated rape into *Blasted*.

second will then consider Kane on rape; its presentation in her plays and its consideration in her subsequent interviews. It has been said that *Blasted* is a play of strategic 'incoherences'.[9] In the third, we will contemplate the consequence of this apparently perplexing supposition. It goes, as we will see, to the very heart of the 'law and literature' enterprise; the capacity of a literary text to elevate our ethical consciousness, and in so doing encourage us to contemplate rather more closely the collateral 'incoherences' of the law.

Rape and Myth

The crime of rape represents something of a touchstone in feminist legal and political theory. According to Robin Morgan, rape is the 'perfected act of male sexuality in a patriarchal culture', the 'ultimate metaphor for domination, violence, subjugation, and possession'.[10] Ann Cahill writes in a similar vein. Rape is 'a crime that epitomizes women's oppressed status', one of 'indisputable violence and loathing.[11] For much of the 1970s and 1980s, it was possible to distinguish two alternative positions. A first, associated commonly with Susan Brownmiller, argued that rape is less about sex, and more about simple violence committed by men against women, 'a brief expression of physical power, a conscious process of intimidation, a blunt, ugly sexual invasion with possible lasting effects on all women'.[12] A second, favoured by many critical legal feminists, followed Catherine MacKinnon in arguing, to the contrary, that rape is a logical extension of heterosexuality.[13] Adopting a position that owed much to the influence of Andrea Dworkin, MacKinnon argued in her *Toward a Feminist Theory of State*, that the 'wrong of rape has proved so difficult to define because the unquestionable starting point has been that rape is defined as distinct from intercourse, while for women it is difficult to distinguish the two under conditions of male dominance'.[14] Accordingly, she famously concluded, 'If sexuality is central to women's definition and forced sex is central to sexuality, rape is indigenous, not exceptional, to women's social condition'.[15]

---

[9] See S. Carney, 'The Tragedy of History in Sarah Kane's *Blasted*', 46 *Theatre Survey* 2005, 279, 292–3.

[10] R. Morgan, *Going too Far: The Personal Chronicle of a Feminist*, (Random House, 1977), 163–4.

[11] A. Cahill, *Rethinking Rape*, (Cornell UP, 2001), 2.

[12] S. Brownmiller, *Against Our Will: Men, Women and Rape*, (Penguin, 1975), 377. Historically, of course, the violence was inflicted by one man upon the property of another, his wife.

[13] For a useful overview of these alternative positions, see Cahill, *Rape*, 18–25, 37–40.

[14] C. MacKinnon, *Towards a Feminist Theory of State*, (Harvard UP, 1989), 174.

[15] MacKinnon, *Towards*, 172.

The problem is that MacKinnon's approach diminishes agency and particularity. As Patricia Williams has observed, sex is not a 'bad' thing. It is how sex is 'done' which can be problematic.[16] The discourse of rape must accommodate differentiation. It is for this reason that Ann Cahill, for example, has suggested that rape should instead be understood 'as something that is taken up and experienced differently by different women but also holds some common aspects'.[17] Carine Mardorossian has said the same, advising the importance of challenging 'paradigms' which suppose a common 'experience' of rape.[18] From within the legal academy, Susan Estrich has likewise argued the case for particularity in rape law reform. In the place of rape defined as a physical 'event' Estrich suggests that the law of rape should be written so that it can take account of rape as 'experience'.[19] Of course, it is just as important here to ensure that the rhetoric of 'experience' does not preclude differentiation; as Mardorossian and more recently still Janet Halley, Karen Engle and Clare McGlynn have all pointed out.[20] Relatedly, it is not just a matter of sex and violence, but of power too, and fear and consequence. And aesthetics and language, as both Halley and before her Carol Smart have argued.[21] Here the

---

[16] P. Williams, 'Alchemical Notes: Reconstructed Ideals from Deconstructed Rights', 22 *Harvard Civil Rights-Civil Liberties Law Review* 1987, 401–34.

[17] Cahill, *Rape*, 4–5, and again at 9 reaffirming that 'every rape experience is unique'.

[18] C. Mardorossian, 'Toward a New Feminist Theory of Rape', 27 *Signs* 2002, particularly 745–7 and also 751–3, distinguishing her work from that of Sharon Marcus who, she argues, despite a more nuanced appreciation of the discursive and differentiated nature of rape experience falls prey to the temptation to fashion peculiarly female 'victims'. See S. Marcus, 'Fighting Bodies, Fighting Words: A Theory and Politics of Rape Prevention' in J. Butler and J. Scott (eds) *Feminists Theorize the Political*, (Routledge, 1992), 385–404.

[19] S. Estrich, 'Rape', 95 *Yale Law Journal* 1986, particularly 1105–21, 1147–57 and 1179–82. The fact that Estrich wrote from personal experience, as a rape victim, necessarily added a further dimension to her argument.

[20] See J. Halley, 'Rape in Berlin: Reconsidering the Criminalization of Rape in the International Law or Armed Conflict', 9 *Melbourne Journal of International Law* 2008, 78–120, K. Engle, 'Feminism and its (Dis)Contents: Criminalizing Wartime Rape in Bosnia-Herzegovina' 99 *American Journal of International Law* 2005, 778–816, and C. McGlynn, 'Rape, Torture and the European Convention on Human Rights', 58 *International and Comparative Law Quarterly* 2009, 565–95. It is notable that Halley, Engle and McGlynn are all writing in the closer context of rape in war, something which as we shall see imports a particular pertinence in regard to the second rape depicted in *Blasted*.

[21] Halley's 'Rape in Berlin' moves around the publication in 2005 of *A Woman in Berlin: Eight Weeks in a Conquered Country* (Philip Boehm). For her necessarily literary analysis of this apparently testamentary account of serial rape experiences, published anonymously, see 'Rape in Berlin', 91–109. See also C. Smart, 'Law's Power, the Sexed Body, and Feminist Discourse', 17 *Journal of Law and Society* 1990, 203–8.

particularity of experience imports impression and perception, gesturing, as it must, to a still more radical subjectivity. The 'politics and aesthetics of rape' are 'one'.[22]

The reorientation of rape towards the particular and the impression-istic reinforces the case for deconstructing the particular historical and culturally embedded 'myths' of rape; an endeavour which has assumed a pivotal place in contemporary rape discourse.[23] Such myths, in Martha Burt's original determination, are represented as 'prejudicial, stereotypical and false beliefs about rape, rape victims and rapists'.[24] Some of these myths, of course, found reinvestment in the universalist assumptions of 'second wave' feminism written into the accounts of Brownmiller and MacKinnon; that all rape is violent, that all sex is a species of rape and that all men, the logic continues, are prospective rapists. The necessary insinu-ations of passivity and inevitability, as critics have observed, does little to diminish female stereotyping.[25] There is a peculiar irony in the supposition that some feminist campaigners and lawyers, so keen to engage the patent inadequacy of rape law, should have reinforced the collective mythology which underpins the 'real rape stereotypes' so regularly pedalled in modern courtrooms.[26]

Four species of rape myth are commonly identified.[27] A first suggests that only women are raped. A second supposes that only certain kinds of

---

[22] See L. Higgins and B. Silver, 'Rereading Rape', in L. Higgins and B. Silver (eds) *Rape and Representation*, (Columbia UP, 1991), 1.

[23] See here J. Burke, *Rape; a history from 1860 to the present*, (Virago, 2007), 24–49, and also D. Cornell, *Beyond Accommodation*, (Routledge, 1991), 115–16 likewise urging the need to 'deconstruct' the mythic discourse of rape.

[24] M. Burt, 'Cultural Myths and Supports of Rape', 38 *Journal of Personality and Social Psychology* 1980, 217.

[25] See I. Anderson and K. Doherty, *Accounting for Rape: Psychology, Feminism and Discourse Analysis in the Study of Sexual Violence*, (Routledge, 2008), 6–9 and also Burke, *Rape*, 143–5, 415–16, 423.

[26] The continuing strength of this stereotyping in the modern legal process, and attendant medical and 'support' networks, has been graphically reaffirmed in the recent UK Government Equalities Office report *Connections and disconnections: Assessing evidence, knowledge and practice in responses to rape*, (GEO, 2010), particularly at sections 5–7. For a further comment on the enduring strength of this 'stereotype' in modern criminal law, see J. Temkin and B. Krahe, *Sexual Assault and the Justice Gap*, (Hart, 2008), 50–1.

[27] See, for example, G. Bohner et al., 'Rape myth acceptance: cognitive, affective and behav-ioural effects of beliefs that blame the victim and exonerate the perpetrator', in M. Horvath and J. Brown (eds) *Rape: Challenging contemporary thinking*, (Willan, 2009), 18–19, 31, and at a marginal variant, Temkin and Krahe, *Sexual Assault*, 43–7.

women are raped; those who 'had it coming', who somehow projected a desire to be raped, consciously or unconsciously.[28] Speaking to these first two myths, and their prevalence in the judicial process, Kimberley Crenshaw observed:

> The routine focus on the victim's sexual history functions to cast the complainant in one of several roles, including the whore, the tease, the vengeful liar, the mentally or emotionally unstable, or, in a few instances the Madonna. Once these ideologically informed character assignments are made, the 'story' tells itself, usually supplementing the woman's account of what transpired between the complainant and the accused with a fiction of villainous female intentionality that misleads and entraps the 'innocent' or unsuspecting male.[29]

No crime, as Jennifer Temkin and Barbara Krahe have recently observed, is more closely concerned with the 'victim's conduct'; not just in her possible incitement to a rapist, and her seeming failure to detect in advance which men might be prone to rape, but also in her subsequent behaviour when reporting the violation.[30] So strong is this myth that victims are commonly seen to accept the insinuation that the responsibility for their rape is their own.[31] Crenshaw's observation also gestures towards the third prevalent rape myth; that alleged rapists are often 'led on' to such a degree that they cannot be held responsible for their actions.[32] The final myth, particularly prevalent in cases of alleged male rape, assumes that rape must be physically violent.[33]

[28] The latter supposition found dubious authority in Freud's *Psychopathology of Everyday Life*, and was then taken on by Helene Deutsch in her 1944 *The Psychology of Women*. Women, Deutsch opined, have a 'masochistic' desire to be forcibly overcome before sex; a desire that is moreover 'necessary'. See Burke, *Rape*, 70–1.

[29] K. Crenshaw, 'Whose story is it anyway? Feminist and antiracist appropriations of Anita Hill', in T. Morrison (ed) *Race-ing Justice, En-gendering Power*, (Pantheon, 1992), 408.

[30] Various such factors, most commonly the manner of the victim in her reporting the violation, and the time lapsed in reporting the violation, are commonly raised in court, and all too commonly accepted by investigating authorities as evidence as to whether there is a case to be prosecuted. See Temkin and Krahe, *Sexual Assault*, 33–4, 38, 43, and also Anderson and Doherty, *Rape*, 36–7, making similar observations.

[31] Bohner et al., 'Rape myth acceptance', 24.

[32] A constituent myth further supposes that middle-class, particularly well-dressed, men are more likely to be able to control themselves in such a situation. See Burke, *Rape*, 97–9 and 145, and also Temkin and Krahe, *Sexual Assault*, 47.

[33] See Anderson and Doherty, *Rape*, 83–4 and 95–7, and also P. Rumney and N. Hanley, 'The mythology of male rape: social attitudes and law enforcement', in C. McGlynn and V. Munro (eds) *Rethinking Rape Law: International and Comparative Perspectives*, (Routledge, 2010), 297, 302–3.

The supposition of necessary violence spawns a series of constituent myths. Victims are expected to resist. At an extreme, it is supposed that no woman who resists can be raped.[34] Rape is a physical, as opposed to merely mental, experience; a prejudice which is, of course, written into the common law of rape.[35] And perhaps one of the most enduring of all rape myths, that 'real' rape is 'stranger' rape.[36]

It is again upon such myths that rapists and their defence counsel rely so commonly and so urgently in court.[37] Rape trials are conducted in terms of a prescribed 'script'.[38] The credibility of either party depends upon their 'performance' in court.[39] And, of course, the chronically low rates of prosecution and conviction in rape cases only serve to sustain the vitality of rape mythology.[40] Most women, it is assumed, must be lying; otherwise, so many more rapists would be in prison.[41] The role of law in addressing rape, as has been frequently noted, is limited and partial. It is limited because it focusses on the 'event' rather than the 'experience' of rape, and it is partial because it is jurisprudential 'script' written by men; and men, as Robin West has observed, have no 'experience' of rape. For the overwhelming majority of men, rape is 'quite literally incomprehensible'.[42]

In this context, advocates of law reform argue the need to look beyond the narrow confines of the legal process and to contemplate rather more closely the cultural and aesthetic dimension of rape. There is, of course, an

---

[34] See Burke, *Rape*, 24–5.

[35] See Anderson and Doherty, *Rape*,7 and Burke, *Rape*, 213.

[36] See Burke, *Rape*, 41, on the historical strength of the myth of 'stranger' rape, and also 143 quoting one US commentator who suggesting that 'comparing real rape to date rape is like comparing cancer to the common cold.'. See also Temkin and Krahe, *Sexual Assault*, 31, suggesting that the 'stranger' rape myth is perhaps the most pervasive of all such myths.

[37] And with good reason. For further and more recent confirmation of the impact that rape 'myths' continue to have in contemporary courtrooms, see Brown et al. *Connections*, 25–32.

[38] H. Frith, 'Sexual scripts, sexual refusals and rape', in Horvath and Brown, *Rape*, 100–1, and also F. Raitt and S. Zeedyk, *The Implicit Relation of Psychology and Law: Women and Syndrome Evidence*, (Routledge, 2000), 88.

[39] See Burke, *Rape*, 398.

[40] Approximately 6 per cent of alleged rapes result in a conviction. See here C. McGlynn, 'Feminist activism and rape law reform in England and Wales: a Sisyphean struggle?' in McGlynn and Munro, *Rape Law*, 139–42, and also comparing UK and US statistics, Anderson and Doherty, *Rape*, 11–13.

[41] A view which can be ascribed most obviously to 'just world' believers, those who assume that law reflects an innate justice in human relations. See Bohner et al., 'Rape myth acceptance'. 26–7, 34, and also Anderson and Doherty, *Rape*, 3–5, confirming the continuing scepticism which pervades incidents of alleged rape.

[42] R. West, *Narrative, Authority and Law*, (Michigan UP, 1993), 247–8.

inherent danger in facilitating the re-shaping of rape discourse in broader cultural media. The myths of rape are cultural expressions, in large part enshrined in this same media.[43] The 'celebration of rape in story, song and science', as Andrea Dworkin observed, 'is the paradigmatic articulation of male sexual power as a cultural absolute'.[44] The alternative, however, is silence.[45] Women must seek to write their own alternative 'scripts'. Here drama, in its combination of text and performance, suggests itself as a credible discursive space. Of course, drama plays with the emotions as much as it does with the faculty of reason; something that might be supposed to exacerbate the danger of contradiction and incoherence.[46] Certainly, the performance of rape will rarely engender emotional indifference. And it will always defy objectivity; presenting as it must a particular experience of rape.[47] But again, this is no reason to deny its strategic value as a space within which women, and indeed men, can articulate personal experiences of violence and violation.

Kane on Rape

Rape is a common feature in Kane's writings. Critical consistency in terms of dramatic presentation is not. For reasons we shall consider shortly, Kane had no interest in subscribing to any particular feminist position on rape. But if there is no critical or political consistency, there are a number of common features; of which the lack of critical consistency is, of course, one. Another is the conspicuous, and inevitable, engagement with rape mythology. It is impossible to read any account of rape, fictive or otherwise, without contemplating these myths. Kane's plays are no exception. Another common feature, very obviously appropriate in the context of rape, is violence. Kane's violations are each violent, and each differently so. Violence is one of the distinguishing features of Kane's writings; something which, as we have already noted, led to her work being

---

[43] See J. KItzinger, 'Rape in the media', in Horvath and Brown, *Rape*, particularly 74–6, 79, and also Anderson and Doherty, *Rape*, 132–3.

[44] A. Dworkin, *Pornography: Men Possessing Women*, (Dutton, 1989), 23. This supposition has found more recent support in Higgins and Silver, 'Rereading Rape', 2–4, and also Burke, *Rape*, at 7, confirming that rape is 'deeply rooted in specific political, economic and cultural environments'.

[45] See S. Ehrlich, *Representing Rape: language and sexual consent*, (Routledge, 2001), 1–2, 12–18.

[46] See R. Giner-Sorolla and P. Russell, 'Anger, disgust and sexual crimes', in Horvath and Brown, *Rape*, particularly 65–6.

[47] See here E. Rooney, 'A Little More than Persuading: Tess and the Subject of Sexual Violence', In Higgins and Silver, *Rape*, 88–9.

commonly presented as paradigmatic of 1990s 'in-yer-face' drama.[48] We have, she surmised, a 'human need for violence'.[49] It was not, of course, the actual violence that troubled critics so much as the presentation in theatre. Kane wanted to unsettle her audience, and she did so by writing at the 'extremes'.[50]

Rape, as we have also already noted, is totemic of the pervasive violence that is written into *Blasted* and indeed *Phaedra's Love*. Kane confirmed that *Blasted* is first and foremost 'a play about violence, about rape, and it was about these things happening between people who know each other and ostensibly love each other'.[51] It is a conspicuously 'de-glamorized' violence. The influence of Shakespeare is undeniable, but there is nothing remotely lyrical about the violation of Cate and Ian, or Phaedra or Strophe in *Phaedra's Love*.[52] The critical temptation, conversely, is to identify Kane's work with that of near contemporaries such Edward Bond, as well as with previous generations of playwrights inspired by Artaud's 'theatre of cruelty'.[53] Kane's rapes are violent, cruel, and ultimately rather too familiar. It is, of course, this which makes them also so unsettling. Kane's rapes are ordinary rapes; except that no rape is really ordinary.

---

[48] Reluctant to see herself as being part of any such 'movement'. See Saunders, *Love Me*, 8.

[49] Here Kane repeatedly acknowledged the influence of Edward Bond. Bond reciprocated his admiration, observing of *Blasted* that it was 'The only contemporary play I wish I'd written, it is revolutionary'. See *Love Me*, 25–7 and 37, and also *About Kane*, 101–2 quoting Kane's confirmation that 'violence is the most urgent problem we have as a species, and the most urgent thing we need to confront'. For an informed comparison of Bond's *Saved* and Kane's *Blasted*, see J. Brannigan, *Orwell to the Present: Literature in England 1945–2000*, (Palgrave, 2003), 152–6.

[50] See *About Kane*, 1, and also 30–1, quoting James Macdonald's view that 'Kane wanted people to experience something emotionally before experiencing it intellectually. *Blasted* hits you so hard that you don't use your head until afterwards'.

[51] Interview with Alex Sierz, given in 1999, and quoted in Saunders, *About Kane*, at 50.

[52] An 'almost puritanical' violence, according to Kane's agent Mel Kenyon. See *About Kane*, 100, and also 140.

[53] Having only started to read Artaud later, after writing *Blasted*, Kane was enraptured. The 'more' she read the more 'I thought this is a definition of sanity: this man is completely and utterly sane and I understand everything he's saying. And I was amazed how it connects completely with my work'. In *About Kane*, 87. For an extended discussion of Artaud's influence, see L. De Vos, 'Sarah Kane and Antonin Artaud: cruelty towards the subjectile', in De Vos and Saunders, *Kane in Context*, 126–38. Other modern influences on Kane, most commonly suggested by critics, are Beckett and early Pinter, as well of course as Bond and Howard Barker. See here Saunders, *Love Me*, 54–70, and also 'The Beckettian world of Sarah Kane', in De Vos and Saunders, *Kane in Context*, 68–79, and also E. Aston, *Feminist Views on the English Stage: Women Playwrights 1990–2000*, (Cambridge UP, 2003), 77–8.

The Rape of Cate

Cate's rape takes place in the first Act of the play, set in a hotel bedroom in Leeds. It is not as such a domestic environment. But it is an environment in which a species of rape familiar in domestic environments can take place. It is not the only familiar aspect of Cate's rape. She is raped by someone she knows. Ian is not a 'stranger'. He is someone with whom has had in the past had sex, sometimes at least consensually (16). And she is equally aware of Ian's paranoid aggression, carrying a gun, consistently articulating images of misogynist and brutal sexuality; very obviously in his dictated report of the murdered 'Scouse tart' who, he decides, must have invited her fate because she was too easily persuaded to 'spread her legs' (13).[54] Undaunted by Cate's early refusal to engage sexual activity when he strips in front of her, Ian then 'cuddles' and 'kisses', at which point Cate merely observes 'Don't put your tongue in' (7, 12). Even Cate senses the danger she is in, observing in self-referential terms 'Have to tell her/ . . . She's in danger' (9). When Ian approaches her again, putting his hand 'under her top' she first 'responds' by kissing him, but then shies away, saying 'don't' (14). 'That wasn't very fair', Ian insinuates, 'Leaving me hanging, making a prick of myself', to which he adds a more threatening advice, 'don't push your cunt in my face then take it away 'cause I stick my tongue out' (14–15). 'It hurts', he reiterates, an observation which elicits an apology from Cate who, as the play progresses, seems only too willing to assume that she is, to some degree, culpable in her own violation (15). Still he persists in asking for sex, still Cate declines, and still Cate stays (22).

All the attendant myths of the victim who should have seen it coming, who failed to take evasive action, who somehow contributed to her own violation, are present; something which Kane later admitted:

> Yes, I think Cate's very fucking stupid. What's she doing in that hotel room in the first place? Of course, she's going to get raped, and it's utterly tragic that this happens to her. I did have nights during rehearsals of *Blasted* when I would go home and cry and say, 'How could I create such a beautiful woman in order for her to be so abused'? I really did feel a bit sick and depraved. Part of that was to do with the fact that there was no sort of overwhelming sense that Cate came out on top.

---

[54] Ian claims, not entirely convincingly, that he is also a hit-man, for which reason he always carries a gun. For a commentary on the uncertainty of this claim, and the possibility that Ian is simply paranoid, see Saunders, *Love Me*, 42.-3. Ian also claims that his phone has been 'tapped' (29).

Had there been I'm sure I would have felt completely exonerated. But I didn't. [55]

The tragedy lies in the predictability.[56] Cate knows Ian, she knows his propensity to violence, and yet she still accepted an invitation to come up to his room simply because he sounded 'unhappy' (4). She is, she confirms on arriving, 'here for the night' (5).

Cate is, furthermore, prone to fits, 'Happens all the time' (9); something which makes her still more vulnerable to abuse, but also something which, it might be implied, should have made her more cautious still with regard to her personal safety. Along with her vulnerability, this condition also seems to reflect, perhaps even enhance, Cate's inability to express her violation.[57] Alongside her failure to complain is Cate's failure to resist. She is raped whilst she is unconscious, only later realising the nature of her violation.[58] In the absence of its initial presentation, the rape of Cate is repeated by simulation. As she fits again, Ian 'puts the gun to her head, lies between her legs, and simulates sex' (27). Kane later confessed that she found Cate's simulated rape to be the 'most disturbing scene' in the play.[59] There is no doubt that Cate was raped, and there is no doubt that she feels violated, to such a degree that she asks Ian to 'shoot' her: 'It can't be no worse than what you've done already' (34). And Ian is left in no doubt too; at least after the event. When Ian suggests that she made 'enough noise' to suggest that she enjoyed it, Cate replies her screams were those of pain and that 'I didn't want to do it'; something which confirms that Cate was raped, but which also casts doubt on the 'guilty mind' of her assailant (31). Interestingly in an initial draft of the play, Kane had Cate directly accuse Ian of rape, to which Ian responded dismissively: 'That wasn't rape. Don't know the meaning of the word'.[60]

Consent is one of the primary 'fictions' with which the law tests the

---

[55] In Saunders, *About Kane*, 58.

[56] Kane's comments are reinforced by Kate Ashfield, who played Cate in the original production. She recalled Kane suggesting that Cate 'is simultaneously the most intelligent person in the play, and at the same time absolutely stupid to walk into that hotel with Ian, because she knows what is going to happen'. In Saunders, *Love Me*, 164.

[57] According to Solga, Cate's illness is reflective of 'her abuse' being 'elided, dismissed, ignored by those around her, leaving her unable to access and deal with it consciously'. See her 'Hysteria', 362.

[58] According to Solga the greater significance of Cate's rape lies here, in its absence, representative of a 'history of effacement, rape as missing-ness itself'. See Solga, 'Hysteria', 347–9, adding at 350 that in his matter, the matter of Cate's rape, *Blasted* 'does not stage what is missing, what we fail to see, so much as it stages the process of our failure to see'.

[59] In Saunders, *About Kane*, 63–4.

[60] See Saunders, *Love Me*, 45.

veracity of rape claims. But it is a blunt instrument, cherished for its simplicity rather than its subtlety. It struggles to deal with the inevitable myths of implied consent, and fares no better when challenged by the realities of inequality and abuse in sexual relations. Human relations are rarely equal. That of Cate and Ian most certainly is not.[61] 'Originally' Kane later testified, 'I was writing a play about two people in a hotel room, in which there was a complete power imbalance, which resulted in the older man raping the younger woman'.[62] The scale and the nature of Kane's endeavour would change. But the basic situation of Cate's rape does not. It is, when all is said and done, an ordinary rape, only too familiar in conception and execution, and only too resonant of so many of its defining myths. The supposition that Cate might be deemed, by way of her various acts and omissions, to have consented to her violation, is just one. As Kim Solga suggests, the significance of Cate's abuse lies in this constant 'challenging' of the audience's 'precepts' as to what constitutes 'real' rape.[63]

Having confirmed that she never wanted sex and that she has been raped, Cate then proceeds to perform 'oral sex' on Ian, biting his penis when he comes and then spitting 'frantically, trying to get every trace of him out of her mouth' (30–1). The symbolism of self-disgust is striking, speaking once again to familiar notions of victim culpability; as does the otherwise seemingly inexplicable decision of Cate, not just to stay with Ian, but to perform a further sexual act. Theirs, as Kane later observed in more general terms, is one of those relationships in which the victim, trapped in a 'completely self-perpetuating circle of emotional and physical violence', manages to emerge feeling 'guilty' herself.[64] There is much that is only too familiar in the rape of Cate, and there is much that does not really make any sense. Kate Ashfield, who played Cate in the original production of *Blasted* observed that when she asked 'why does Cate give Ian that blow job, at that point in the play?' Kane admitted that 'I didn't know what to do at that point in the play, and I remember Joe Orton saying something about if you didn't know what to do at a given moment in writing then shock your audience – that's why I put it in'.[65]

---

[61] As Patricia Holland observed, in her review published in the *Independent*, the rape of Cate is 'shown not as a single brutal act, but as structured into a deeply unequal relationship, and performed with whingeing self-pity'. In Saunders, *Love Me*, 45.

[62] In A. Sierz, 'Looks like there's a war on: Sarah Kane's *Blasted*, political theatre and the Muslim Other', in De Vos and Saunders, *Kane in Context*, 49.

[63] Solga, 'Hysteria', 350 and also 365 referring to the 'host of questions' which Kane asks of her audience with regard to rape in *Blasted*.

[64] In Saunders, *Love Me*, 4–6.

[65] In Saunders, *Love Me*, 164. Saunders suggests that this apparent lack of reason in Cate's behaviour might be ascribed to the influence of Beckett on Kane. See his 'Beckettian world', 69.

The Rape of Ian

The second rape, that of Ian, takes place after the outside world, in the person of the Soldier, has quite literally blasted its way into the play.[66] The play pivots around the 'huge explosion' and the gaping hole it leaves. When challenged as to her motivation in writing this scene, Kane replied 'I think that what happens in war is that suddenly, violently, without any warning whatsoever, people's lives are completely ripped to pieces. So I literally just picked a moment in the play: I thought 'I'll plant a bomb and blow the whole fucking thing up'!'[67] The immediate motivation, she later confirmed, lay in pictures of Srebrenica which were, on the day she began to write *Blasted*, being relayed around the world. Moved to tears by the images, 'I started to want to write about that pain. That was probably when I had the idea that I wanted a soldier in it'.[68] It is the Soldier who rapes Ian, as he apparently has done a number of other victims, male and female, during his wartime experiences in the Balkans (43, 50). The fact that the Soldier further insinuates that he was 'ordered' to rape speaks to another familiar rape myth which seeks to explain, if not exonerate, the prevalence of rape in war (45).[69]

Subsequent comments again confirmed the extent to which rape played a pivotal role in refining this motivation:

> In terms of Aristotle's Unities, the time and action are disrupted while unity of place is retained – which caused a great deal of offence because it implied a direct link between domestic violence in Britain and civil war in the former Yugoslavia. *Blasted* raised the question: 'What does a common rape in Leeds have to do with mass rape as a war weapon in Bosnia?' And the answer appeared to be 'Quite a lot'. The unity of place suggests a paper-thin wall between the safety and civilization of peacetime Britain and

[66] A moment which, in its disregard for the classical unity of place, caused especial critical concern. Michael Billington later confirmed that the 'difficulty' with *Blasted* 'was always structural: that it yoked together two apparently irreconcilable worlds'. In Solga, 'Hysteria', 351. See also Saunders, *Love Me*, 40–51 and Sierz, *in-Yer-Face*, 101–3, discussing the problem of structure in *Blasted*.

[67] In *About Kane*, 91. Kane also confirmed that the moment was, unsurprisingly, intended to cause the audience maximum disturbance. See Solga, 'Hysteria', 352.

[68] The siege of Srebrenica was in 1992. Kane's Interview was given in 1995. Quoted in Saunders, *About Kane*, 49–50.

[69] Sierz suggests that the final draft of *Blasted* addresses, as a principle theme, the idea that 'the seeds of war lie in men's psychology' and that rape is the primal expression of this seeding. See his 'Muslim Other', 54–5.

the chaotic violence of civil war. A wall that can be torn down at any time, without warning.[70]

Critics have commonly referred to the 'thinness' of the line between instances of individual private and larger 'catastrophic' suffering as a dominant theme in Kane's work.[71] The extent to which there may be any credible distinction between the experience of rape in domestic environment, or a hotel bedroom, and the experience of rape in a devastated war-zone has long exercised lawyers and feminists.[72] Ian certainly assumes there is a difference. As a local journalist, he reports 'Shootings and rapes and kids getting fiddled by queer priests and schoolteachers. Not soldiers screwing each other for a patch of land' (48). But he is about to be disabused of such a simple demarcation. 'The logical conclusion of the attitude that produces an isolated rape in England', Kane later confirmed, 'is the rape camps in Bosnia'.[73] 'You don't know fuck all about me', her Soldier observes in response. 'Turn over', he orders Ian, 'Going to fuck you' (48–9).

Critics have tended to focus on Ian's rape as the 'real' rape in *Blasted*, partly because the physical event is actually presented on stage, rather than merely simulated, because it is overtly violent and partly too because the Soldier is a stranger.[74] It is also, of course, an instance of male rape; something which imports a series of particular constituent myths. A first is the supposition that male rape only happens to homosexuals. Ian alludes to precisely this in his response to the Soldier's question, 'You never fucked a man before you killed him?' No, Ian replies, because 'I'm not queer' (47). A second is an intense version of the myth that no one who resists can be really raped. Ian does not resist, something which the Soldier assumes counts as consent (49). But then Ian has a gun pointed to his head, reciprocating precisely the imagery which accompanies his simulated rape of Cate.[75] As Kane observed:

---

[70] In *About Kane*, 90.

[71] See Solga, 'Hysteria', 348, Iball, 'Room Service', 323–4, Sierz, 'Muslim Other', 47 and also Aston, *Feminist Views*, 81, suggesting that Kane here presents a quintessential 'connection between the personal and the political, the intimate and the epic'.

[72] Something which Alex Sierz found 'troubling', adding 'In other words, if you ever met someone who's just been raped domestically and tell her that it's the same thing as being raped in Bosnia its unlikely to be of any use to that person. And simultaneously, when dealing with rape victims in a war situation, it probably doesn't help to tell them that all men are potential rapists'. In *About Kane*, 129.

[73] In Aston, *Feminist Views*, 85.

[74] Solga, 'Hysteria', 348.

[75] For a commentary on the obvious significance of this parallel, see Saunders, *Love Me*, 47–8.

I was reading all these reviews and thinking, 'But that's not what I wrote at all!' What was being described was that a soldier comes in and randomly rapes Ian. And what they kept ignoring was the fact that the Soldier does it with a gun to his head, which Ian has done to Cate earlier – and he's crying his eyes out as he does it. I think both these things have changed that theatrical image entirely.[76]

Kane explicitly denied the critical supposition that she was somehow engaging a larger 'crisis of masculinity' thesis.[77] Ian's rape is not defined by gender, but by circumstance and by violence.

The Rapes of Phaedra and Strophe

Blasted may be Kane's most notorious play and her most notorious depiction of rape. But it is not the only. Her second play, *Phaedra's Love*, was based, if loosely, on Seneca's *Hippolytus*.[78] In its portrayal of a degenerate royal family riven by internal hatred and sexual scandal, it was clearly intended to import a contemporary resonance in the minds of late-twentieth-century British audiences.[79] And, following Seneca's original, the plot moved in considerable part around the alleged rape of Phaedra, Hippolytus's step-mother. The key difference in Kane's version of the story lies in Hippolytus's active sexuality and the consummation of sexual relations with Phaedra.[80] Seneca's Hippolytus was chaste and morally virtuous. Kane's is not.[81] Kane's Hippolytus lives for

---

[76] In Saunders, *About Kane*, 65.

[77] Saunders, *About Kane*, 17–18. The idea that the 'crisis of masculinity' emerged as dominant theme in 1990s drama was strongly pressed by David Edgar, and finds critical echo in Alex Sierz, *Rewriting the Nation: British Theatre Today*, (Methuen, 2011), 19, and also Aston, *Feminist Views*, 3–4.

[78] According to Graham Saunders, Kane's interest in Seneca was not 'surprising' given the 'thematic similarities' the two shared, most obviously in the nature of human suffering. See his *Love Me*, 72.

[79] The presentation of a 'sexually corrupt royal family', Kane admitted, was consciously intended to give the play a 'highly contemporary' resonance. In Sierz, *In-Yer-Face*, 109. At one moment Hippolytus declares: 'News. Another rape. Child murdered. War somewhere. Few thousand jobs gone. But none of this matters 'cause it's a royal birthday' (74). For Kane's comment, and a critical appraisal of the play's assault on the 'crass sentimentality' which characterises popular devotion to the modern royal family, see Saunders, *About Kane*, 23–4, 67, and also *Love Me*, 74 noting the particular parallel, necessarily later drawn, between the fates of Phaedra and Princess Diana, both of whom were posthumously granted an iconic status as wronged women, which in both cases was barely deserved. For an overview of the royal family theme, see Giannopoulou, 'Staging power', 58–9.

[80] Though active in a conspicuously passive and indolent sense. See Giannopoulou, 'Staging power', 60.

[81] Though Kane maintained that in his embrace of death, her Hippolytus did pursue 'honesty'.

sex and gratification.[82] In the absence of having a 'life', it is his 'main interest' (77, 79). All he does, as Phaedra informs the doctor in the very first scene, is 'Watch films. And have sex' (66). If he has people round to visit, it is only so 'They can have sex and leave' (66). Unsurprisingly, Hippolytus hates 'people' (77).

Phaedra, effectively abandoned by her husband Theseus, whom she has not 'seen since we were married', seeks solace with her step-son (68). As her daughter Strophe, who has also had sex with Hippolytus, suggests, she is 'Obsessed' with him (68).[83] 'There is', Phaedra confesses, 'a thing between us, an awesome fucking thing' (71). Phaedra is fully aware of the risks, but the obsession is all-consuming. Declaring her love, she performs oral sex on Hippolytus as a kind of birthday present; a gesture that meets with scarcely veiled contempt and the crushing observation 'I've had worse' (81). Angered, Phaedra counters with the accusation that Hippolytus has 'disappointed' her. The reason, he responds, is that he could not be bothered to 'try'. Strophe, he adds, altogether more 'practiced' than her mother was worth a greater effort (83–4). Phaedra leaves.

And then accuses Hippolytus of rape, before hanging herself (86, 90). There can be little doubt that Phaedra was abused, at least emotionally. But there is nothing in Kane's play to suggest that she was raped in any sense that might be recognised in law. When Strophe seeks to establish whether the claim is true, Hippolytus is evasive and ironic. 'You should have been a lawyer', he derisively replies (87). As Kane later observed, in disregard of jurisprudential pedantry:

> There was something about the inadequacy of language to express emotion that interested me. In *Phaedra's Love*, what Hippolytus does to Phaedra is not rape – but the English language doesn't contain the words to describe the emotional decimation he inflicts. 'Rape' is the best word Phaedra can find for it, the most violent and potent, so that's the word she uses.[84]

See Saunders, *Love Me*, 76. We shall revisit the peculiarity of Hippolytus's death, and its possible moral dimension, in due course. In Seneca's play, Hippolytus is characterised by his pursuit of truth. Kane later suggested that the inspiration for her Hippolytus came, in large part, from the notorious womaniser and Tory politician Alan Clark. See *About Kane*, 71.

[82] Something which, as critics have noted, creates an immediate parallel with Ian in *Blasted*. See Saunders, *Love Me*, 73.

[83] Kane later observed that she personally understood the possibility of 'obsessional love for someone who is completely unlovable'. See Saunders, *Love Me*, 31.

[84] In Saunders, *About Kane*, 73. Graham Saunders agrees that Hippolytus's abuse of Phaedra might be 'likened to a form of mental rape'. See his *Love Me*, 77.

Strophe articulates precisely this when she later challenges Hippolytus, observing 'There aren't words for what you did to me' (87). The problem, of course, is that in presenting the 'rape' of Phaedra, Kane risks reinforcing another of the more enduring myths; that some women are prone to having sex and then, if they feel rejected, crying rape. If this was not the case, the myth runs, there would not be so many failed prosecutions.

There is a subtlety in Hippolytus's observation; that if a rape victim feels she was raped then so, disregarding legal nicety, in a sense she was (90). Hippolytus rather relishes the irony of his fate. Rather than seeking to refute Strophe's charge, he responds 'Then perhaps rape is the best she can do. Me. A rapist. Things are looking up' (87). It is, after all, 'better' than being known as 'a fat boy who fucks' (88). The same sense of irony is articulated to the Priest, who visits his cell in order to urge confession and repentance. When a recalcitrant Hippolytus replies, 'Admit, yes. Confess, no. I admit it. The rape. I did it', the Priest urges him instead to 'deny the rape' and 'confess the sin', the 'unforgiveable sin' of perjuring his soul (94). Hippolytus is unmoved: 'I have no intention of covering my arse. I killed a woman and will be punished for it by hypocrites who I shall take down with me' (96–7).[85]

The second rape in *Phaedra's Love* is that of Strophe, Phaedra's daughter. If less challenging in terms of engaging rape mythology, Strophe's rape is perhaps the most striking in the casual as well as the extreme nature of its violence.[86] As Hippolytus is taken through the streets on the way to what the crowd suspect will be a 'Show trial', unrest turns to violence (99). Theseus has returned and mingles with the crowd in disguise. The crowd calls for vengeance on the 'Royal raping bastard' (100). Theseus obliges, disembowelling Hippolytus whilst the 'children cheer', and then entertaining the assembled crowd by seizing a woman, raping her and cutting her throat (100–1). It is only moments later that he realises that the woman he has raped and killed is his own step-daughter. It is a supremely random rape, by a supremely violent stranger, who just happens to be the victim's step-father. The ironies abound; not least that presaged by Hippolytus in his observation that he will be 'punished' by 'hypocrites' (96–7).[87] Hippolytus appreciates the poetic

[85] For a comment on Hippolytus particular rejection of hypocrisy in the person of the Priest, something which inevitably impresses a sense of anti-clericalism in the play, see Saunders, *Love Me*, 78=9.

[86] See here P. Campbell, 'Sarah Kane's *Phaedra's Love*: staging the implacable', in De Vos and Saunders, *Kane in Context*, 178–9, 182–3.

[87] For a comment on Hippolytus's particular rejection of hypocrisy and the extent to which it might justify Kane's suggestion that he is, thereby, a figure of 'honesty', see Saunders, *Love Me*, 79

justice inherent in his fate.[88] It might be surmised that a similar justice is inflicted upon Strophe, who has already had sexual intercourse not just with Hippolytus but with her step-father.[89] She is certainly aware of the likely consequences if the populace discovers the sexual degeneracy at the heart of the royal family: 'We'd be torn apart on the streets' (73). But she might not, it can be reasonably assumed, have expected to be ravaged by her own step-father.

The Consequences of Contingency

Rape assumes a prominent place in Kane's writing. But Kane did not write about rape, at least not in the sense that a lawyer or a committed feminist might write. She had no position on rape to reinforce. Later critics have liked to place Kane within a tradition of radical contemporary feminist theatre.[90] According to Kim Solga, the rape of Cate, for example, must be 'viewed through the lens of contemporary feminist critique'.[91] But it is not a view that Kane shared:

> I'm not writing about sexual politics. The problems I'm addressing are the ones we have as human beings. An over-emphasis on sexual politics (or racial or class politics) is a diversion from our main problems. Class, race and gender divisions are symptomatic of societies based on violence or the threat of violence, not the cause . . . I have no responsibility as a woman writer because I don't believe there is such a thing. When people talk about me as a writer, that's what I am, not on the basis of my age, gender, class, sexuality or race. I don't want to be a representative of any biological or social group of which I happen to be a member. I am what I am. Not what other people want me to be.[92]

Time and again, as Robert Lublin observes, Kane presents her female characters with 'feminist possibilities' only to then take them away again.[93] Aleks Sierz argues that Kane's scepticism drove her to consciously distance 'herself from a whole collection of women writers because of their ideological feminism'. In Kane's perception, the feminism represented in the work of

---

[88] A species of 'martyrdom' according to Ken Urban. See his 'An Ethics of Catastrophe: The Theatre of Sarah Kane', 23 *PAJ: A Journal of Performance and Art* 2001, 42.

[89] A thought pondered by Saunders, in *Love Me*, 75.

[90] See here Saunders, *About Kane*, 7–8, and also Aston, 'Fabric', 21–3.

[91] Solga, 'Hysteria', 347.

[92] In Saunders, *About Kane*, 106, and further discussed in Aston, *Feminist Views*, 80.

[93] R. Lublin, 'I love you now: time and desire in the plays of Sarah Kane', in De Vos and Saunders, *Kane in Context*, 117.

Sarah Daniels or Timberlake Wertenbaker 'didn't really make much sense to young women living in the so-called post-feminist age'.[94] On first reading Andrea Dworkin, Kane confessed that her first response was to think 'how can someone be filled with such hatred – be so blind and this politically stupid?'[95]

Such an attitude necessarily coloured Kane's personal views on rape. She was particularly contemptuous of the simplistic notion that all men are rapists. The crude binary, in which the world is divided into male 'perpetrators' and female 'victims', is not, she affirmed, a 'constructive' one.[96] All men might have the 'equipment to be rapists', but then again all people have the 'equipment' to be killers. But the vast majority are not.[97] Kane returned to this theme when discussing rape in war; a subject stimulated rather obviously by the role of her rapist Soldier in *Blasted*. Contemplating why rape was prevalent in the Balkan wars, but why it was eschewed by Vietcong fighters in the Vietnam war, Kane concluded that the urge to rape was 'something cultural', rather than something innate.[98] Such a generic impression reinforces the sense of critical incoherence gleaned from her comments on the particular rapes of Cate and Ian, Phaedra and Strophe. Rape, as Kane wrote it, is a differentiated experience.

There is an immediate resonance here with the 'new feminist theory of rape' advanced by the likes of Carine Mardorossian:

> It is time that we stop thinking that subjecting the same experience – that is, the violation of a woman's body – to different explanations is a suspect genre . . . Victim's accounts of their experiences do not exist in a vacuum of authenticity awaiting a feminist revolution to be able to safely express themselves, since victims, like all of us, get their cues from the intersecting and conflicting discourses through which the world is understood and shaped.[99]

---

[94] See Sierz's comments in Saunders, *About Kane*, 128. The view is reiterated in Sierz, *In-Yer-Face*, 244–5.

[95] In Saunders, *About Kane*, 62. On the subject of pornography, Kane's 'problem' with Dworkin's uncompromising denunciation lay in what she perceived to be an implicit reluctance to allow people to distinguish 'fantasy and reality' for themselves.

[96] In Saunders, *About Kane*, 104.

[97] In Saunders, *About Kane*, 63, and also 103–4 reaffirming, in a slightly different context, 'I fail to understand how there can be a gene for criminality at all since crime is culturally defined'.

[98] In Saunders, *About Kane*, 64. For an interesting discussion of rape as a military strategy consciously adopted by the US in the Vietnam war, see Burke, *Rape*, 366–9.

[99] Mardorossian, 'Rape', 747.

There is resonance too with Richard Rorty's broader critique of 'comprehensive' theories of justice.[100] Whilst sharing considerable sympathy with the aspiration of radical feminism, and more particularly that of feminist lawyers such as MacKinnon, Rorty expressed a like scepticism of strategies founded on assumed commonalty of experience.[101] Rorty did not deny the possibility of a coherent narrative. He merely denied the possibility that such could be shaped by anything other than human creativity. 'The world does not speak. Only we do'; a conclusion with which it might, once again, be supposed that Kane would have agreed.[102] In the absence of a 'comprehensive' ethics, Rorty famously argued that human relations should be better understood in terms of contingency and cruelty, in the 'wish to be kind' and to 'diminish suffering', rather than the injunctions of the categorical imperative.[103]

Kane repeatedly rejected the idea that her plays were written as 'moral' texts; preferring instead to suppose that she was more of a 'romantic'. The evident Lear-inferences, especially apparent in *Blasted*, encouraged critics to imagine something more [104] John Peter detected an 'unleavened, almost puritanical outrage'. Annabelle Singer appraised a 'moral hardass'; a choice of vocabulary which seems apposite to the genre.[105] But not Kane. To the contrary:

---

[100] Whilst making no explicit reference to Rorty, Julie Waddington has noted the extent to which Kane shares the same post-humanist sympathies, meaning a belief that beyond classical metaphysical humanism there may be a space for an alternative 'ethics' of the 'human'. See her 'Posthumanist identities in Sarah Kane', in De Vos and Saunders, *Kane in Context*, 139–48. In slightly different terms, Karoline Gritzner has suggested that Kane follows Howard Barker in embracing postmodernism, but without the 'irony'. See her '(Post) Modern Subjectivity and the New Expressionism: Howard Barker, Sarah Kane and Forced Entertainment', 18 *Contemporary Theatre Review* 2008, 340.

[101] See his *Truth and Progress*, (Cambridge UP, 1998), 202–27.

[102] See R. Rorty, *Contingency, Irony, and Solidarity*, (Cambridge UP, 1989), 5.

[103] Rorty, *Contingency*, 91.

[104] For Kane's assertion, that the 'issues of personal and spiritual redemption' so resonant in the final passages of *Blasted* made it a 'romantic' rather than 'moral' play, see Saunders, *About Kane*, 5, 61, and 104–5. The Lear-inferences are evident throughout *Blasted*, the very title of which alludes to the 'blasted heath'. According to Kane, the blinding of Ian by the Soldier is his 'Dover Scene'. Unsurprisingly she likewise attested to the influence of Bond's *Lear*, not least because 'suddenly you see all that violence for what it really is all over again'. For commentaries on the alternative Lears, presented by Bond and Shakespeare, and their influence on Kane see Saunders, *About Kane*, at 39–41 and 45–6, and also 'Out Vile Jelly: Sarah Kane's *Blasted* and Shakespeare's *King Lear*', *New Theatre Quarterly* 2001, 69–78.

[105] Benedict Nightingale also detected a 'moral, social vision' that bore comparison with that articulated by Priestley's Inspector Goode. See Sierz, 'Muslim Other', 48, and also Saunders, *Love Me*, 23 and A. Singer, 'Don't want to be this: the elusive Sarah Kane', 48 *Drama Review* 2004, 131.

I don't think *Blasted* is a moral play. I think its amoral, and I think that is one of the reasons people got so terribly upset because there isn't a very defined moral framework within which to place yourself and assess your own morality – or distance yourself from the material. I think there's a great deal of moral manoeuvre in the play and that's probably one of the distressing things. I suppose that ultimately it's not only about social breakdown – it's about the breakdown of human nature itself.[106]

In the place of the moral philosopher, Rorty preferred the 'strong poet'; someone who sought to reconcile their audience with the radical contingency of life, dramatically and metaphorically.[107] We have already noted Martha Nussbaum doing much the same. The 'strong poet', writing in defiance of simplistic narrative coherence, embraces the inconsistencies which attend human experience. Kane certainly did. *Blasted* may not be a moral play. But it is a play about the contingencies of human experience.[108] As she contemplates her violation, Cate accuses Ian not of the physical act of rape, or indeed of acting violently, but of being 'cruel' (32).[109] As Saunders observed, the violence that Kane prescribed in her plays was, more than anything, a violence of 'love and cruelty'.[110]

'All good art', Kane once observed, 'is subversive'.[111] The presentation of rape in *Blasted* and in *Phaedra's Love* is certainly subversive; at the least, to echo Elaine Aston's observation, it 'defamiliarises' the 'feminist story' of rape.[112] It defies the consistency preferred by moral and political ideology, feminist or otherwise, and by positive law. The law, as Stanley Fish famously declared, aspires to a 'formal existence'; no matter how futile the

---

[106] Interview given to *Start the Week* in 1995, and quoted in Saunders, *About Kane*, at 61.

[107] Rorty, *Contingency*, 60–1.

[108] Ken Urban suggests that it was not the violence alone which defined 'in-yer-face' drama, but 'cruelty' too. See his 'Cruel Britannia', 360–1, and also 362–3, suggesting the particular influence of Artaud.

[109] A distinction that Graham Saunders notes, in *Love Me*, 44–5, noting that Ian assumes the role of a 'torturer' rather than an 'ex-lover', as skilled in the arts of mental as physical 'cruelty'.

[110] See Saunders, *About Kane*, 1 and also *Love Me*, 15. Stefani Brusberg-Kiermeier suggests that 'cruelty', more particularly a ritualised cruelty, is the primary dynamic that Kane uses in place of reason and morality in each of her plays. See her 'Cruelty', 80–1, and also Clare Wallace, 'Sarah Kane, experiential theatre and the revenant avant-garde', in De Vos and Saunders, *Kane in Context*, at 95 observing that for Kane, following Artaud, 'Cruelty then is a primary tool, utilised to affect the audience to achieve an experiential goal'.

[111] In Saunders, *About Kane*, 89.

[112] Aston, 'Fabric', 24, suggesting parallels with Franca Rame's monologues, most obviously *The Rape*.

aspiration.[113] Edward Bond, writing about Kane, concurred. The law 'cannot give justice'. It merely 'administers' degrees of 'injustice'.[114] The law of rape is no exception. In the absence of legal redress, Kane directs the attention of her audience towards the enduring force of myth in the shaping of rape discourse, challenging it to contemplate the prospective veracity of familiar prejudices; that Cate may have 'had it coming', that her rape was not 'real' rape; that Ian should have resisted a bit more; that Phaedra is another of those women who are too ready to cry rape when it suits them.

When asked why she wrote, Kane replied that she did so in order to stimulate conversation and to 'change' people.[115] And in order to stimulate, she shocked. It is impossible to read the rapes of Cate and Ian and Phaedra and Strophe, still more witness them in the theatre, without appreciating their cruelty and their violence, and the intensely 'visceral' nature of their experience.[116] The power of her writing, as Aston confirms, lies precisely here in her 'ability to touch hearts, minds and nervous systems', in offering her audience the 'experience of suffering'.[117] Recalling the actor's difficulty in performing the simulated rape in the first production of *Blasted*, Kane urged him to focus on pure 'stimuli' rather than rationale. Rapists do not act rationally, and neither should actors who pretend to be rapists.[118] Divested of the sanctity of reason, the audience like the actor is left with their own impressions and emotions, their own experiences of cruelty and violation.[119] It is an unsettling place to be. But if we wish to contemplate the reality of rape, as opposed to the simple caricatures written into political ideology and positive law, it is also a necessary place to be. As Kane confirmed 'My responsibility is to the truth, however difficult that truth happens to be'.[120]

[113] See S. Fish, *There's No Such Thing as Free Speech: and it's a good thing too*, Oxford UP, 1994), ch. 11.
[114] Bond, 'Kane', 211.
[115] In Saunders, *About Kane*, 82.
[116] See Saunders, *Love Me*, 15.
[117] Aston, *Feminist Views*, 82–3.
[118] In Saunders, *About Kane*, 63–4.
[119] There are, as Ken Urban concludes, no 'solutions' in Kane. See his 'Ethics', 37.
[120] In Sierz, *In-Yer-Face*, 121.

7

Tears in the Fabric

In February 1993 a two-year-old boy named James Bulger was led away from Bootle shopping centre by two other boys, Robert Thompson and Jon Venables. Thompson and Venables were both aged ten. A short while later they began torturing Bulger, before finally killing him, and leaving his body alongside a nearby railway line. There was some further evidence of sexual molestation. At the end of the year, the two boys were put on trial, convicted and sentenced. We shall consider the legal process in due course. As we shall see, the law did not come out of the experience well. But then it was an exceptional case, the hardest of the 'hard'. And it was not the kind of situation where it was ever possible to conceive an ending that might ever be termed, however flatly, satisfactory. A parallel might be made with another event of comparable horror, and seeming pointlessness, eight years later; the destruction of the Twin Towers in New York. The image of the burning towers has embedded itself in our collective imagination in much the same way as the grainy CCTV images of Thompson and Venables leading James Bulger to his death in the Bootle shopping centre. In a controversial essay on the subject of '9/11' and its consequence, the so-called 'war on terror', Martha Nussbaum suggested that there was some slight consolation which might be extracted from the violence. At such moments we are compelled to think a little more deeply about what it means to be compassionate.[1]

Ten years after the murder of James Bulger, Mark Ravenhill gave a lecture at Goldsmiths College in London. At the time, Ravenhill was emerging as a leading figure amongst the 'in-yer-face' dramatists who were presently storming the London stage. His suggestively entitled *Shopping and Fucking*, first performed in 1996, would be a defining contribution to the genre. It would be a mistake to suppose that in his lecture Ravenhill sought to explain, still less excuse, the essence of 'in-yer-face' drama. But he did present an

---

[1] See M. Nussbaum, 'Compassion and Terror', in J. Sterba (ed) *Terrorism and International Justice*, (Oxford UP, 2003).

intellectual context and a series of unsettling surmises. He recalled a meeting with another author in which they discussed the concept of 'evil'. The conversation started to make 'sense' when they turned to consider the 'case' of James Bulger, more especially 'the deep sense of sorrow, the ugliness, the pointlessness, the bleakness of it all'.[2]

There was a lot of talk about 'evil' in the weeks and months which followed the discovery of James Bulger's body. It was easy to ascribe everything to a necessary evil; far easier than thinking hard. The *Sunday Times* had reassured its readers on precisely these terms: 'We console ourselves that there are no general lessons to be drawn from such events'.[3] But for Ravenhill it was at that moment when he thought about James Bulger that the 'penny' dropped; perhaps there was something to be said for thinking a little harder. His very first attempt to write a play, a decade earlier, had been inspired by precisely the same event. It was not a 'particularly good play'. In fact, it was 'pretty terrible'.[4] But it was the moment that mattered, not the play. Ravenhill had sensed a moment of 'national grief', a collective abjuration. 'I think that something happened in Britain the day James Bulger died', he concluded, 'somehow something had shifted, a tear in the fabric had happened'.[5] And it was for a new generation of playwrights to provide a necessary testament; to 'evil' perhaps, to the reality of life in urban Britain for sure, but above all to the responsibilities of 'judgement'.[6]

Cultures of Abuse

We have, of course, been here before. In due course, we will encounter a play entitled *Monsters* written by Niklas Radstrom. He makes the point. To say that children have been killed 'before' is not to diminish the tragedy of what happened in Bootle in February 2003. But it has 'happened before', on many occasions (46–8).[7] What varies is how such an event is accounted, and read; for crime is written as a cultural as well as a jurisprudential narrative.[8] As a consequence, the history of crime becomes a chronicle of narrative construction, shaped by all the peculiar instances and prejudices of

---

[2] M. Ravenhill, 'A Tear in the Fabric: the James Bulger Murder and New Theatre Writing in the Nineties', 20 *NTQ* 2004, 307.

[3] In D. Green, 'Suitable vehicles: Framing blame and justice when children kill a child', 4 *Crime, Media, Culture* 2008, 204.

[4] Ravennill, 'Tear', 308.

[5] Ravennill, 'Tear', 310.

[6] Ravenhill, 'Tear', 313.

[7] N. Radstrom, *Monsters*, (Oberon, 2009). All references given internally.

[8] See here D. Green, 'Ravenous Wolves: Punitiveness and Culture', 6 *European Journal of Criminology* 2009, 519.

the moment. Child murder is no exception. The more particular murder of children by their mothers was, for centuries, the subject of a specific statutory offence, that of infanticide. The 1623 Infanticide Act, which was directed exclusively at 'lewd', or unmarried, women, was only repealed in 1803, with the passage of the Offences Against the Person Act. The statute passed into history. But the anxiety did not. Victorian England was repeatedly beset with so-called infanticide 'scares', as often as not stimulated by newspaper stories which inferred that thousands of babies were being murdered by their desperate, and unscrupulous, mothers. A great deal of jurisprudential energy was invested in trying to devise means of more effectively policing these mothers, and deterring their murderous intent; and a great deal of newspaper copy too. But then scares are rarely legislated away, and few editors were inclined to minimise the anxiety, not really. It was true in Victorian England, and it is just as true today.

Muckrakers

In 1885 the pioneering investigative journalist W. T. Stead published a series of articles entitled *The Maiden Tribute to Babylon* in the *Pall Mall Gazette*. The articles, which purported to reveal widespread child prostitution in London, were political dynamite.[9] Politicians were named, members of royal family inferred. And there were priests, needless to say. Stead was driven by a genuine desire to bring home to his middle-class readers the horror of child abuse. Much of what he reported was true, but much was also made up. He took a certain pride in being condemned as a 'muckraker', and like any good journalist, he knew what his audience wanted. And it was not just the Victorian journalist who had to wrestle the necessary paradoxes which attend to satiating readers. Poets and novelists were drawn to the same themes, and for the same necessarily conflicted reasons. The murder and abuse of children sold copy. The sorry tale of Hetty Sorrel in *Adam Bede* went a long way to sealing George Eliot's literary reputation. No doubt the many admirers of Eliot's novel would have been just as familiar with Frances Trollope's *Jessie Phillips*.[10] And they probably shared a common admiration for Wordsworth's iconic *The Thorn*. The haunting tale of Martha Ray may not be so familiar today. But the Victorians loved it.[11] And then, of course, the 'sensation' novel arrived on the literary scene at the end of the 1850s, full to the brim with murderous mums. Victorian infanticide 'scares' were not located on

---

[9] The veracity of Stead's claims was immediately contested, and remains a matter of some controversy.

[10] See I. Ward, *Sex, Crime and Literature in Victorian England*, (Hart, 2014), 98–108.

[11] See I. Ward, 'The Voice of Martha Ray', 8 *Polemos* 2014, 345–57.

the streets of London but in its drawing rooms and libraries. It is what made them so scary.

The anxiety which Ravenhill detected is then familiar. The cultural narrative might be written differently today; but not that differently. In prosaic terms, nothing sells copy better; nothing ever has. Crises are discursively created.[12] More recently public attention has been diverted towards an aligned offence, that of child abuse. It is our current 'moral panic'.[13] Allegations of child abuse in public institutions have regularly appeared in the newspapers, with the names of various priest and politicians and so-called media 'personalities' in particular adding a relatable dimension to the mingled sensation of disgust and fascination. In some cases, it is evident that the allegations are true. In others, it is just rumour. The imperatives of journalism have changed little since Stead's day. Newspaper editors rarely worry too much about the distinction. That is left to prosecuting authorities and their barristers. It would be easy, as a consequence, to suppose that child abuse is prevalent in our society; much as mid-Victorians presumed that infanticide was prevalent in theirs. It is not prevalent; though it is evidently more common than we might have previously liked to suppose. And whilst the tone of so much of the newspaper reporting might be decried, it remains true that without their endeavour many of those now shamed and incarcerated might still be abroad in public life, groping their way around the various care homes and televisions studios of middle England.

It is, of course, a balance. It always is. Public disapproval runs alongside legal regulation. They are not always consonant. Sometimes the law does not seem to reach far enough. Sometimes it seems to reach too far. But in the end, they are constitutive. Taken together, they prescribe what we deem to be acceptable, and unacceptable, behaviour. We will turn our closer attention to alternative theories of justice and retribution in cases of child murder and abuse shortly, as we will more closely the legal proceedings which attempted to deal with the cases of Robert Thompson and Jon Venables. But first, we should note the broadening context. Crimes are rarely discrete. The case of James Bulger is no exception. It was never just a case of murder. There was a prequel, as we shall see, a story of child abuse, petty theft, casual violence and

---

[12] See P. Bruck, 'Crisis as Spectacle: Tabloid News and the Politics of Outrage', in M. Raboy and B. Dagenais (eds) *Media, Crisis and Democracy: Mass Communication and the Disruption of Social Order*, (Sage, 1992), 108.

[13] For a broader discussion of 'moral panic' and its legal consequence in modern society, see D. Haydon and P. Scraton, 'Condemn a little more, understand a little less: The Political Content and Rights Implications of the Domestic and European Rulings in the Venables-Thompson Case', 27 *Journal of Law and Society* 2000, 426–7.

drugs. And there would be a sequel, inevitably. Fleet Street was never going to allow the case of 'Jamie' Bulger, as he had been re-christened in the press, to come to a close with a couple of convictions and the quiet despatch of his assailants to a young offenders institution.

Much was invested in the sanctification of little 'Jamie', as it was in the demonization of Thompson and Venables. Their spectres would be raised time and again in the years which followed. Rumours of this and rumours of that; in 2007 *The People* declared itself incredulous at reports that the 'evil' Venables had become a born-again Christian; news that Thompson had fathered a child was greeted with barely concealed horror; and when there was not much else going on pages could be filled with variously credible estimates of the cost of incarceration, and then the measures which put into place to ensure their anonymity following release.[14] The backdrop to the sequel, which ran and ran, painted a gruesome picture, of a Britain sliding inexorably towards social and moral collapse. It depicted, according to the *Sunday Times*, a 'new brutality about Britain'.[15] The British reading and voting public like nothing more than to wallow in the prospect of pending doom.[16] The shadow Home Secretary and future Prime Minister, Tony Blair projected a grim prognosis. 'There is something very wrong and very sick at the heart of our society', he warned readers of the *Daily Mirror*.[17] There was some consolation, though. He at least had spotted the malaise and might be able to sort it all out, if he got the chance. Meanwhile, the incumbent Prime Minister, John Major, was already embarked upon a 'crusade against crime', and particularly against younger criminals.[18]

And the sequel would be told in terms of consequential crimes too; of which, for our particular purposes, two have an especial resonance. The first extends a familiar affinity. The relation of child murder and child abuse is well-established in criminological literature. And so is the coincidence of child pornography with each; except, as we shall see, it is not really coincidence at all. In 2010 it was reported that Venables was returned to prison in early 2010 for breaching the terms of his licence, allegedly for accessing child

---

[14] Green, 'Suitable vehicles', 199.

[15] Green, 'Suitable vehicles', 202.

[16] Or at least so it presently does. It has not always been so. In a notorious 1861 case, which involved very similar facts, the trial judge ascribed the murderous consequence to 'babyish mischief' gone wrong. History, as Green surmises, provides a further context, suggesting that our present age is one of peculiarly intense 'ontological insecurity'. See Green, 'Suitable vehicles', 207, 212.

[17] Green, 'Suitable vehicles', 198.

[18] In Haydon and Scraton, 'Condemn', 426.

pornography on the internet. News that was met with glee by editors up and down the land. There was nothing surprising in this; though it suggests that the capacity for rehabilitation in prison is somewhat limited. We will again take a closer look at the myriad complexities of child pornography in the next chapter, and more particularly still the peculiar facility offered by modern technology and the internet. The law, as we shall see, has struggled to deal with the various challenges presented by the internet; much as it has struggled to work out what to do with ten-year-old children who kill.

A second context comes at a tangent. The unlawful interception of communication or 'phone-hacking', as it is more commonly known, is proscribed in Section 1 of the Regulation of Investigatory Powers Act 2000. Unfortunately, Section 1 is another bit of law which does not really work; as became very apparent at the time of the phone-hacking scandal which engulfed News International between 2005 and 2007 and then again in 2011–2012, the consequence of which was the subsequent setting up of the Leveson Inquiry into press standards and regulation.[19] Amongst the most egregious incidents uncovered by the Metropolitan Police was the hacking of the phone of the Dowler family, whose daughter Milly had been abducted and murdered in 2002. The Dowlers eventually sought damages for breach of privacy, and no one thought fit to demur.[20] A further layer of irony is, however, revealed in the case of Jon Thompson, one of James Bulger's killers. When his phone was hacked, and reports emerged that he intended to pursue civil redress, the newspapers swung behind the Bulgers in campaigning to have his suit prevented. It is difficult to chart a sure path through the associated moral and jurisprudential paradoxes. The former CEO of News International, Rupert Murdoch, was not inclined to bother. Such breaches of propriety are, he observed, just part of 'Fleet Street culture'. It may be that

---

[19] The problem with the 2000 Act is the stipulation that a criminal offence is only committed if there is an interception of communication 'in the course of transmission'. It was commonly supposed that this meant that the offence was only committed prior to the communication being heard by intended recipients. It is now thought that the offence might be committed regardless of whether the communication has been heard. But the matter remains unclear. Perhaps as a consequence of this uncertainty prosecutions were, initially at least, rare. There have, as a consequence of the News International investigation, been some prosecutions and convictions, most notably of the former managing editor of *News of the World*, Andy Coulson, and two journalists Glenn Mulcaire and Clive Goodman, both of whom were convicted of intercepting communications at Clarence House.

[20] Though there was in the end no police prosecution. It was however revealed that the Dowler phone had been hacked by Mulcaire, who was subsequently convicted of phone-hacking following a different investigation. The Dowler family instead pursued a civil suit against *News International*, for breach of privacy and, it was reported, had settled for a sum of £2 million.

there is indeed little else to conclude from the paradox, except of course that the two cases confirm the desperate relation of craving reader and craven editor, the thin line which can lie between abuser and abuse-hunter; and of course the peculiar difficulties which the law has encountered in trying to police the margins.

Before the Law

It was not long before the killers of James Bulger were in custody, after which the ordinary course of the law proceeded. And this was the problem. It was not an ordinary case. The victim was not ordinary, and neither were the alleged offenders. The process reached a kind of resolution, if conviction and sentencing count as resolution. After a seventeen-day trial at Preston Crown Court in November 1993, the two boys were convicted of murder and ordered to be detained at Her Majesty's pleasure, the normal substitute sentence for life imprisonment when the offender is a juvenile. It was already slightly incongruous as a consequence. But along the way, there were so many discomforting moments, so many occasions when the formal legal process seemed not just incongruous but dysfunctional.

Six years later, the European Court of Human Rights passed down a judgement which detailed precisely which breaches of the European Convention on Human Rights had occurred during the original trial and subsequent sentencing process. The jurisdiction of the Court had been affirmed by the passage of the 1998 Human Rights Act. But disquiet had been articulated for some time, especially in regard to the process of setting an appropriate 'tariff', a minimum period during which an offender convicted of murder must serve in prison before being considered for release on license. The trial judge, Mr Justice Morland, had set a tariff of eight years for the two boys. This was increased to ten by the Lord Chief Justice. In July 1994, having received a petition with 278,000 signatures, which asked that the two boys should never be released, the Home Secretary Michael Howard increased the tariff further to fifteen years. Whilst the gesture might have gone some way towards satiating the 278,000, it attracted immediate criticism from within judicial circles. The Master of the Rolls Lord Donaldson termed it 'institutionalized vengeance' inflicted by a 'politician playing to the gallery'. Three years later, the House of Lords struck down the Home Secretary's increased tariff on the grounds that it was *ultra vires*. Parliament had vested the Home Secretary with duties which were clearly granted on condition of their impartial exercise. And the Home Secretary had not acted in accordance.[21]

---

[21] For an overview of the domestic proceedings, see Haydon and Scraton, 'Condemn', 431–3.

The opinion of the European Commission in March 1999, that Thompson and Venables had been denied a fair trial was a sure indication that the European Court was likely to express a similarly dim view. And in December of the same year, it did. Lawyers for the two boys had argued the breach of three particular Articles of the Convention: Article 3, which prohibits inhuman or degrading treatment, Article 5, which enshrines the right to liberty, and Article 6 which confirms the right to a fair trial.[22] The Article 3 argument, which moved around the fact that the two boys as a consequence of their age had been given an indeterminate sentence, was dismissed by the Court. A tariff does not *per se* amount to degrading treatment.[23] The Article 5 argument was similarly rejected, at least in the main. The detention was clearly lawful under English law. The Court did however find breaches of Article 6. Both the accused would have felt inhibited by the process, and both were denied proper access to legal counsel as a consequence of 'their immaturity and disturbed emotional state', for which reason it is quite probable that neither was capable of providing information necessary for the 'purposes of their defence'.

The Court further held that the role of the Home Secretary in the resetting of tariffs was a breach of Article 6. In doing so, it confirmed that this particular breach also incorporated a collateral breach of Article 5.4, on the grounds the appellants had no opportunity to have the lawfulness of their detention assessed by a judicial body. The incumbent Home Secretary expressed his misgivings but confirmed that, as a consequence of the 1998 Act, he had no alternative but to accept the ruling.[24] Shortly after, the Lord Chief Justice reinstated the original tariff, which paved the way for the release of the two boys. It was not, however, quite the end. In anticipation of

---

[22] *T v UK* (Application 24724/94) and *V v UK* (Application 24888/94), parallel judgement given 16th December 1999.

[23] Though to might be noted that this constituent decision was only reached by a majority of ten to seven. And doubts remain in regard to whether the Court reached the right decision. Psychiatrists who examined Venables suggested that the indeterminate nature of the offence, which inferred the possibility that he might never being released, could amount to inhuman treatment. It was further suggested that, as a consequence, Venables had intimated thoughts of suicide.

[24] According to the Home Secretary, who reported to Parliament, the judgement of the Court was likely to 'cause great disappointment and offence to many people in this country'; as if that should be a factor in reaching a legal resolution. The reaction of both Houses of Parliament to the judgement can be found in Hansard. See <http://hansard.millbanksystems.com/lords/1999/dec/16/echr-judgment-thompson-and-venables> (last accessed 26th June 2020), and <https://api.parliament.uk/historic-hansard/commons/2000/mar/13/echr-judgment-thompson-and-venables> (last accessed 26th June 2020).

their release, the boys' lawyers secured an unprecedented High Court order granting anonymity for the rest of their lives. The claimants, it was held, were 'uniquely notorious' and thus at 'risk of serious harm.' Their case was 'exceptional'.[25] Newspaper editors, some of whom has opposed the application in court, expressed their dismay.

There is not much positive that can be gleaned from the Bulger case. The law did not come out of it well, neither did successive Home Secretaries, and neither most certainly did the press; for reasons we have already explored. Amongst the headlines which greeted their conviction in November 1993 could be found 'Freaks of Nature' and 'How Do You Feel Now You Little Bastards?' In his book on the case, Blake Morrison concluded that the trial and what followed 'shamed Britain in the eyes of the world – not because the murder itself was so shocking (though it was) but because the media circus, the court process, the inability of the boys to instruct their lawyers and the public's opposition to the possibility of them being rehabilitated'.[26] But it was the legal failure which is the most shaming and the most troubling. It must be admitted that the Bulger case was hard. But then it is the 'hard' case which tests the integrity of a legal system. It is for this reason that we must pause to consider the limitations of the law, precisely indeed because the situation was so peculiar and the failures to discomforting; and perhaps more importantly because there are alternatives. It is perhaps understandable if carceral punishment presented itself as the obvious solution to the cases of Jon Thompson and Robert Venables. Public opinion would have tolerated nothing less, and the common law is obliging.

It is worth, however, pausing to consider the case of Silje Redergard. Silje was five when she was beaten to death by two six-year-old boys in Trondheim in 1994. There were certain differences between Silje's death and that of James Bulger. But the parallel between the two cases was close enough to bear critical comparison. As to the immediate differences, most obviously perhaps Silje had known her assailants. They had been playing together, and the game had gone horribly wrong. They were much the same age as Silje too, significantly younger than Thompson and Venables who were much older than their victim. But perhaps the more remarkable, and most remarked, difference was the respective reaction of the different communities and their judicial systems. The age of criminal responsibility in Norway is

[25] *Venables & Thompson v News Group Newspapers Ltd* [2001] EWCC 32 (QB); [2001] Fam 430; [2001] 2 WLR 1038; [2001] 1 All ER 908; [2001] EMLR 255; [2001] 1 FLR 791.
[26] See Haydon and Scraton, 'Condemn', 426–8, discussing the 'moral panic' which evolved around the case, and also <http://www.theguardian.com/uk/2013/feb/11/james-bulger-20-years-on> (last accessed 26th June 2020).

fifteen. So there was no prospect of a criminal trial. But most notable perhaps was the conceptualisation of the case in the press, in terms not of 'criminal justice' but of 'child welfare'.[27] The public mood was anyway different; in large part perhaps as a consequence. As the senior police officer tasked with investigating the incident observed, there were 'no suspects' in the case, 'only victims'.[28] Once it was known that the killers were little boys, the 'lynch mob mood' dissipated [29] There were no haunting CCTV images to fuel public animosity. Nobody mused on the concept of 'evil'. It could do no good. Instead, attention was focussed on rehabilitation, for all parties. It was, Silje's step-father confirmed, 'important to take care of all those who are parties in the case, and to have compassion for all the victims'.[30] The identities of the two boys remained anonymous and respected. The murder was not forgotten. But neither was it deployed as an excuse to keep selling newspapers. And twenty years on neither killer has re-offended. The murder of Silje Redergard was, in sum, characterized as a 'horrible aberration'.[31] It did not betoken apocalyptic social collapse.

It would be a mistake to paint too bright a picture here. The scars remain, as Silje's mother has more recently testified. An appreciation of compassion does not diminish the sorrow or the anger. At least one of the assailants has reported ongoing psychological trauma. There are again no easy conclusions, certainly no happy endings. And the Redergard case, like indeed that of James Bulger, is exceptional in so many ways. That said it is suggestive of something more. Justice can be done differently. One of the jurors who had convicted Thompson and Venables subsequently reflected in terms that approach regret: 'We should have gone back into court and said yes, we do have a verdict: our verdict is that these boys are in urgent need of social and psychiatric help'.[32] Which is what, in effect, transpired in Trondheim. But it was not an option in Britain in 1993, or at least it was not the preferred option. And it is still not. As the lawyer who originally represented Venables has recently confirmed 'nothing has really changed'. Sentencing of children might be a little 'more sympathetic' today; but not much. And society is just

---

[27] Green, 'Suitable vehicles', 202.

[28] See <https://www.independent.co.uk/life-style/somethind-died-with-silje-does-the-killing-of-five-year-old-silje-marie-redergaard-by-her-own-1444162.html> (last accessed 26th June 2020).

[29] See <https://www.theguardian.com/theguardian/2010/mar/20/norway-town-forgave-child-killers> (last accessed 26th June 2020).

[30] In Green, 'Suitable vehicles', 204.

[31] Green, 'Suitable vehicles', 208.

[32] Quoted in <http://www.theguardian.com/uk/2013/feb/11/james-bulger-20-years-on> (last accessed 26th June 2020).

as 'venomous', newspapers just as egregious, politicians no less craven to the whims of public opinion.[33]

Ghosts and Monsters

In May 2009 a play opened in London entitled *Monsters*. It was written by a Swedish playwright Niklas Radstrom. It had already courted some controversy following its initial production in Copenhagen in 2004, and was anticipated by UK critics with a 'good deal of preliminary disquiet'.[34] *Monsters*, its subtitle confirmed, is 'a play about the killing of James Bulger'. Some thought it to be in 'very bad taste, at the very least.[35] Child murder on stage is always likely to provoke the most intense of emotions. It is not, however, unfamiliar. Classical and modern stage is soaked in the blood of slaughtered children; from the *Medea* of Euripides to Shakespeare's *Titus Andronicus* and *Macbeth*, to Edward Bond's *Saved*.[36] For dramatists such as Ravenhill, the writing of *Saved* was a pivotal moment in post-war British theatre. Of the many things which so troubled contemporary reviewers of Bond's play was the scene in which a bunch of bored and disaffected youths torture and then stone a baby to death. Bond twisted the tale by presenting his audience with a singularly unapologetic ringleader of the baby-killers, Fred, who spends much of his oddly brief time in prison complaining about how much the wider public appears to misunderstand him. The play closes with the gang back together, the baby's mother still holding out a hope that she might be able to get together with Fred. Bond is as unapologetic as his protagonist. The ending, he suggested, is 'almost irresponsibly optimistic'.

Theatre, of course, facilitates contention. It is the place for abrasion. And the murder and abuse of children, which so obviously excavates the depths of human emotion, is abrasive. Ravenhill attributes his first three plays, including *Shopping and Fucking*, to the immediate inspiration of the Bulger killing, noting that none of his earlier protagonists, or the victims of their violence,

---

[33] Public reaction to the Edlington 'case', in which two brothers, aged ten and eleven, stabbed and sexually assaulted two boys, aged nine and ten, is only too suggestive. The same headlines, the same desperate struggle amongst the authorities to work out what seemed the most appropriate response. Quoted in <http://www.theguardian.com/uk/2013/feb/11/james-bulger-20-years-on> (last accessed 26th June 2020).

[34] Michael Billington's review in <https://www.theguardian.com/stage/2009/may/09/monsters-michael-billington-theatre-review> (last accessed 26th June 2020).

[35] In the words of the founder of Mothers Against Murder and Aggression, a charity founded as a consequence of the Bulger murder.

[36] Interestingly Radstrom confirmed in his Afterword to *Monsters* that it was written in the 'form' of classical Greek tragedy.

were 'fully adult'.[37] In doing so he acknowledges the same unsettling conclusion which is articulated in his lecture; that however convenient, responsibility for what happened in Bootle in February 1993 cannot be left to the two boys alone. It is just too simple to consign the tragedy to the presence of pure 'evil'; too simple and too complacent. Sections of the media had already begun to countenance a sense of collective responsibility; at least to 'fight' the evil that was abroad in the land, to halt the kind of moral decay which Tony Blair had identified.[38] But it was not the kind of responsibility that helped much.

Monsters implicates the audience from the very start, stage instructions emphasising that the setting should be 'so relaxed that it is impossible to distinguish between the audience and the actors' (15). And then again in the very opening scene, the Chorus wonders not just what the audience expects to see, but what it intends 'to do about it' (17). The various interviews with Thompson and Venables and their parents is interleaved with scenes which affirm the broader familial and social context; a sub-narrative of depravity, violence, drug-use, petty theft (28–34, 52). The implication is patent. Thompson and Venables were not born evil. They certainly exhibited pathologies of dissociation. But they were pathologies nurtured by the society within which they lived. Thus, when an investigator relates an attempt to console Venables, it is the look of sheer incomprehension which is so striking, 'as though he simply could not understand what I was doing' (37). Later the Chorus ventures the thought: 'Yes, perhaps that is what evil is./ When we are in a place where there is no love,/ then we are the monsters' (65). And then, at the very end, the inference is made most explicit: 'We are all guilty of what we did or didn't do./ Where there is evil/ it thrives on indifference, contempt,/ self-complacency, arrogance' (78).

The suggestion that responsibility for the fate of James Bulger might be shared amongst the audience certainly troubled Michael Billington in the *Guardian*. This is not, he emphasised, to deny the value in reminding us of 'things we might prefer to forget', such as the fact that thirty-eight witnesses saw a two-year-old boy being abducted by two ten-year-olds who very obviously should have been in school (38). But the play, according to Billington at least, was at its weakest when it strayed into 'metaphysical speculation'.[39]

---

[37] Ravenhill, 'Tear', 311–2, further adding that whilst he has tried subsequently to 'shift' this particular 'set of obsessions' the 'imprint' remains, in more recent plays such as *Mother Clap's Molly House* and *Some Explicit Polaroids*.

[38] See Green, 'Suitable vehicles', 206, quoting an early comment in the *Times* from February 1993.

[39] See <https://www.theguardian.com/stage/2009/may/09/monsters-michael-billington-theatre-review> (last accessed 26th June 2020).

Conversely, it is at its strongest when it adopts the necessarily more sober tones of a documentary drama. As Radstrom confirms in his Afterword to *Monsters*, much of the play is derived from primary documents, most obviously in the form of the police transcripts of the many interviews with Thompson and Venables. The strategy is entirely understandable; for reasons we have already explored in an earlier chapter. The extensive, even exclusive, deployment of primary material should lend to the veracity of the piece. Pol Heyvaert's *Aalst* similarly adopts a quasi-documentary form, in re-presenting another notorious case of child murder, this time in Belgium in 1999. Radstrom's determination to minimise what he termed 'characterisation' is affirmed in the opening stage instruction (15). Of course the insistent interrogation of 'truth' and its meaning, most obviously in the interviews with Thompson, infers a necessary irony; the use of document to attest the limits of metaphysical speculation (25). And here again, it is a familiar irony; one that commonly attaches to docu-drama. It is never quite what it would like to seem.

Interestingly it is precisely this scepticism which underpins Dennis Kelly's acclaimed *Taking Care of Baby*.[40] Kelly's play purports to chronicle the case of another alleged child murderer named Donna McAuliffe. The play opens with the statement 'The following has been taken word for word from interviews and correspondence'.[41] It seems to be a documentary drama. But it is not. The reviewer in *Timeout* settled alternatively for 'quasi' or 'pseudo-documentary'.[42] But it is not even that. There is no real Donna McAuliffe; though the name is calculated to insinuate a vague remembrance.[43] In fact, none of the characters exist outside the script. *Taking Care of Baby* is, in fact, an interrogation of truth or rather the fabrication of different kinds of truth; in the media, in the theatre, in the family, and in the mind of Donna

---

[40] *Taking Care of Baby* was first performed at Birmingham Repertory Theatre in May 2007, three years after the first performance of *Monsters* in Copenhagen. There is no suggestion that it was written as a direct repost in any sense. *Monsters* was first performed in England in 2009.

[41] Each scene opens with the same affirmation, adding in each case 'Nothing has been added and everything is in the subject's own words, though some editing has taken place'. The exception, partial, is the final scene, which opens with the same affirmation, but chronically misspelt.

[42] Which of course might be said to be a contradiction in terms, and which if true infers that all supposed documentary drama is so compromised. See <http://timeout.com/newyork/theater/taking-care-of-baby> (last accessed 26th June 2020).

[43] In the *Telegraph*, Charles Spencer was minded to recall the case of Sally Clark, who was sentenced for similar crimes, and then later acquitted. See his review, available at <https://www.telegraph.co.uk/culture/theatre/drama/3665620/In-a-labyrinth-of-heartbreak.html> (last accessed 26th June 2020).

McAuliffe.[44] Aleks Sierz detected a constitutive strategy, in part a 'satire on verbatim theatre', in part a 'serious inquiry into the nature of truth'.[45] If there is a lesson to be learnt from Kelly's play, it is, as the reviewer in the *New York Times* concluded, 'that there is no such thing as a truly true story'.[46] As Kelly's Dr Millard concludes, the key to understanding truth is to appreciate that it is always 'relative', or at least 'we have to think that to live'.[47] Truth ultimately is 'just people saying things'; at least that is Dr Millard's truth, and it is not obvious that Kelly thinks any different.[48]

Documentary drama is only one dramatic strategy, of course. There are alternatives. In his recent study of generic trends in contemporary drama, Simon Shepherd has identified at least three further; the 'readable', the poetic and the realist.[49] Whilst the latter remains identifiably distinct, the margins between the first two have become ever more blurred over the last century or more. In effect poetic drama, characterized most obviously by its verse or quasi-verse form, has been squeezed out, in large part by the continued popularity of the 'readable'. Bartlett's *King Charles III*, which we encountered earlier, is a fine example of poetic drama. But it is also a rare example. Interestingly Shepherd identifies Alan Ayckbourn as a prominent example of the 'readable' writer, whose work imports a certain poetic tone, if not form.[50] Ayckbourn is familiar as one of the most acclaimed comic writers of his generation, his most common subject-matter being the peculiarities of contemporary middle-class suburban life. Child abuse would not seem an obvious topic, or at least it might not until very recently. But Ayckbourn comedies are rarely quite as light as they might at first glance seem. They are, after all, only 'tragedies which have been interrupted'.[51] And the middle-class home is frequently a place of tragedy and cruelty, of 'private lacerations'.[52] The home

[44] See Lyn Gardner's review, available at <http://www.theguardian.com/stage/2007/may/16/theatre3> (last accessed 26th June 2020).

[45] Sierz, 'Introduction' to *Dennis Kelly: Plays 2*, vii.

[46] See <http://www.nytimes.com/2013/11/20/theater/reviews/taking-care-of-baby> (last accessed 26th June 2020).

[47] D. Kelly, *Plays 2*, (Oberon, 2013), 21–2.

[48] Kelly, *Plays 2*, 60.

[49] S. Shepherd, *Modern British Theatre*, (Cambridge UP, 2009), 125–39.

[50] Shepherd, *Theatre*, 125–8.

[51] See D. Wu, *Six Contemporary Dramatists*, (St Martins Press, 1995), 117–19, quoting Ayckbourn, and also M. Page, 'The Serious Side of Alan Ayckbourn', 26 *Modern Drama* 1983, 37, noting his subject's earlier confession that the characters in his later plays are getting 'sadder' if not 'nastier', and also P. Allen, *Alan Ayckbourn: Grinning at the Edge*, (Methuen, 2001), at 134–43, inferring that critical acclaim arrived when Ayckbourn's writing darkened.

[52] See B. Dukore, 'Seriousness Redeemed by Frivolity: Ayckbourn's *Intimate Exchanges* 53

of Annabel and Miriam Chester certainly is. Annabel and Miriam inhabit Ayckbourn's 2002 play *Snake in the Grass*, a tale of murder and ghosts and terrifying memories, of 'demented' characters inhabiting a 'sinister' world.[53] It is also a play about the consequences of child abuse. Miriam might have murdered her father as a consequence of her abuse.[54] There again, she might not.[55] Rumour and insinuation are pervasive. The only evidence is testamentary. They call them 'ghost' stories.[56] As to being abused by her father, it was, Miriam confirms, 'worse than anything. Ever. In my whole life'.[57]

A different kind of rumour, and a different kind of tragedy, characterises Simon Stephens's play *One Minute*. *One Minute* can be readily placed within the dominant genre of expressionist realism. It tells the story of a missing child named Daisy Schults. The play was inspired by the case of Milly Dowler.[58] The central figure is Daisy's mother, and much of the play moves around her shifting emotional state, as she reconciles herself first with Daisy's disappearance, then the suspicions of the police, the false hope of inconclusive witness sightings and the discovery of a body. Three moments in the play import a particular resonance for our purposes, each occurring towards the close. A first resonates with one of the recurring themes in Radstrom's play, that of collective responsibility. One of the detectives reflects on Daisy's disappearance: 'I want to find the cunts who saw Daisy go and did nothing'.[59] The pertinence of the second and third moments will become more apparent

Modern Drama 2010, at 467, citing Clive Hirschhorn's original comments in his review of *Intimate Exchanges*.

[53] See <http://guardian.co.uk/culture/2011/feb/15/snake-in-the-grass-review/> (last accessed 26th June 2020), Ayckbourn characterises the play as a contribution to a genre of 'small-scale frighteners'. In A. Ayckbourn 'Introduction' to *Alan Ayckbourn: Plays 5*, (Faber and Faber, 2011), at vii.

[54] 'Darker, deeper lying themes', as Ayckbourn confirms, born of 'all too solid human origins'. In *Plays 5*, at viii

[55] Here again Ayckbourn touches on an issue of contemporary interest. Miriam admits to increasing her father's medicine in order to alleviate his suffering. It might be interpreted as a 'little push'. It was also, she is quick to confirm, an 'accident'. There again both sisters look to inherit a considerable estate, and in Miriam's case there is very clearly a further motive, vengeance. It is interesting to surmise how, if at all, a prosecutor might have wished to proceed.

[56] Annabel recounts being abused by her husband. Interestingly Ayckbourn is on record as suspecting that his own mother was abused by his step-father. See Allen, *Ayckbourn*, 18–19, and also 257–8 noting the 'instinctive' feminism that is commonly attributed to so much of Ayckbourn's writing.

[57] In *Plays 5*, 66.

[58] S. Stephens, 'Introduction' to *Plays 2*, (Bloomsbury, 2009), xi.

[59] Stephens, *Plays 2*, 69.

shortly. At one point in conversation with the same detective, Daisy's mother observes: 'Gary, if you find him, when, when you find him. I don't ever want to see him. Because I know I could, I, I could actually *kill* him'.[60] And then there is the end of the play, an incomplete sentence and 'Very, very long pause'.[61] It is only an end insofar as there is nothing else to be said. In the final analysis, *One Minute* is a 'meditation on grief', as Stephens asserts.[62] In their different ways the same is true of *Monsters*, *Taking Care of Baby* and *Snake in the Grass*. The genres may vary, but the aspiration is shared. Radstrom alludes to a peculiar facility of theatre; to nurture our collective contemplation of the 'unbearable'.[63] And the same is true of another play to which we will now turn, Bryony Lavery's *Frozen*. But before we turn to Lavery's play, we should briefly pause, to consider an alternative way of reaching judgement, of getting done what critical lawyers like to term the 'law job'.

Restoration Play

The meaning of justice has haunted moral and legal philosophers since Aristotle distinguished the two species of 'particular' justice in his *Nichomachean Ethics*, distributive and rectificatory. The redress for an injustice suffered as a consequence of a criminal act, which Aristotle characterised as an 'involuntary transaction', lay in the latter.[64] It does not mean that the redress must be punitive. But in cases involving violent crime it generally is; at least in the Anglo-American tradition of criminal jurisprudence. The best interest of the victim, it is assumed along the way, lies with the punishment of the offender.[65] But it is only assumption. Criminologists commonly ascribe this tendency to a neo-liberal appetite for contention; though it can, of course, be traced long before the emergence of a society which might be termed neo-liberal. In similar terms, it is sometimes ascribed to a collateral consequence of democracy; of giving an argumentative society what it wants. David Green terms it 'penal populism'.[66] And it is getting worse, as each successive gen-

---

[60] Stephens, *Plays 2*, 66.

[61] Stephens, *Plays 2*, 71.

[62] Stephens, 'Introduction'., xii. For the same conclusion see Rachel Lynn Brody's review of the original production at the Traverse Theatre in Edinburgh, available at <http://britishtheatreguide.info/reviews/oneminutetour-rev> (last accessed 26th June 2020).

[63] Radstrom, 'Afterword', 80.

[64] Aristotle, *Ethics*, (Penguin, 1976), 176–7.

[65] For commentaries here, both from the particular perspective of gender-based crime, see D. Martin, 'Retribution Revisited: a Reconsideration of Feminist Criminal Law Reform Strategies', 36 *Osgoode Hall Law Review* 1998, 153, and also C. McGlynn, 'Feminism, Rape and the Search for Justice', 31 *Oxford Journal of Legal Studies* 2011, 837.

[66] Green, 'Feeding wolves', 521, 527–8, and 'Suitable vehicles', 214.

eration of politicians seeks to curry popular favour by pretending that it is tougher on crime than its predecessor.[67] Here again, of course, punitive sanction for criminal activity long predates the development of anything resembling modern liberal democracy. The urge to punish is firmly embedded in our jurisprudential mindset. But this does not preclude the possibility of alternative responses, in particular situations. Responses to crime, as we have already noted, are susceptible to myriad social and political imperatives. It is why those who killed Silje Redergard were treated so differently from those who killed James Bulger.

Raising Voices

As a consequence of its punitive prejudice, our criminal jurisprudence tends to show rather greater interest in the offender than it does the victim of crime. In recent years, however, a debate has arisen in regard to the efficacy of one particular alternative, or in certain circumstances complementary, species of justice; what is commonly, if sometimes loosely, termed restorative justice.[68] The broad principle is relatively uncontested. An influential 1999 Home Office paper suggested that restorative justice 'is a process whereby parties with a stake in a specific offence come together to resolve collectively how to deal with the aftermath of the offence and its implications for the future'.[69] The appreciation of specificity is critical. The concern is with the harm suffered, and the sufferer, rather than simply the crime and the culprit. It is as Susan Miller has concluded in her extensive study of the Victims Voices Heard programme in Delaware, about the 'violation of people' and about how to rebuild 'relationships' of trust.[70] The victim is at the centre of the process, though in many cases programmes import a collateral desire to assist in the rehabilitation or 're-integration' of offenders too.

Most significantly though, as the name of the Delaware programme infers, it is about 'having a voice and being heard'.[71] The listening empowers,

---

[67] See G. Johnstone, *Restorative Justice: Ideas, Values, Debates*, (Routledge, 2011), 9, and also L. Snider, 'Towards Safer Socities: Punishment, Masculinities and Violence Against Women', 38 *British Journal of Criminology* 1998, 5–8.

[68] Loose insofar as there is such a variety of restorative justice practices, notwithstanding certain commonly identified features. See J. Shapland et al., 'Situating restorative justice within criminal justice', 10 *Theoretical Criminology* 2006, 506.

[69] T. Marshall, *Restorative Justice: an overview*, Home Office Occasional Paper, 1999, at 5.

[70] S. Miller, *After the Crime: the power of restorative justice dialogues between victims and violent offenders*, (New York UP, 2011), 7, and also 185–7.

[71] Miller, *Crime*, 163. See also Johnstone, *Justice*, 51–5, 62–4, Christie, 'Conflicts', 4–5, 13, and S. Juelich, 'Views of justice among survivors of historical child sexual abuse – implications for restorative justice in New Zealand', 10 *Theoretical Criminology* 2006, 131.

making victims feel constructively engaged in the process of healing and restoration. Most commonly, restorative justice programmes take the form of conferences and mediated engagements between those deemed to be part of the 'offence community', in other words, victims and offenders, and in some cases other interested parties.[72] Whilst some argue the case for 'diversionary' programmes, most are 'situated' within the conventional processes of 'retributive' criminal justice, for which reason the 'parameters' of the engagement will be, to a considerable degree, already 'fixed'.[73] We will revisit these various alternatives, and contentions, shortly.

In its broader sense, the principle of restorative justice is not new. Species of restorative justice are a common feature of numerous legal anthropologies, and many studies of contemporary practice like to alight upon the reinvestment of 'aboriginal' initiatives in Australia and New Zealand.[74] And the underlying principles can be traced in medieval canon law; finding occasional and spectacular contemporary articulation in venues such as the South African Truth and Reconciliation Commission.[75] In its more contemporary guise, however, the re-emergence of restorative justice is commonly aligned with the strengthening of victims-rights movements in North America during the 1970s and 1980s.[76] Whilst victim support groups had become a familiar presence during the same period, the broader principle of restorative justice began to gain significant political traction in the UK during the 1990s, as the opposition Labour party focussed its anti-crime policy around a perceived need to 'rebalance' criminal law in order to promote 'victim's justice'.

The 1999 Home Office paper provided further impetus, and the Youth Justice and Criminal Evidence Act of the same year gave statutory credence to the idea, establishing three 'principles' of restorative justice for youth offender panels: making restitution to victims; achieving re-integration into the law-abiding community; and taking responsibility for the consequences of

---

[72] See Johnstone, *Justice*, 1.

[73] See Shapland et al, 'Situating', 508–12, Miller, *Crime*, 12–13, and also Johnstone, *Justice*, 134–7.

[74] See here N. Christie, 'Conflicts as Property', 17 *British Journal of Criminology* 1977, 2–3, and also 10–11 discussing the idea of 'neighbourhood courts' and also Johnstone, *Justice*, 3–4, 30–40.

[75] According to its first Chair, Archbishop Desmond Tutu, the Commission was established on Christian principles derived from New Testament scripture. See Johnstone, *Justice*, 149–51, 161–2, Miller, *Crime*, 185, and also I. Ward, *Law, Text, Terror*, (Cambridge UP, 2009), 87–9.

[76] See Johnstone, *Justice*, 2–3 and C. Hoyle, 'Victims, the Criminal Process, and Restorative Justice', in M. Maguire, R. Morgan and R. Reiner (eds), *The Oxford Handbook of Criminology*, (Oxford UP, 2012), 405.

offending behaviour. Collateral initiatives, such as victim impact statements, appeared in the years which followed.[77] Further statutory recognition came in the form of the 2008 Criminal Justice and Immigration Act, and then more importantly perhaps in Schedule 16 of the 2013 Crime and Courts Act which established guidelines for the 'deferring' of 'sentence' in certain situations 'to allow for restorative justice'.[78] There is an evident trajectory; so much so that some commentators have credited an 'enormous success' in persuading politicians to contemplate the implementation of alternative criminal justice schemes.[79] There again, for the present it must be admitted that statutory recognition, in the UK at least, remains fragmentary; restricted in practice to a relatively limited number of chiefly youth-related crimes.

In some ways, the intellectual debate assumes a similar shape; a contentious trajectory. Modern restorative justice critics typically pay homage to the work of 'founding fathers' such as Nils Christie and Howard Zehr.[80] They also, just as typically, tend to shy away from the 'evangelism' which is perceived in much of this earlier work, instead preferring a more 'nuanced' approach, with a greater appreciation of the demerits as well as the merits of the many and various restorative justice programmes.[81] This does not diminish the original aspiration; to provide a means by which to raise the 'voices' of the victims of crime. Indeed, as Carolyn Hoyle has recently suggested, the need has never been greater. In a 'hot criminological climate', restorative justice recommends itself as a thoroughly desirable 'cooling device'.[82] The shifting mood is, however, significant and is the consequence of practice.

---

[77] Family Impact Statements, which can be read out in court by counsel on behalf of the victim's family, were first introduced in 2006. The ongoing determination to press forward with practical programmes in the UK is further evidenced in the *Breaking the Cycle* green paper and the new anti-crime strategy document *A New Approach to Fighting Crime*. Many of the victims support groups were concerned more particularly with gender-based violence, or violence directed towards children. See Hoyle, 'Victims', 405–8 and, more generally, M. Wright, 'The Court as a Last Resort: Victim-Sensitive, Community-Based Responses to Crime' 42 *British Journal of Criminology* 2002, 661–3.

[78] There is further an overlying European Union Directive of 2012, Article 10 of which validates restorative justice programmes where considered 'appropriate', by member states.

[79] See Johnstone, *Justice*, 13–14, 142–3.

[80] Zehr's work is, in these histories, especially revered. The two sacred texts are *Retributive Justice, Restorative Justice*, (Mennonite Central Committee Office of Criminal Justice, 1985), and *Changing Lenses: A New Focus for Crime and Justice*, (Herald Press, 1990). For a commentary see Johnstone, *Justice*, 139.

[81] See Hoyle, 'Victims', 418, Shapland, 'Situating', 523, McGlynn, 'Feminism', 833 and also J. Stubbs, 'Beyond apology? Domestic violence and critical questions for restorative justice', 7 *Criminology and Criminal Justice* 2007, 171–2.

[82] Hoyle, 'Victims', 419.

Aside from the larger, still contested, question of principle, a range of prosaic concerns have emerged; including those of environment, personnel, timing, and of course consequence.

Restorative justice programmes remain largely operational within the criminal justice system and its institutions.[83] As noted before, the most common forms are victim-offender mediation and restorative or family group conferences. Most commonly, the offenders are younger, the crimes of a less violent nature.[84] Shaping the appropriate 'offence community' can be contentious.[85] Victim and offender are necessary participants. Conferences can be wider, speaking to a larger supposition, that crime is a shared community experience and responsibility; though this necessarily opens up questions of how such 'micro' communities might be described.[86] It is a precept of criminal justice that even quasi-legal processes should be open and transparent, and accountable.[87] There again, for reasons that are obvious, there is much to be said for enhanced privacy in regard to restorative justice meetings. There is certainly much to be said for precluding a prurient media. Environments should be unthreatening, to all concerned parties. This particular consideration engages the matter of location too. Options are often limited, most obviously where an offender is already incarcerated. Otherwise, whilst there is an evident convenience in using police facilities, not least in terms of security, many commentators recommend more relaxed, less institutional environments.[88] As regards 'professional' support, the presence of facilitators is rarely disputed; though here again there is a debate as to whether they are better drawn from police, probationary or lay personnel.[89] Mediation must be voluntary, but it also needs to be managed, to some extent at least. The extent to which facilitators should intervene in order to shape conversations

---

[83] Although commentators note the coincidence of similar schemes in alternative environments, such as schools and the workplaces.

[84] Johnstone, *Justice*, 95, 137–8, and Shapland et al., 'Situating', 506.

[85] Dignan et al. 'Staging', 18–21.

[86] See variously Johnstone, *Justice*, 25–7, 40–5, 64–6, 124–30, and J. Braithwaite, 'Shame and Modernity' 33 *British Journal of Criminology* 1993, 12–14, and 'Repentance Rituals and Restorative Justice' 8 *Journal of Political Philosophy* 2000, 121–2.

[87] And a strict reading of Article 6 ECHR might be said to reinforce this perception. For a broad discussion of accountability in restorative justice, see Braithwaite, 'Standards', 563–77, and also Zehr, *Changing Lenses*, 194–5, admitting that the 'justice process' can never be 'fully private'.

[88] See J. Dignan et al. 'Staging restorative justice encounters against a criminal justice backdrop: a dramaturgical analysis', 7 *Criminology and Criminal Justice* 2007, 11.

[89] Current practice suggests that about 50 per cent of facilitators are 'professional' and about 50 per cent are not. Se Dignan et al., 'Staging', 14.

remains a matter of debate too, with a number of commentators decrying a tendency on the part of many to 'coach' either or both parties, to provide more or less directive 'scripts' or to ensure 'compliance'.[90] There again, it is vital that facilitators are sensitive to the dynamics of the conversation, and most obviously alert to the risk that particular participants might seek to dominate dialogue.[91]

The presence of the offender is obviously vital to a restorative justice programme; permitting victims to 'vent feelings of bitterness and hurt directly to the one who caused them'.[92] The venting is commonly presented as a necessary first step in a 'core sequence' of moments which will chart a process of 'symbolic reparation'; followed by reciprocal expressions of regret, remorse and forgiveness.[93] Ideally, the reparation will lend to a sense of 'healing' in the victim. But aside from the further responsibility to apologise, there remains considerable debate regarding the constructive role of the offender. As noted before, some programmes share a larger aspiration, not simply wishing to empower victims, but also enhance the possibility of offender re-integration or rehabilitation, to help offenders make 'good again'.[94] But to achieve this aspiration, it is commonly supposed, it is not merely a matter of presence, but of inclusion. The offender must be encouraged to participate. At this point, however, further questions arise. Some commentators express a concern that too much focus on the offender might distract from the 'voice' of the victim.[95] Others conversely are troubled by the thought that offender apologies might be forced, and that attendant 'shaming' rituals might serve to hinder the possibility of social re-integration. The distinction between 're-integrative' shaming and dis-integrating stigmatisation is critical but fine.[96]

---

[90] See Dignan et al. 'Staging', 9–17, and also Johnstone, *Justice*, 112–14.

[91] See J. Braithwaite, 'Setting Standards for Restorative Justice', 42 *British Journal of Criminology* 2002, 565–7, and also Miller, *Crime*, 167–8, 173.

[92] N. Baker, 'Mediation, reparation and justice', in J. Burnside and N. Baker (eds) *Relational Justice: Repairing the Breach*, (Waterside Press, 1994), 75.

[93] The 'core sequence' model found original expression in S. Retzinger and T. Scheff, 'Strategy for Community Conferences: Emotions and Social Bonds', in B. Galaway and J. Hudson (eds) *Restorative Justice: International Perspectives*, (Criminal Justice Press, 1996), 315–36.

[94] See Christie, 'Conflicts', 9. Many rehabilitation programmes are designed, of course, to aid the offender's return to society, for which reason much research moves around the functioning of 'circles of support' and similar initiatives. See Johnstone, *Justice*, 78–9, 87–8, and Miller, *Crime*, 199–200.

[95] Johnstone, *Justice*, 17–19

[96] See here N. Harris et al., 'Emotional dynamics in restorative conferences', 8 *Theoretical Criminology* 2004, 191–2, 197–204, B.van Stokkom, 'Moral emotions in restorative justice conferences: managing shame, designing empathy', 6 *Theoretical Criminology* 2002, 341–7, and Johnstone, *Justice*, 97–101, 109–11.

It might accordingly be better to focus on feelings of guilt or remorse.[97] But the lines are always thinly drawn. The balance of interests, between victim and offender, requires considerable emotional sensitivity; something which emphasises once again the critical role of the facilitator.[98]

A different question, which necessarily touches on that of rehabilitation, relates to timing. Programmes can be ante-conviction or post-conviction, or indeed 'parallel'.[99] The former, more common in the context of youth crime, are commonly termed 'diversionary'. Post-conviction programmes, conversely, are essentially 'therapeutic'; and raise the collateral issue as to how soon after the offence or conviction a programme should commence.[100] According to Miller, post-conviction 'therapeutic' programmes, incorporating 'elements of both retributive and restorative justice', are more appropriate to crimes of violence.[101] Others take a different view. According to Clare McGlynn post-conviction programmes, even in the instance of violent crime, merely enhance 'the status of conventional' criminal proceedings. What matters is practice, not principle.[102] The debate, however, remains moot, with the likes of Barbara Hudson reaffirming that a formal criminal process reinforces the fact that violent crime is something that 'society' takes 'seriously'.[103]

And it is ultimately a matter of practice. The question of efficacy can be reduced to the relatively simple question: does it work? The answer is not, however, so simple, not least because the aspiration is so uncertain. Whilst it is possible to objectify a crime, it is not so easy to calibrate harm suffered. It all depends on the victim. And much the same is true in regard to consequence or outcome. Research suggests that many victims do gain some measure of satisfaction from participation in restorative justice programmes.[104] But the picture is very far from uniform. Some evidently do not.[105] The very idea of a

---

[97] See van Stokkom, 'Moral', 347–51.

[98] This is, of course, especially so in those programmes geared towards youth offenders; and most are. For an overview, see Shapland et al., 'Situating', 510–12.

[99] See Johnstone, *Justice*, 135–7, discussing the 'parallel but interlinked' model of restorative justice familiar in Japan, and also L. Zedner, 'Reparation and Retribution: Are They Reconcilable?' 57 *Modern Law Review* 1994, 228–50.

[100] See Miller, *Crime*, 12–14, and also Wright, 'Court', 658–9.

[101] Miller, *Crime*, 12, 160.

[102] McGlynn, 'Feminism', 826, 830–2, citing particular, and successful, diversionary programmes in both the US and New Zealand, and also 841–2.

[103] B. Hudson, 'Restorative Justice and Gendered Violence – Diversion or Effective Justice', 42 *British Journal of Criminology* 2002, 629. The same is argued in A. Duff, 'Punishment, communication and community', in M. Matravers (ed) *Punishment and Political Theory*, (Hart, 1999). 51–3.

[104] See Hoyle, 'Victims', 418, and McGlynn, 'Feminism', 834.

[105] See here K. Daly, 'Restorative Justice – the real story', 4 *Punishment and Society* 2002, 69–71.

restorative justice conference is to facilitate greater human engagement. But human activity is precisely subjective and unpredictable. Especial doubts are voiced in regard to the suitability of restorative justice in cases of domestic violence and other 'gendered harms'.[106] Much depends on the empathetic capacity of particular parties, as well as the skill of particular facilitators.[107] It can be hard to predict quite how a given meeting might go, and what measure of risk is tolerable. Each dialogue is unique. To calibrate expectation is not to dampen it. But it is to admit a necessary caution.[108]

Victim response is especially hard to gauge. The world of 'shattered assumptions' defines prediction.[109] There can be no doubting the trauma which a restorative justice meeting can induce, in both victim and offender. At the same time, it is unarguable that a facilitated encounter between victim and offender is far preferable to a non-facilitated encounter. In 2004 it was reported that James Bulger's mother Denise had tracked down Robert Thompson but had not confronted him, in large part because she was 'paralysed with hatred'. Radstrom deploys the same sentiment: 'I didn't know I had that much hate in me . . . / But now I'm burning with hate, fury and fear' (73). It is not surprising. Existing research on restorative justice programmes affirms that many relatives of victims find it impossible to detach themselves from such feelings. Beathe Redergard felt still more conflicted. In her case, the anger deepened over time. At first, she had managed, quite extraordinarily perhaps, to feel 'bad' for her daughter's killers. But their continued presence in her community was hard to bear, and the hatred grew.[110]

It is tempting to suppose that a restorative justice programme might have helped Beathe. It might. But it might not. The same research commonly suggests that restorative justice is only effective where victims have

---

[106] Typically in such cases offenders prefer to trivialise the significance of their actions, whilst victims commonly seek to assume guilt, whilst also evincing almost too great a desire to forgive. See Stubbs, 'Beyond', 173–8 and K. Daly, 'Mind the Gap: Restorative Justice in Theory and Practice', in A von Hirsch et al. (eds), *Restorative Justice and Criminal Justice: Competing or Reconcilable Paradigms?* (Hart, 2003), 220. The limitations of traditional retributive penalties in such cases is conversely discussed in Snider, 'Societies', 2–8.

[107] See here J. Braithwaite, 'Restorative Justice and a New Criminal Law of Substance Abuse', 33 *Youth and Society* 2001, 228, Harris et al., 'Emotional dynamics', 202–4, Stubbs, 'Beyond', 171–2, 178–80, and Shapland, et al., 'Situating', 507–8.

[108] See here Wright, 'Court', 659–60 and Miller, *Crime*, 103, 184.

[109] Miller, *Crime*, 3–5.

[110] See <https://www.theguardian.com/theguardian/2010/mar/20/norway-town-forgave-child-killers> (last accessed 26th June 2020); <http://news.bbc.co.uk/1/hi/uk/8577458.stm> (last accessed 26th June 2020).

moved 'beyond' their anger.[111] Moreover, the situation in Trondheim, where the continued presence of the killers in the community was considered a necessary part of rehabilitation, is itself peculiar. There are few universals, and it is for this reason just as difficult to speculate on how a restorative justice programme might have helped Denise Bulger. It is just as impossible to speculate as to whether it might have helped Thompson or Venables. Restorative justice is about the particular, always. Put simply, it would have depended. The debate as to the merits and demerits of 'restorative' justice programmes remains contentious, in cases involving children no less than any other. But it can at least be supposed that if restorative justice does have a role to play in our criminal justice system, or indeed outside, it might well be in cases such as that of Thompson and Venables; not just in their immediate regard, but in regard to those who suffered as a consequence of what they did that day in Bootle in February 1993.

Frozen

There is an immediate resonance between the aspirations of restorative justice and the 'strategies' of law and literature scholarship; so evident that it might easily import a sense of undue confidence, even complacency. Most obviously there is the shared interest in 'voice', and how best it might be facilitated.[112] There is also a common emotional currency.[113] The faculty of law is commonly a faculty of reason, or so it likes to suppose. Restorative justice, however, trades on therapeutic potential as opposed to rationalist pretence. Those who embark upon a restorative justice programme embark upon an 'emotionally intense journey'.[114] And they tell 'stories', as do their chroniclers who assume the particular responsibilities of 'storytellers'. The language is different, the need to convey emotional intensity admitting nuance and situation.[115] The endeavour is inherently poethic and dramatic.

The theatrical or dramaturgical aspect of restorative justice has been noted by a number of commentators. Dignan has analysed generic restorative justice programmes in terms of theatrical 'production', replete with a 'cast of actors', a facilitator serving as 'master of ceremonies', various front and 'backstage' functions, and an 'audience'.[116] Of course, to an extent all

---

[111] Miller, *Crime*, 177
[112] See here McGlynn, 'Feminism', 827.
[113] See Shapland et al., '513–14.
[114] Miller, *Crime*, 172.
[115] Miller, *Crime*, 8, 159.
[116] See Dignan et al. 'Staging', 5–31.

criminal justice proceedings, especially trials, are theatrical.[117] But the peculiar nature of restorative justice practice makes this theatricality different,
and seemingly more intense, in a number of significant ways. Deploying a
methodology familiar to anthropological studies of 'interaction ritual' and
related associational practices, Meredith Rossner has analysed participant
'performance' in a filmed restorative justice programme. In her opinion, the
success of any programme is heavily dependent on the micro-contingencies of
the conversations which evolve; something which can make the responsibility
of facilitators all the more critical. The rhythm comes and goes as control of
the conversation moves from one participant to another.[118] And it is of course
so contingent because there is no text, merely a set of actors placed together in
a room with a shared experience to discuss. It might almost resemble a species
of 'improvised' theatre.

Bryony Lavery's *Frozen* does not invite improvisation in quite this way.
There is a text and three actors on stage. And there is, of course, a particular
context. The play was first performed at Birmingham Repertory theatre in
1998. The moment was transitional, in terms of both politics and theatre. A
Labour government had been recently returned to power, with a reformist
agenda which included a declared intention to 're-balance' the criminal justice system. The new Home Secretary promised a 'root and branch' reform of
youth justice.[119] The 1998 Crime and Disorder Act sped through Parliament.
Theatre-goers meanwhile, still coming to terms with the kind of 'in-yer-face'
plays that Ravenhill was writing, were about to encounter a revitalised species
of 'docu-drama' too. Norton-Taylor's *The Colour of Justice* was nearing first
production. But *Frozen* was neither documentary nor 'in-yer-face.'[120] For the
sake of generic place, it might be termed realist, perhaps expressive. A number
of Lavery plays are more poetic in tenor. A number are more obviously
political too in their engagement with the question of gender and sexuality;
and Lavery has developed a critical reputation on these terms.[121] *Frozen* does

[117] As Howard Zehr noted a 'kind of theatre in which issues of guilt and innocence predomi-
nate'. See his *Changing Lenses*, 72.

[118] M. Rossner, 'Emotions and Interaction Ritual: A Micro Analysis of Restorative Justice', 51
British Journal of Criminology 2011, 95–119.

[119] In Haydon and Scraton, 'Condemn', 427.

[120] Though by way of passing coincidence, and possibly no more, she did briefly teach Sarah
Kane in a drama class at Birmingham University.

[121] Whilst remaining, in the words of Kate Kellaway, one of the 'most consistently underrated
playwrights in the country'. See her comments in <http://www.theguardian.com/theob-
server/2002/jun/23/features.review27> (last accessed 26th June 2020). Earlier plays were
written for companies such as the Gay Sweatshop, with whom she served for a period as
artistic director, and Monstrous Regiment. For a commentary on Lavery's earlier writings

this, to an extent. It is about human sexuality, albeit in its darkest form. But there is much more.

The play moves around the agonies experienced by a mother whose daughter is abducted, sexually assaulted and murdered. Critics noted evident similarities between its plot and the subsequent case of Sarah Payne, another girl abducted and murdered, in 2000. It was, as Kate Kellaway put it, a discomforting instance of 'reality turned into a dire impersonator of art'. Lavery recognised the curious 'synchronicity'. In her brief acknowledgements to the printed edition of the play, she actually made reference to another notorious murder case, expressing her 'gratitude' to Marian Partington who had written a heart-rending piece for the *Guardian* about the murder of her sister Lucy.[122] Her acknowledgements also paid tribute to the inspiration of two neuropsychiatrists Dorothy Otnow Lewis and Jonathan Pincus, whose work was highlighted by Malcolm Gladwell in a 1997 article in the *New Yorker*. The latter interest finds dramatic form in *Frozen* in the character of Agnetha who is conducting research into the pathology of serial killers.

Whilst *Frozen* is about much more than a restorative justice programme, the idea is pivotal in terms of both theme and plot. The possibility of facilitating a meeting between Nancy and Ralph, the man convicted for the murder of her daughter, has been suggested by a 'Restorative Justice Lobby', and whilst their encounter does not proceed as might have been originally intended, it very obviously simulates the kind of meeting which is chronicled in much of the empirical research on restorative justice programmes (173).[123] And in doing so, of course, it encourages an audience to reflect intellectually on the merits and demerits of generic restorative justice schemes. Most of all, however, *Frozen* is intended to stimulate an emotional, possibly even an empathetic reflection. In this, it articulates an aspiration which is common in much of Lavery's work. It is written first from the 'heart'.[124] A play such as *Frozen*, according to Lavery, should certainly encourage intellectual contem-

on the subject of women and sexuality, see S. Carlson, 'Self and Sexuality: Contemporary British Women Playwrights and the Problem of Sexual Identity', *Journal of Dramatic Theory and Criticism* 1989, 162–4, and also her own affirmation in Stephenson and Langridge, *Rage and Reason*, 107 and 110–13.

122   Lucy was a victim of the notorious murderers Fred and Rosemary West. The article was entitled *Salvaging the Sacred*, and was published in May 1996. It was later revised and published in book form as *If You Sit Very Still* in 2012. Partington's essay also inspired a film entitled *Frozen*, written and directed by Juliet McKeon. Lucy was the cousin of Martin Amis, who also wrote about her disappearance and murder in his memoir *Experience*.

123   B. Lavery, *Plays 1*, (Faber and Faber, 2007). All internal references are taken from this edition.

124   Stephenson and Langridge, *Rage and Reason*, 110.

plation of the larger political context, but only after it has first embraced the human dimension. The poethical aspiration is here again resonant.

The meeting between Nancy and Ralph occurs later in the play, much of which takes the form of preparatory monologues, some stretching back twenty years, to the moment when ten-year-old Rhona disappeared, abducted whilst walking to her grandma's house doing an errand. The first three scenes introduce the three principle characters; Agnetha rushing to the airport to catch a flight to London in order to give a lecture on her research, Nancy in the garden saying what will, in the end, be a final goodbye to her daughter, and Ralph in his room reflecting on it being 'one of those days' when he feels like molesting a young girl. In their different ways, each character and each place seems so very ordinary. It is the conjunction, as ever, the contingency, which is so extraordinary. As Ralph observes 'sometimes you're fucked by/ circumstances/things don't go your way' (109). It is most ordinary of sentiments, and the most dreadful of ironies.

As the play unfolds, Agnetha assumes a shifting presence. She should contribute a necessary certainty to an otherwise distinctly uncertain prospect. But she does not, perhaps cannot. Despite her intellectual and clinical pretence, Agnetha is overcome by uncertainty and a lack of confidence, in her science and herself. It transpires that she too is struggling to deal with tragedy, and is as a consequence 'frightened of everything' (118).[125] She is also struggling to make some sense of her work, which moves around the question of criminal culpability. The title of her thesis is 'Serial Killing – A Forgivable Act?' The question mark is critical. Agnetha wants to think that there is a scientifically determinable difference between 'crimes of evil' and 'crimes of illness' (132). She wants to 'examine/ what goes wrong with that humanity . . . /which can make certain individuals appear inhuman'. To do so, she will take a closer look at the functioning of the human brain and at lots of 'data' (133). The Victorians, of course, did much the same. The Victorian age was the first to take statistics seriously, whilst the likes of Arthur Conan Doyle and Charles Dickens were both famously fascinated by the emergent 'science' of phrenology.[126] Agnetha harbours much the same hopes, of both the science and the statistics. It will all help to understand Ralph.

So she conducts a series of tests, tapping Ralph on the nose, getting him to walk around, do a series of image and word association tests. And, as

---

[125] A close married friend with whom she had just started an affair has died in a traffic accident.

[126] Queen Victoria even had the heads of her children measured in order to give her a better sense of how each might be expected to cope with their prospective responsibilities. Her eldest Prince Bertie had, it transpired, a disappointingly small brain cavity.

she does so, Ralph relates a series of accidents from his youth, crashing cars and falling down mineshafts, of being abused by his 'mom' (147–9). The petty crimes and petty trespasses might be interpreted as a narrative of social dislocation. Agnetha is, however, more interested in the possible longer-term physical consequences, of how Ralph might have incurred incidental brain damage, of how the abuse and 'neglect' might have limited the growth of his 'cortical regions' (154–5). In the end, she reaches the conclusion that Ralph 'can't help it' (157). At the end of her lecture on Ralph, she concludes that he is 'abnormal' (143). In an unguarded moment, she reaches the vernacular conclusion that he is just 'crazy' (164). It amounts to much the same. It also advances the still unresolved question of what might be considered normal. Science gets so far, but only so far; as Agnetha comes to realise. And then there is the human. In the final of the scenes which interweave Agnetha's lecture on Ralph, she concludes that there is no such thing as necessary 'evil'. Killers like Ralph 'are driven by forces beyond their control'. But there is a time, she concedes, when science has to stop, and 'living' has to start (177).

Nancy presents a very distinct contrast, the poetry as opposed to the prose. In the earlier scenes, she is still clinging to the diminishing hope that Rhona might be found. She has 'Faith' (121). She must be 'somewhere' (112). She may ring on her birthday, perhaps. And then Rhona's body is found, and the lingering hope is replaced by the inevitable cocktail of conflicting emotions, feelings of blame and guilt and hatred, but also increasingly a desire to know more, to speculate further, on her daughter's final moments, on the mind of her killer. At first, she would:

> like to see him die.
> Watch him
> Suffer
> he wouldn't suffer like she suffered
> but it would be something.
> An eye for an eye
> tooth for a tooth. (137–8)

She imagines what it might be like to attend his execution, as victim's families can in America. Feelings of revenge are, however, tempered by an incipient urge to forgive; a conflict which, as we have seen, is common in so many restorative justice cases.

Just as familiar is Nancy's contempt for formal legal process, for all the 'red tape' (158). The 'trial starts to happen'. Ralph's solicitor prevents the release of Rhona's body. Her remains are his 'exhibits' (151). Nancy can visit the mortuary and even touch her daughter's 'skull'; a scene that parallels Agnetha's physical examination of Ralph's head. But whereas Agnetha is focussed on the size of Ralph's cortex, Nancy is transfixed by the beauty of the 'skull' and all the other fragmentary remains which she finds in the box (158–9). The science might be enough for Agnetha, just as the law might satiate the formal demands of justice. But neither helps Nancy. There has to be something more, something human; a resolution confirmed by her other daughter Ingrid. It is time to 'let go', Ingrid supposes, but they can only do that if they are able to 'forgive', and in order to forgive, Nancy has to meet Ralph (160–1).

Ralph's pathology unfolds from the early scene in which he reflects on his dreary existence, his alcoholism and his predilection for little girls. All he wanted to do was 'get in the van' and 'keep her for a bit' (107). He is a resentful man, given to blaming others for his condition, his landlady for throwing him out, and the 'law' for not guaranteeing his 'security' money, his tattooists for making his skin sting, the police interrogators for their bad 'language' and their wilful destruction of his extensive collection of child pornography (114, 119). He is also very tidy. His flat is as clean as a 'pin', the collection of child pornography videos, his 'investment' as he calls it, meticulously 'organised' (114–15, 168). It might be supposed that Ralph has retreated from the outside world of 'rage' to an inside world of order; except of course that the 'rage' is his, and it is consuming (123). Everyone is to blame, except himself; a view which Agnetha reinforces when, following a long scene in which she seeks to explore his brain function whilst he tries in turns to grope her 'pussy', she concludes 'it's okay Ralph./It's not your fault./You can't help it' (157).

As we have already noted the meeting between Ralph and Nancy occurs towards the end of the play. Nancy is the animator. She is 'up to speed' with all the 'data vis-a-vis the use of/ Victim Offender Communication in the/ Treatment of Sexual Abuse and Violent Crime Trauma', and the operation of various 'Victim-Sensitive Offender Schemes' in the US. She is, she assures herself, 'impeccably prepared' (167).

All she needs, apparently, is Agnetha's support. Agnetha, however, is not convinced. She is even less sure that Ralph is ready. He feels no 'remorse', no 'compunction'. He is only 'sorry' that 'killing girls' is 'not legal' (169–70). No one, Agnetha suspects, is really ready for a meeting; least of all herself. She is barely in control of her own emotional state and is certainly not trained to mediate or facilitate. She informs the 'Restorative Justice Lobby' that she 'would not be comfortable in recommending' a meeting between Nancy and Ralph, the 'experiment is unviable/the components unstable' (173–4). Nancy is not, however, going to be stopped by a 'bloody American doctor' (173). She knows the 'Right People', and Ralph confirms his willingness in correspondence (174, 177).

And Lavery has dramatic license on her side, and so the meeting happens.

In reality, it would never have taken place. Not least because there is no facilitator present, just Nancy and Ralph, and a silent guard, sat in a prison room. The conversation is stilted as a consequence. Lavery wants it to be. 'For a long time', the stage direction confirms 'they look, they really look, at each other', and Nancy and Ralph repeatedly sink into long periods of silent contemplation (177). Lavery has attested to her interest in writing characters who struggle to articulate their feelings, to 'find the language to express that anger or that hurt or that love'.[127] Nancy and Ralph are precisely such characters. But they must communicate because Nancy's anger can only 'vanish' at the moment when it finds expression.[128] Here again, in the absence of a facilitator, Nancy animates the conversation, opening with the affirmation: 'I want you to know/ I forgive you for killing my daughter' (178). In doing so, she disrupts the 'core sequence' which is commonly adopted in facilitated mediations. As yet Ralph has expressed no remorse.

'I don't hate you', she adds, 'I used to./ But I don't any more' (179). Ralph remains taciturn, the stage direction confirming that he is 'not interested' in Nancy's explanation why, that she wants to move on. Nancy then proceeds to show Ralph various photographs of Rhona. Such a practice is not unknown in facilitated mediations. The direction adds that, as she does so, Nancy's 'body indicates leaning' (180). Finally, Ralph begins to talk about Rhona, and there is again a predictability and a familiarity in what he says. 'I don't think I hurt her', he opens. And when Nancy responds with disbelief, his adjustment is just as familiar: 'I don't think she was frightened at all' (181). Dialogues such as this are commonly found in recorded case-studies of facilitated mediations. The offender appears to want to reassure the victim, or the victim's family, but is primarily driven by a desire to attenuate his or her own responsibility.

The absence of a facilitator, and the consequence, becomes increasingly apparent. Desperate to get Ralph to move towards a stage of admission, and then remorse, Nancy reaches out to touch his arm. Ralph stops her. And then the direction of the conversation begins to turn. Ralph begins to talk, not about Rhona, but about himself and his upbringing, especially the abuse he suffered at the hands of his father. Nancy allows him to continue, repeatedly expressing her sympathy, in the hope that she might be able to convince Ralph of the evident parallel between the abuse he suffered and the abuse he inflicted upon Rhona. A 'long' pause ensues, and then Ralph finally breaks down in tears, and admits that she must indeed have been 'frightened' and

---

[127] See her comments on writing 'dumb' characters in Stephenson and Langridge, *Rage and Reason*, 110.

[128] In Stephenson and Langridge, *Rage and Reason*, 100.

'hurt'. It might be thought that the meeting thus ended on a satisfactory note. Nancy hands Ralph a tissue. His response, however, suggests that there is still some way to go: 'Don't come and bother me again./ Cunt' (184–5).

Five short scenes follow. They track the consequences of the meeting. In the next Ralph is writing a letter of apology to Nancy, and evidently enduring a mental breakdown as he does so. He keeps lining up his stationery and pens 'And again. And again'. He tears up the letter, then tries to reassemble the pieces (185–6). A little later Ralph meets Agnetha. She tells him that it will be the 'last time'. He tells her that he thinks he has cancer, but that the doctor thinks it is just 'stress'. The pain is around his 'heart', and it started the 'night after that mother of that girl Rhona I done came' (189). At least she has forgiven him, Ralph observes, so they are 'straight on it' (190). Agnetha suggests that he tries to speak to a psychiatrist, and maybe give it a bit of a rub'. And then she leaves, whilst Ralph rearranges his desk 'And again. And again' (190–1). In the next scene, Ralph hangs himself. The final scene, which follows, is set at Ralph's graveside. Agnetha has returned, and Nancy is present. It is another scene in which the conversation is, understandably, stilted. Agnetha confirms that Ralph probably killed himself as a consequence of the meeting. When Nancy wonders if she should be 'sad or glad', Agnetha suggests maybe 'both'. But Nancy is really just 'glad'. Crimes have consequences, and those who commit them must expect to 'suffer' (194–5).

The sentiment is entirely understandable, and again familiar in a number of recorded restorative justice cases. There are no happy endings; indeed, there are no endings, not really. Emotions are likely to remain raw and conflicted. All that can be hoped for is that some of those who participate as part of the 'offence community' might be better placed to move on as a consequence. But there are no guarantees; as the case of Nancy and Ralph makes evident. By the end, Ralph is dead, Nancy only barely forgiving, and as an entirely unconvincing in her assertion that she might now be able to experience 'happiness' again (195). As we have already noted, in reality their meeting would never have taken place; regardless of what the 'Restorative Justice Lobby' might have recommended. Agnetha's suspicions were correct. Neither Ralph nor Nancy was prepared for what transpired. The absence of a facilitator is stark, the unplanned dialogue runs contrary to the familiar and recommended 'core sequence'. Only at the bitter end of the conversation does Ralph appear to proffer an essentially forced apology, after which it seems that he is unable to complete a letter of remorse. If he was shamed, it was clearly in the more 'dis-integrating' sense. His death seems to furnish Nancy some grim satisfaction. But it is hardly the kind of satisfaction which advocates of restorative justice are inclined to recommend. This is not to denigrate restorative justice programmes. This is not Lavery's purpose. But it is to stress just how fragile the emotional experience, and how sensitively the process must be directed. *Frozen* is a lesson in precisely what can go wrong if the respective parties are left to work it out for themselves.

Frozen was generally well-received by the critics.[129] The reviewer in the *Evening Standard* cast a slightly more cautious note, concluding that the 'vivid eloquence' of the writing redeemed the play from the incipient tone of 'liberal wish-belief'. Charles Spencer in the *Telegraph* was more fulsome in his admiration for a 'truly outstanding play'. So was Michael Billington. *Frozen*, he affirmed in a review of a 2002 production, is a 'remarkable play'. *The Times* was no less impressed. A 'major play', it concluded, 'thrilling, humane and timely'. A 2014 revival was just as well-received; a play of 'immense compassion', according to one reviewer.[130] It is all of this, humane, compassionate, thrilling. But it is also unsettling, even disturbing. And it is supposed to be. According to Lavery, her specialist subjects are 'grief, death, sex and anger'.[131] But the reach is larger still. *Frozen* provokes like Bond's *Saved* provoked, and indeed Radstrom's *Monsters*. It is not just about presenting an audience with a flawed restorative justice meeting and its consequence. There is a greater ethical responsibility. As we noted earlier, Radstrom suggests that theatre might be the 'only' place where 'we can meet one another, to really talk about the unbearable'. In reply to critics, he reaffirmed: 'I wanted to use theatre to talk about things we find unbearable and hard to understand: the fact that our child may be murdered by another child; that our child may be a murderer'. Theatre facilities 'conversation'; indeed, it is defined by conversation, by making 'space for dialogue'. It may be 'quite an uncomfortable conversation' at times. But it is a vital one. It is certainly difficult to conceive a more uncomfortable series of conversations than those raised in both *Monsters* and *Frozen*.[132] It is thus hardly surprising that the implicit conversation fashioned between text, author and audience, might be every bit as discomforting. Sometimes it has to be; which is of course precisely what Ravenhill infers in his reflective lecture on why dramatists sometimes feel impelled to contemplate what happens when there is a sudden tear in the fabric of our otherwise ordinary lives.

---

[129] The New York production of *Frozen* earned four Tony nominations.

[130] Maddy Costa at <https://www.theguardian.com/stage/2014/mar/06/frozen-review-finger smith-deaf-signing-language> (last accessed 26th June 2020).

[131] Quoted in <http://telegraph.co.uk/culture/theatre/drama/3620193/Sexndrugsnpoetry. html> (last accessed 26th June 2020), adding that she was 'ricocheting from grief' when she wrote *Frozen* following the death of her mother in a 'botched' hospital accident.

[132] Quoted in Lyn Gardner's review of the play in <http://theguardian.com/stage/2009/ may/06/monsters-james-bulger-arcola-niklas-radstrom> (last accessed 26th June 2020)·

8

A Revenger's Tragedy

As we have already noted, 'law and literature' scholarship is as much concerned with what happens in the classroom as what happens in the courtroom. When we revisited David Hare's *Murmuring Judges* in the first chapter of this book, we further noted that some texts are more immediate than others. *Murmuring Judges* is immediate in this sense, a play squarely about the law. Others are more allusive. We have to dig a little deeper to extract the jurisprudential ore. Our final play is a bit of both. Evan Placey's *Girls Like That* is about the use, and misuse, of social media. In experiential terms, it is very immediate. Every law student sat in a lecture theatre is familiar with social media; as any law teacher will most probably realise as they glance across the room. It is an addiction, the consequences of which, on young minds, and young emotions, are well-documented. Placey's play is about this. But it also, at a slightly deeper level, about the law. More particularly, it is about an area of social media activity which has continued to present serious jurisprudential problems for lawyers and regulators. That activity is what is called, sometimes controversially, 'revenge porn'.

Girls Like That was jointly commissioned by Birmingham Repertory Theatre, the Theatre Royal Plymouth and the West Yorkshire Playhouse, and was first produced on stage in 2013. It was commissioned specifically for youth theatre; something which necessarily impacts upon questions, not just of performance, but of audience reception. The plot of *Girls Like That* moves around the experiences of a secondary school pupil, Scarlett, a naked picture of whom is circulated online following the break-up of a relationship. As such she becomes victim to what has become known as 'revenge porn', a peculiarly vicious and virulent species of online harassment. The victims of 'revenge porn' are not always younger women. But most commonly they are. And they are growing in number. In summer 2014 the Safer Internet Centre identified between 20 and 30 revenge porn internet sites operating in the UK alone. The global figure is considerably greater, estimates running to hundreds of such sites, some transitory, others more permanent, many notorious. There is a much larger context within which 'revenge porn' must be comprehended; a pervasive and thoroughly engendered 'visual economy of nudity' that 'flourishes online'.[1] According to ChildLine, 25 per cent of thirteen to eighteen-year-olds have admitted sending a sexual image of themselves to another person. And the law, very obviously, has struggled to comprehend the sheer magnitude of the regulatory challenge. In regard to incidences of 'revenge porn', for example, 149 incidents were reported to eight police forces between 2012 and 2014. But only six of these cases resulted in either a police caution or a prosecution.[2] Addressing the harms of 'revenge porn' cannot, it seems, be left to the law alone; nor should it be.

The first part of this chapter will set the jurisprudential context, taking a closer look at the evolving legal regulation of 'revenge porn', as well as the critical debate which this regulation has stimulated. The second will then consider the dramatic presentation of the same issues and arguments in Placey's play. According to Placey, any 'time we write a script, we're hoping in some way people will listen, that our words might have an effect, that they might shake people'.[3] The final part will contemplate the extent to which this aspiration is realised in *Girls Like That*.

Pornographies

The regulation of pornography has emerged as one of the defining issues in modern feminism. It is not simply a matter of regulating the creation, distribution or possession of pornographic imagery. Pornography expresses a larger cultural misogyny, one which permits, even encourages, the emotional and physical violation of women. The law should prevent this. But it does not, at least not convincingly. As a consequence, the campaign to rewrite pornography regulation has assumed a still greater semiotic significance within critical

---

[1] See here M. Salter and T. Crofts, 'Responding to Revenge Porn: Challenges to Online Legal Impunity', in L. Comella and S. Tarrant (eds), New Views on Pornography: Sexuality, Politics and Law, Praeger Publishing, Westport, 2015, at 5–6, discussing the notoriety of sites such as *Is Anyone Up?* which at its height was attracting up to 240,000 visitors a day.

[2] See here a report discussed in *The Independent*, 30th September 2014, quoting Laura Higgins, from the UK Safer Internet Centre, suggesting that the known figures were probably 'just the tip of the iceberg'. The Chief Constable in charge of the College of Policing freely admitted that dealing with various species of online harassment was a 'real problem for people working on the frontline of policing'. See *The Daily Telegraph*, 2nd July 2014, and also 7th October 2014. The difficulties which the police were encountering in regard to 'revenge porn' were acknowledged in Parliamentary debates which preceded the passage of the 2015 Criminal Justice and Courts Act, Section 33 of which was specifically targeted. We will take a closer look at Section 33 in due course.

[3] See <http://nickhernbooksblog.com/category/nhb-author/evan-placey> (last accessed 26th June 2020).

feminist movements. Catherine MacKinnon, for example, famously placed pornography and rape along the same jurisprudential continuum, whilst noting a further fundamental violation; that pornography militates against the political equality of men and women. And in this violation pornography, for reasons that are only too obvious, infringes a collateral principle of human dignity.[4]

The reason for the failure of law is various. There is, of course, the familiar terminological and conceptual confusion. Law has always struggled to define pornography. A second problem flows from this definitional confusion. Liberal legalism loves rights, and the regulation of pornography appears, rather obviously, to contravene one of the most cherished of all liberal rights, that of free expression. And then there is the problem of trying to balance alternative rights to equality, privacy and freedom of expression. These collected difficulties have been long felt across the Atlantic, Supreme Court justices and reform campaigners alike struggling to make sense of their conflicting presence in the US Constitution. And now since 1998 and the enactment of the Human Rights Act, the same frustrations have loomed in the UK, most obviously around the scope and meaning of 'privacy'. The emergence of tortious actions based on an alleged breach of confidentiality is a further consequence of this latter confusion.

A third specifically jurisprudential problem is similarly formalist, and again speaks to the broader situation of women who come 'before the law' as victims of male violence. Liberal legalism is as obsessed with procedural formality as it is with rights. As such, it is concerned almost exclusively with the factual 'event' of the alleged crime rather than the 'experience' of the victim, or indeed the perpetrator. The consequence of this disinterest is disarticulation. The law silences its victims. As MacKinnon observed 'No law imagines what happened to you, the way it happened. You live your whole life surrounded by this cultural echo of nothing where your screams and your words should be'.[5] Silencing matters, because silencing means, in effect, exclusion. It is not just men who violate the rights of women. It is the law, or more specifically the procedural prejudices of liberal legalism.

The legal regulation of pornography in the UK is a mixture of statute and common law. The governing statutes are the Obscene Publications Acts, which treat the creation and distribution of pornographic imagery, and a series of Criminal Justice Acts, wherein can be found a range of provisions intended

---

[4] As also noted by the likes of Martha Nussbaum, to whose ideas we shall return in due course, and Jeremy Waldron. For the latter's observations, see his *The Harm of Hate Speech*, (Harvard UP, 2012), 105–9, 138.

[5] C. MacKinnon, *Only Words*, (Harvard UP, 1993), 3.

to expressly address the possession of the same. The jurisprudential landscape is constantly shifting, in large part a consequence of the emergent challenges of new media and technology. Pornography predates the internet. But it has never been so easy to sell and to distribute. And, with each passing tech-toy, it just gets easier. Global sales of smart-phones in 2014 topped 1.2 million, up by 28 per cent on the previous year. The implications here in regard to the circulation of online imagery are patent, as Derek Bambauer observes:

> Creating an explicit photo can be done easily, impulsively. And the device that snaps the photo can share it as well. The cost of distributing analog photos was an effective barrier to most non-consensual sharing; it was simply too much to work . . . But, as sexting proves, the smartphone has made intimate media ubiquitous.[6]

Concern is greatest where the technology appears to promote the circulation of imagery which is thought to be especially reprehensible, and so especially deserving of the most intense jurisprudential attention, and perhaps, more importantly, a comprehensive and effective regulatory legal regime. Here two particular species of pornography immediately come to mind. A first is child pornography.[7] A second is 'revenge' pornography.

At first glance, it might be supposed that 'revenge' pornography is relatively easy to determine. Most commonly it is characterised as an act in which one ex-partner exerts revenge on another by maliciously, and without consent, distributing sexually-explicit photos online, most commonly by either uploading onto a revenge porn website or simply distributing by email or smart-phone. But first glances can deceive. For a start, the very term 'revenge porn' is problematic, and can be something of a distraction. Much of the Parliamentary debate which accompanied the passage of the 2015 Criminal Justice and Courts Act, Section 33 of which we shall shortly encounter, was spent agonising over the meaning of 'revenge'. Lord Marks, for example, one of the two Liberal Democrat peers who tabled the specific amendment which became Section 33, suggested that the focus of the legal regulation should be against the 'widespread publication of such images' that was 'intended to cause distress, humiliation, and embarrassment for the victim'.[8] Yet it can just as readily be argued that the non-consensual distribution of sexual images is no less reprehensible for not being maliciously intended.

---

[6] D. Bambauer, 'Exposed', 98 *Minnesota LR* 2014, 2092.

[7] On the latter see here M. Johnson and K. Rogers, 'Too far down the Yellow Brick Road - Cyber-hysteria and Virtual Porn', 4 *Journal of International Commercial Law and Technology* 2009, 61–2, 66–7.

[8] Hansard 21st July 2014. The second peer was Baroness Grender.

In this context, it is sometimes argued that a focus on the 'harm' suffered by the victim would be more profitable. Amongst the most obvious of these harms can be listed shame, loss of dignity and sense of equal worth, the limitation of personal aspiration, as well as various consequential emotional and physical harms, to include an array of self-inflicted harms such as anorexia nervosa, depression and suicide.[9] And it inflicts a further familiar harm, familiar at least to critical feminists and readers of MacKinnon. As an extreme species of online harassment 'revenge porn' silences, as well as shames, its victims.[10] As such it could then be characterized as a species of cyber-terrorism.[11]

But just as there can be little doubt regarding the devastating effect of online harassment, so too is there little doubt in regard to the extent to which society, and its legislators, have tended to 'trivialize' it.[12] Legal regulation could play a significant role in combating online harassment, deploying a range of both criminal and civil sanctions. Remedies in the latter context could, of course, include both damages and injunctions. There again civil law actions, particularly those founded on supposed privacy breaches, are notoriously difficult to establish, aside from being prohibitively expensive to mount. There is moreover a question of state responsibility here, and legal principle. Individuals should not be left to counter cyber-terror themselves.[13] This is what the government, and the criminal law, is for. The latter especially possesses 'an important expressive character beyond its coercive one'.[14] Its disapproval can help to shape social norms.[15] Thus far, however, criminal law has failed to properly comprehend the harms of 'revenge porn'; just as it has more broadly struggled to engage so many of the challenges presented by the internet revolution.[16]

---

[9] See here D. Keats Citron, 'Law's Expressive Value in Combating Cyber Gender Harassment', 108 *Michigan Law Review* 2009, 388–90, and also 'Civil Rights', 66–71, and more particularly on the theme of dignity, J. Waldron, *The Harm of Hate Speech*, (Harvard UP, 2012), 105–9, 138.

[10] D. Keats Citron, 'Cyber Civil Rights', 89 *Boston University Law Review* 2009, 64.

[11] See here Citron, 'Civil Rights', 75–6 and 81–6.

[12] See here Citron, 'Harassment', 374–6, 395. And also 378–9 discussing the implications of recent surveys which confirm that between 60 and 75 per cent of reported victims are female. The figure is likely to be higher still for unreported victims.

[13] Though it might be noted that a number of anti-porn activists have developed cyber-strategies designed to counter-attack 'revenge porn' websites.

[14] Citron, 'Civil Rights', 86–8 and 104–5, and also 'Harassment', 376–7 and 404–7. In regard to law's 'expressive' character, Citron cites its ability to reshape society's attitudes to domestic violence and workplace harassment.

[15] See here, discussing more closely the American experience, Citron, 'Harassment', 401–4.

[16] See here Citron, 'Civil Rights', 67, Johnson and Rogers, 'Cyber-hysteria', 61–2, and McGlynn and Rackley. . .

Critical anxieties in regard to the limitations of legal responses to 'revenge porn' have been expressed in various jurisdictions, most especially in those where there have been initial attempts to devise some kind of statutory response or where there has been controversial case-law. Canada, Israel, Japan and Germany have already passed legislation which criminalises 'revenge porn', as have a number of US states. In California, for example, the Penal Code has been recently amended so that s.647.j.4 now makes the distribution of images of another person's body, with the intent to cause distress, a criminal misdemeanour. This provision can be added to those found s.649.9 which criminalise various other forms of harassment. Whilst in Australia, the case of *Giller v Procopets* established the principle that a victim might recover damages for emotional distress under the tort of breach of confidence.[17] The Australian Commonwealth Criminal Code already prohibits the use of the internet to menace or harass or otherwise cause offence, by virtue of a 2004 amendment; a provision which the Commonwealth Attorney-General has stated could, and should, be used to prosecute instances of 'revenge porn'.[18]

Section 33 of the Criminal Justice and Courts Act 2015 represents a first attempt in the UK to directly address the phenomenon of 'revenge porn'. Pre-existing legislation provided only piecemeal regulatory cover; a 'mishmash' as one MP concluded in parliamentary debate.[19] Section 1 of the Malicious Communications Act 1988 makes it an offence to send electronic communications which are indecent, grossly offensive, threatening or false, provided there is intent to cause distress; which means that it cannot apply in situations where the offender does not inform the victim or argues that they were never intended to know. Section 127 of the Communications Act 2003 makes it an offence to send or cause to be sent through a 'public communications network' a message that is 'grossly offensive' or of an 'indecent, obscene or menacing character'; which seems more useful perhaps, but which fails to effectively distinguish between the distribution of images that were taken consensually or otherwise. More promising perhaps is the 1997 Protection from Harassment Act which criminalises incidents which amount to a 'course of conduct'. Two recent cases, *AMP* and *ABK*, have suggested that courts are sympathetic to its application in cases which might be categorised as 'revenge porn'.[20] However, the Act still requires the harassment to be 'oppressive',

---

[17] *Giller v Procopets* [2008] VSCA 236.

[18] Section 474.17.

[19] Maria Miller in Hansard 1st December 2014. For similar observations see 19th June 2014 and 30th June 2014.

[20] *AMP v Persons Unknown* [2011] EWHC 3454 (TCC) and *ABK v KDT & FGH and Anor* [2013] EWCR 1192 (QB).

and to 'go beyond annoyances or irritations, and beyond the ordinary banter and badinage of life', whilst further requiring repeat publication of images.[21] Thus whilst the classic 'revenge porn' scenario might well fall within this jurisprudence, it would not seem to cover cases where pictures were posted as a joke, or for money, or where they were intended to be retained for personal use, or simply where there is no evidence of harassment.

Section 33 of the 2015 Act is more specific in regard to the regulation of 'revenge porn'. Sub-section 1 states that 'It is an offence for a person to disclose a private sexual photograph or film if the disclosure is made (a) without the consent of the individual who appears in the photograph or film, and (b) with the intention of causing that individual distress'. There are certain defences articulated in Sections 4 and 5, respectively where disclosure is 'necessary for purposes of preventing, detecting or investigating crime', and where publication of 'journalistic material' was 'reasonably believed' to be in the public interest'. But the test here will, as Lord Faulks affirmed, be 'stringent'.[22] The offence carries a maximum sentence of two years imprisonment.

Statutory enactments invariably introduce particular definitional concerns, and section 33 is no exception. The nature of disclosure is immediately contentious. Possession of imagery is clearly not the concern of Section 33. Distribution might be. Certainly, the mere taking of photographs cannot be sufficient grounds for legal regulation or response; for the obvious reason that such images might have been originally made by victims. Then there is the determination of 'private' and 'sexual' imagery. The common law determination of 'private' tends to the tautological, in that it is something not ordinarily seen in public. It also fails to provide much clarity in instances where private sex acts are performed in public.[23] Section 35 meanwhile attempts to define the 'sexual' as 'exposed genitals or pubic area', or 'something that a reasonable person would consider to be sexual because of its nature' or 'its content, taken as a whole, is such that a reasonable person would consider it to be sexual'. As ever, therefore, judges will look not to the real harm suffered by the victim but to the virtual reality of the so-called 'reasonable person'. Finally, there is the matter of disclosure with 'intent to cause distress'. Intent is clearly central to the operation of Section 33. Yet the absence of such intent does not necessarily reduce the harm suffered. Moreover, there may be a different,

---

[21] *Majrowski v Guys and Thomas NHS Trust* [2006] UKHL 34, and *Iqbal v Dean Manson Solicitors* [2011] EWCA Civ.123.

[22] *The Times* 19th February 2015.

[23] An instructive example here is the case of a woman who performed an act of oral sex as a part of a competition organised whilst on holiday in Magaluf. The video was posted online last year.

most obviously perhaps commercial, intent. The harm would be just as great. It might thus be reasonably wondered if the final five words of Section 33 serve much useful purpose. Time will tell, as it will of the wider effectiveness of Section 33, both in regard to the proscription of 'revenge porn' websites and the prosecution of those who use them. In the meantime, hundreds of such sites continue to operate around the world, and hundreds of victims fall prey to a very peculiar and very cruel species of sexual harassment.

Placey's Girls

Drama, ancient and modern, has long engaged with, even deployed, pornography; or at least the presentation of the sexualised body in order to stimulate physical or emotional arousal. Classical tragedy is full of violated men and women. So is Shakespeare. Of course, from a strictly legal perspective, plays like *The Bacchae* or *Titus Andronicus* are only pornographic if they were intended to stimulate sexual arousal, and indeed were successful in doing so. The dramatic determination of pornography is no easier to resolve than the jurisprudential. And in the closer context of modern drama, the same problems pervade. Most famous perhaps is the furore which surrounded the depiction of male rape in Howard Brenton's *The Romans in Britain* in 1980. Brenton was certainly hoping to shock, but it was not clear that he intended to arouse anyone, at least not sexually. Much the same might be said of Sarah Kane's *Blasted*; a play we encountered in the previous chapter. *Blasted* might seem at first glance to be pornographic. Many of its critics thought so on first witnessing its performance in 1995. But on closer inspection, it is not obviously written to be sexually arousing. And, as we have already noted, Kane was keen to deny that such was her intent.[24]

For obvious reasons the various difficulties, conceptual and definitional, assume centre-stage in plays which specifically address pornography, such as Sarah Daniels's *Masterpieces*. Daniels has long enjoyed a reputation as a writer determined to probe 'the fault-lines of contemporary society', most especially those which address the female condition.[25] *Masterpieces*, which

---

[24] For a commentary on the presentation of sexuality and violence in *Blasted*, see I. Ward, 'Rape and Rape Mythology in the plays of Sarah Kane', 47 *Comparative Drama* 2013, 225–48.

[25] Daniels has written a number of similarly issue-based plays, many of which move around questions of gender and prejudice, including perhaps most famously *Beside Herself* and *Byrthrite*. For critical commentaries see C. Dymkowski, 'Breaking the Rules: The Plays of Sarah Daniels', 5 *Contemporary Theatre Review* 1996, 63, 75, and also L. Gilleman, 'Drama and Pornography: Sarah Daniels's *Masterpieces* and Anthony Neilson's *The Censor* ', 25 *Journal of Dramatic Theory and Criticism* 2010, 76.

was first performed in 1983, was consciously written as an 'issues-based' play inspired, as Daniels made clear in her prefatory essay, by the work of the anti-pornography campaigners such as Andrea Dworkin and Catherine MacKinnon.[26] The political message is uncompromising. Men violate women, by what they say and do, by what they look at, and by what they imagine; and the violation is pervasive. *Masterpieces* traces the experiences of three women afflicted, in different ways, by the consequences of pornography; and notably by the complicity of the law. This latter 'issue' is most evident in the case of Rowena.[27] Traumatised by a 'snuff' movie she has recently watched, Rowena kills a man who she fears might be about to attack her.[28] Rowena is brought to trial as a consequence but refuses to plead. In this way, Daniels moves the attention of the audience away from the narrower concern with Rowena, and her victim, and towards the greater limitations of law and legal process. In doing so, she invokes the binary which, as we have noted, is so familiar in feminist critique of rape law; between event and experience.[29] Critics reacted variously to Rowena's case, as they did Daniels's play. Particular concerns were advanced in regard to the perceived weakness of Rowena's character; her peculiar naivety making for an uninspiring caricature of neurotic femininity. A few wondered about the fate of her unfortunate, and entirely innocent, victim; noting that neither Daniels nor Rowena did. More broadly, many concluded that the political intensity detracted from the poetry. It was too 'strident', perhaps even too 'feminist', for which reason it seemed too 'cold, passive' and too 'controlled'.[30] The clarity of the argument was both a virtue and a vice. Whilst *Masterpieces* is uncompromising in its central message, that pornography is violent and pervasive to the female condition, it evaded its own 'dark, unexamined centre'; in other words, it neglected to consider what pornography actually is and, more importantly perhaps, what it does.[31]

Girls Like That is a very different play, more subtle, more evasive, and

---

[26] See Daniels's prefatory observations in her 'Introduction' to *Plays: 1* (Methuen, 1997), at xi. See further Gilleman, 'Drama', 76–80.

[27] The pivotal moment in the play according to Luc Gilleman. See 'Drama', 81.

[28] Daniels was inspired to write *Masterpieces* by the long delayed appearance of the film *Snuff* in the UK in 1982.

[29] Gilleman, 'Drama', 78–9, 82.

[30] See Gilleman, 'Drama', 76–7, noting further the 'mockery' evinced in many critical reviews, and 81–2, and also T. Davis, '*Extremities* and *Masterpieces*: A Feminist Paradigm of Art and Politics', in H. Keyssar (ed) *Feminist Theatre and Theory*, (Macmillan, 1996), 145, 152, ultimately concluding that the criticism is largely unfair.

[31] See Dymkowski, 'Rules', 73, and also Gilleman, 'Drama', 81–2 referring to the play's 'oppressive sense of inevitability', and also 92 commenting on its 'all-encompassing' sense of 'masculine evil'.

more poetic too. It can still be characterised as an 'issue-based' play. Indeed, precisely because it is so much more subtle, it can make a much greater claim to experiential reality. Few in its audience are likely to have watched snuff movies or pushed men under trains, or indeed appeared in court accused of murder. But many are likely to have encountered the kind of problems advanced in Placey's play; or if they have not, their children very probably have. There is an adult presence in the play, as we shall see. But *Girls Like That* is, very obviously, about the experiences of teenagers. And it is intended to be acted by teenagers too, at least in the main part. The fact that *Girls Like That* was written expressly as a piece of youth theatre adds, as we noted before, a particular contextual dimension.

The plot of *Girls Like That* moves around the experiences of Scarlett, a 'naked' picture of whom goes viral during a history lesson. As such, it might be supposed that she is the central character in the play. But only in a sense; for there is a critical ambiguity which attaches to Scarlett. For much of the play, she says virtually nothing and does virtually nothing. Indeed for much of the play, she is not even on stage. Her silencing is, of course, resonant. Unable to erase the image, Scarlett erases herself. In due course, she disappears. In the later stages of the play, a police officer turns up at school to confirm that Scarlett has gone 'missing'; thus providing a figurative complement to the defining metaphor (59). Rumours spread that she may even have killed herself. A body is found in the river. It transpires that the body is not that of Scarlett, but of a Latvian prostitute, another disappeared. The fact that the authorities circulate another image of Scarlett, her 'school photo', is again suggestive (61). Whilst the 'real' Scarlett might have disappeared, there is any number of 'virtual' Scarletts around. As well as the school photo there is, of course, the original image of Scarlett that went viral, and then there is the culturally retained Scarlett, familiar from novels and films such as *Gone with the Wind* and Hawthorne's *The Scarlet Letter*. Scarlett is everywhere and nowhere, her absence like her silence speaking volumes.

Scarlett's problem, of course, is that whilst she can delete the image, she cannot be sure that everyone else will. In fact, she knows that they will do quite the opposite. So she panics and starts pressing buttons, manically sending and forwarding and tweeting, and three minutes later 'everyone in the school' has it. And the torment begins. If Scarlett articulates the critical silence, the noise is provided by the chorus of tormentors, classmates and erstwhile friends. There is a minor chorus of boys. But they spend most of their time just posing and 'smirking', casting 'furtive glances' and occasional aspersions regarding Scarlett's sexuality. Meanwhile, they cling to the 'straps of their rucksacks as if they're cords of a bomb and they might combust' (24). Inevitably they start turning on themselves. When Jay suggests that they should not really be looking at Scarlett's picture, he is taunted with being 'gay' (25). To say they lack 'social awareness' is something of an understatement (26). 'Lusty Russell' is possessed of conspicuously more muscle than vocabulary, his articulation amounting to nothing more than the occasional vicious joke. When Scarlett casts him a glance in the dining-hall, he eschews, predictably enough, the chance to save her just a little bit of her reputation. 'Again?' he says for all to hear, 'I'm a bit worn-out Scarlett' (28). The boys have a good laugh. They are 'such dicks' (28). And later, when his girlfriend attacks Scarlett, he just stands and watches. Predictably enough 'he doesn't say anything' (46). In due course, another image goes viral, this time of a naked Russell. The consequences are, however, very different. Russell 'goes to the gym' and 'plays rugby'. His 'body is what you would expect' (37). Rumour supposes that it must have been circulated by Scarlett. Scarlett 'obviously doesn't get it's fine for boys to be, you know' (38). Russell becomes a 'legend' (38).

It is the female chorus which provides the real energy in the play. It is the female chorus, not Russell or any of his boorish mates, which sets out to destroy Scarlett. The very first scene opens with it chanting a string of sexual aspersions, thirteen in all: 'Slut/ Skank/ Sket/ Ho/ Prossie/ Whore/ Slag/ Tart/ Tramp/ Hussy/ Floozie/ Ho-bag/ Slapper'. And then it becomes more personalised: 'Skanky Scarlett/ Slutty Scarlett/ Scarlett the Harlot' (11). Later in the play, noting Scarlett's disappearance, they decide to call her. There is a sense that they want reassurance, to know that she has not done anything 'stupid'. But the concern is overcome by the greater desire to continue the torment, and so they leave a series of messages purporting to be from editors of pornographic magazines. There is a necessary paradox. The need to torture demands communication, but the principal means of torture is exclusion and dis-communication. She has given them all a 'bad name' (27). Association is dangerous. Scarlett must be cast out:

> The problem with girls like that is that their reputation is contagious. And if you hang around girls like that, it's not necessarily that you'll start behaving like she does – we are intelligent young women, we have minds of our own – but people will think you do. And that's worse really. (27)

The irony is patent. And there is insight too; only it is nothing like strong enough to counter the panic. What is happening to Scarlett, in a very small way, is what happened during the Holocaust. Everyone 'stood by' and watched. The girls know this because they studied it in class. And they evidently learnt something too; though not perhaps enough.

The role of Placey's chorus was applauded by critics; most especially its tangible hostility. In classical Greek theatre the chorus was intended to reflect, and shape, the attitudes of the audience; serving indeed as a kind of interior audience.[32] If this is Placey's intention, it does not say much for either the gang of taunting teenage girls who set about terrorising Scarlett, or the generation which produced them. The function of the chorus in *Girls Like That* is not simply to make Scarlett's life miserable. At a deeper level, it reinforces a range of associated connotations regarding hierarchies, institutions and exclusivity; all the darker aspects of communal dissociation identified by troubled chroniclers of contemporary liberal society such as Nussbaum and Waldron. In the opening scene of the play, Scarlett is back in her primary school St. Helens. Her mother calls it 'special'. Scarlett calls it 'hell' (13). Others, perhaps as a 'joke', or perhaps not, call it 'Satan Hell' (15). She compares it with a 'prison', and then with the farm where she lives, with all the chickens fighting it out to determine their 'pecking order' (13). And so it will continue from one institution to another: 'Positioning themselves in the order that will determine the rest of their lives' (14).

In a couple of later scenes, both set at the local swimming pool, the girls now aged eight and eleven all stare anxiously at each other's bodies, trying to work out who is fattest and who is thinnest, who has already got 'boobs', who is wearing a bra (41–2). Aged eight, Scarlett prefers to think of herself in 'the middle', the best 'place' to be. No one wants to be different. But in reality 'Scarlett is at the bottom. Full stop' (14). At least they are all friends; 'twenty chuckling bellies' in the pool (32). 'We are indestructible'; except of course they are not. The age of innocence will pass. Aged eleven, Scarlett is the first to get 'boobs' and wear a bra, for which reason the boys have started to 'swarm', like 'bees to honey'. The pubescent 'Maneater' has become a figure of envy and fear (43). The circulation of her image online merely adds a virtual dimension to a process which is already well underway. How fat is she now? How big are her nipples, and how short her arms? Is that a mole on her right breast or a freckle? Judging Scarlett makes the other chickens 'feel good' in comparison. But it is not just Scarlett who is being judged; it's all the little 'mermaids' (32). And so, as soon as the image appears during the history lesson:

> Then the chickens start attacking each other, like really going for it, they can draw blood, and that's when, that's when you need to be really careful. Because if they see blood, the other chickens, they can turn into murderers. They'll keep pecking until there's blood and more . . . I don't know why. But I think it's maybe cos a vulnerable chicken is putting the whole flock at risk. (17)

---

[32] See here M. Nussbaum, *Political Emotions: Why Love Matters for Justice*, (Harvard UP, 2013), 258.

The mechanics of cyber-terrorism are only too apparent. The terrorisers ter-rorise because they are themselves terrified. Scarlett is not punished merely for being a 'skank', but for realising a shared nightmare. What has happened to her might have happened to any of them. The metaphorical violence is replaced by something altogether more real when Scarlett returns to school and is assaulted by Russell's girlfriend. Now 'You can taste the blood' (47).

The fact that Scarlett's image went viral during a history lesson imports an obvious significance; as is the fact that her torment was in effect authorised by her history teacher, who forces Scarlett to confess her guilt in front of the whole class. The classmate who relates the scene compares it with the moment in Arthur Miller's *The Crucible* when John Proctor charges his wife with telling the 'truth' (40). History and law have long conspired to punish women like Elizabeth Proctor, and Scarlett; a point which Placey reinforces by means of a series of historical interludes which interweave throughout the play. Each of the interludes introduces figures from Scarlett's family history, something she has been researching for a school project. In the first, a Girl in a Flapper Dress is assaulted by her brother at a pool party. She is laughing too loud. Her brother worries that she might, as a consequence, be mistaken for a 'whore'. Her mother may have 'fought' for the rights of women, but not 'so you could behave like this' (20–1). There is no right to laugh or not be slapped in the face. In a later scene, set in 1945, a Girl with Aviator Helmet and Goggles experiences a familiar misogyny when a putative co-pilot refuses to fly with her because he is not 'taking orders from a lass' (36). The next generation moves forward to 1968 and finds a Girl With Flowers in her Hair discussing the fact that she is sixteen and pregnant. Her lover wants them to keep the baby and move in with his parents. But she will decide for herself what to do with her 'body'. So she gets up and walks away, passing a dancing girl who whispers in her ear 'Us girls need to stick together' (51). A final flashback returns to 1985, to Scarlett's mother, aspiring to a legal career, working as a 'runner' in a solicitor's firm and getting fondled by a partner (62–3). She might make a formal complaint to an employment tribunal. Or she could just put up with it.

One critic supposed that the historical interludes were written principally for adults, providing breaks from the torrent of 'teenage witterings'.[33] It might, in less pejorative tones, be supposed that they provide an oppor-tunity for deeper reflection, perhaps adding a measure of continuity, even some much-needed stability. But *Girls Like That* does not really do stability,

---

[33] See <https://www.behindthearras.com/reviewsam/ReviewsAMjul-oct2015/girls-like-that-S207–15.html> (last accessed 26th June 2020).

certainly not reassurance. It can just as readily be concluded that the interludes simply confirm that, whilst the situation of women might have improved from generation to generation, the progress is slow, the journey uneven and the destination still some way distant. In a later scene, set in a McDonald's, Scarlett is spotted by her former classmates who start, inevitably, to torment her again. One of them wonders 'why she doesn't say something. Speak up! Its 2013! Women have earned the right to speak!' But she just keeps 'staring' at her new boyfriend (55). She might have any number of constitutional rights to freedom of expression and so on. But in practice, Scarlett knows that there is nothing she can do right now that will save her. So she cries. And if there is such a thing as female solidarity, it is fragile. It has certainly not taken a firm root amongst the girls of St. Helens.

It might be supposed that the final scenes are more uplifting. Scarlett's disappearance invokes a measure of contrition amongst her classmates, and compassion. At first, perhaps inevitably, this contrition finds an online expression, through the facility of Facebook. Later the girls are gathered at school to hold a more personal 'vigil'. More particularly it is the appearance of her school photo on the TV which has finally touched their consciences. This is a different Scarlett, a safer de-sexualised Scarlett, the kind of Scarlett who might be re-integrated into the family of St Helens girls, if only she can be found again. Of course, when Scarlett duly appears, 'like a ghost', and asks permission to give her presentation, they immediate revert, feeling that they have been somehow 'duped' (65). The real Scarlett is so much more frightening, on this occasion because she is about to turn the tables. Her presentation, which recounts 'the history of women' in her family, shames. It transpires that it was her mother who was fondled in the solicitor's office. She is now a FTSE 100 chief executive. Her grandmother, who chose to decide for herself whether to keep her baby, became a teacher. Her great-grandmother flew planes during the war, and it was her mum who so scandalised her brother, and readers of the *Daily Mail*, by 'dancing to Negro music and drinking in cocktails' (66).

Scarlett's presentation invites a series of connected reflections, and just as many complexities. In one sense it is uplifting, perhaps even empowering. In another, it is bitter and contemptuous, and hardly calculated to enhance any sense of solidarity amongst her female peers:

> I have basically learned that in my family history there were always boys who were arseholes who made things shit for the girls in my family. But things have moved on for my generation. Because for me, it is not so much that boys are arseholes – they are – but more that the girls have become the arseholes that boys used to be. (66)

And there is little that can be said to be ameliorating, or hopeful, in her closing expression of reciprocal contempt:

> There is a big bad world out there where St Helen's means nothing. There is a big bad world that is just ready to swallow you up. But when it swallows up you lot, it will vomit you back up. Because you are indigestible girls. That's the kind of girls you are. You are food poisoning. And the world will know you are girls like that. And you will be alone. Together, but alone. Do you see?
>
> And I will forget you. (67)

A similar tone affects the mood of the girls on their last day at the school; a range of conflicting emotions about the fragility of friendship, the uncertain future, and the tyranny of image.

This latter tyranny is reinforced by a series of musical interludes which, like the historical, interweave through the play. There is nothing particularly light or reassuring about Taylor Swift's *Better Than Revenge* or Hall and Oates's *Maneater*, still less perhaps Rihanna with her taste for 'chains and whips', and her ex-boyfriend Chris Brown with his taste for beating her up (51–2). The world outside St Helens is just as intimidating as the world within, full of conflicted messages, allusions of violence and cruelty. And full of images and impressions and evasions; a place where nothing is quite what it seems. The question of authenticity cuts, as it must, across any piece of dramatic writing. At a more existential level, as we noted before, the different images of Scarlett engage questions of essentiality. Who is the real Scarlett? Is there a 'real' Scarlett, or just a series of images and impressions, and actors, all infinitely interpretable? But these are metaphysical questions, and they defy resolution.

Shaking

Girls Like That is an urgent play. It is supposed to invite pause for reflection. But the pause should not be for too long. As we noted earlier, according to Placey, the hope is that in writing drama 'our words might have an effect, that they might shake people'. The observation was made in an interview which followed the performance of *Girls Like That* at Westminster in January 2014; just as Parliament was considering early drafts of what would become the 2015 Criminal Justice Act. The question of audience was obviously pertinent, and here Placey emphasised a duality of purpose. On the one hand, *Girls Like That* was intended to 'shame' its adult audience, to 'tell' them 'what it is that needs to change, the obstacles they are facing, and the realities of being a young person in the UK at the moment', and to emphasise the inevitable consequences of 'collective inaction'. On the other, as a piece of youth theatre, Placey hoped that his play would educate its younger audience 'about feminism and empowering'.[34] Here Placey took the opportunity to confirm once again the wider 'importance of having creative arts for young people's expression, to ask the questions no one else is asking'.[35]

The plea struck a resonant note amongst critics. Reviews of *Girls Like That* were uniformly positive, glowing even. A 'sensational staging of a brilliant play', said one speaking more immediately of its production at the Crescent Theatre in Birmingham, 'in fact' one of the 'cleverest youth productions I have seen in years'.[36] An 'energetic and dazzling piece' and 'incredibly interesting', in the words of another, engaging a series of 'strong, relevant issues and themes that young people today go through'; and most importantly a piece which speaks to different generations.[37] Even the more ambivalent, such as *Time Out*, concluded that whilst the subject is 'grim' the 'piece is refreshingly optimistic'.[38] Lyn Gardner in the *Guardian* noted that it was 'viciously funny', and 'urgent'.[39] It is this latter quality which perhaps matters most. *Girls Like That* was written, above all, to engage immediate experience, the kinds of things which, as Placey observed, really happen to real girls in contemporary society. Gemma Woffinden, who directed the play when it was performed at the West Yorkshire Playhouse, recalled one cast member observing that she had not, until then, thought there was anything especially original about the 'issues' raised in the play. It just portrayed 'normal life and I didn't believe it could be different'.[40]

In many ways, law functions to delineate the extraordinary; identifying and prohibiting behaviour which is not, by definition, considered normal. It is here that alternative forms of cultural expression exert such normative, and didactic, power. It might be reading newspaper reports of celebrities expe-

---

[34] Placey's comments in <http://nickhernbooksblog.com/category/nhb-author/evan-placey> (last accessed 26th June 2020).

[35] Placey's comments in <http://nickhernbooksblog.com/category/nhb-author/even-placey> (last accessed 26th June 2020).

[36] Roderick Dunnett in *Behind the Arras*, available at <https://www.behindthearras.com/reviewsam/ReviewsAMjul-oct2015/girls-like-that-S207–15.html> (last accessed 26th June 2020).

[37] See <http://www.ayoungertheatre.com/review-girls-like-that-west-yorkshire-playhouse> (last accessed 26th June 2020).

[38] See <http://www.timeout.com/london/theatre/girls-like-that> (last accessed 26th June 2020).

[39] See <https://www.theguardian.com/stage/2014/nov/13/girls-like-that-review-esther-baker-feminism> (last accessed 26th June 2020).

[40] In <http://nickhernblogs.com/category/nhb-author/even-placey> (last accessed 26th June 2020).

riencing the same kinds of abuse.[41] Or it might be attending performances of plays such as *Girls Like That*. The idea that literature might serve such an educative purpose is familiar to 'law and literature' teachers. But it is not just a matter of education, or tracing the margins of the ordinary. Literature, as Martha Nussbaum has repeatedly argued, is also good at deepening our collective sense of what justice might mean, of leavening the rigour of liberal legalism with a vital measure of feeling and emotion. Most importantly, a properly liberal theory of justice should be founded on a 'compassionate and generous attitude towards the frailties of human beings'.[42] It should make us kinder, more sensitive to the pain of others, their shame and sadness. Literature can help in fashioning this sensitivity, for 'compassion' is the principal 'emotion aroused by tragic spectatorship'.[43] And, as a consequence, we should better appreciate the suffering of girls like Scarlett, and indeed the girls who terrorise girls like Scarlett, and the boys; for we all have the capacity to be terrorised, just as we all have the capacity to terrorise.[44]

This movement from spectatorship to self-reflection is at the very heart of Placey's play. Why, one of the girls wonders, did Scarlett take the photograph? Did it make her 'feel special'? Was it 'just a bit of fun'? Did it make her 'feel pretty'? Or maybe she let Russell take it, because otherwise, he might 'lose interest'. And anyway 'Why does a photo make someone a slut?' The answer is 'too complicated to explain', the girl records, when challenged by her little sister on the subject, 'so I don't' bother (45). Much the same can be said of a later reflection at a 'pimps 'n' hos' party, when one girl is accused of being a 'prick-tease' and bursts into tears. Why should it be assumed that just because she dressed according to the theme and wore a bit of mascara that she would have sex with whoever asked her? The paradox is only too obvious: 'Cos she's a prick-tease cos she didn't, and she'd be a slut if she did, so how does she get to the space between?' (53)

Gradually reflection refines sensitivity. The girls begin to contemplate how Scarlett might feel, how they might feel if the same happened to them. And they begin to think in terms of harms suffered rather than simply of things done. Here Placey writes in a couple of pointed allusions. A first is to the tragic case of the Canadian schoolgirl Amanda Todd, who committed

---

[41] Most famously perhaps in 2012 the X-Factor judge Tulisa Contostavlos was victimised by a former boyfriend who posted sexually explicit images. Three years earlier the pop-star Rihanna was similarly victimised. Both spoke out about their experiences, and attracted considerable media attention as a consequence.

[42] Nussbaum, *Emotions*, 22.

[43] Nussbaum, *Emotions*, 261.

[44] Nussbaum, *Emotions*, 195.

suicide in 2012 after a webcam video of her exposing her breasts went viral; 'pretty grim', as one of the Placey's girls reflects, 'I thought Canadians were nice. I'm not so sure any more' (59–60). A second is to the equally tragic case of the New Jersey student Tyler Clementi who took his own life, two years earlier, when his room-mate circulated a video of him with a gay date. When the girls gather for a school reunion many years later, it transpires that one of Scarlett's chief tormentors, a boy named Tyler, now has a 'boyfriend who is a model' (73). The case of Tyler Clementi confirmed that there does not need to be a vengeful motive for the online circulation of sexual images to destroy young lives.

Finally, more prosaically, but no less importantly, literature can progress political and social as well as legal reform. Speaking in Parliament during the debates which accompanied the passage of the 2015 Bill, Baroness Thornton rightly emphasised that a specific legal response would not itself be sufficient. There must also be a 'strong political will to tackle the underlying culture that creates and legitimises sexual violence, abuse and harassment in all its forms'.[45] The internet plays a vital role in shaping social attitudes to sexual violence, as it does social attitudes to much else. It is estimated that as high as 20 per cent of under-18s have engaged in sexting.[46] It is not, of course, the only species of online sexual abuse. Towards the end of *Girls Like That*, the scene shifts back just a couple of years to an evening when the girls sit around watching a pornographic film, for most of them for the first time. The scene is not cruel or violent. Indeed, there is a conflicting sense of cosy togetherness, perhaps even solidarity, amongst the girls as they sit on each other's laps eating Doritos (57–8). But it is no less disturbing. The internet revolution presents a lot of challenges to the law, 'revenge porn' is just one of the most concerning.

The question of solidarity returns in the very final scene of the play. At first glance, it is a simple scene. Gathered together for the school reunion, now aged in the mid-forties, the girls exchange gossip, about Tyler and his boyfriend, about the fact that 'lusty' Russell is now fat and bald and working in IT. The future, it seems, will be just as ordinary as the past. A new generation has arrived, just as confused and just as confusing. 'My three are all boys', one of the girls observes, 'I still don't know what to do with them' (73). But when they see a small boy trying to 'destroy' a snowman in the playground, they all link arms in order to protect it: 'Think you can break through us, boy? Go on. Just you try' (74). It would be easy, and reassuring, to suppose a

---

[45] Hansard 21st July 2014
[46] Hansard, 1st December 2014.

happy ending. Time and maturity have made something genuinely empowering out of the 'St Helens girls'. Except that there is no Scarlett present. And the little boy is only in reception class; not much of triumph in bullying five-year-olds, and it is still a kind of bullying. Where was the solidarity when it might have meant something? And how many girls are inside the school now, all suffering the way Scarlett suffered? Happy endings may be nicer, but they rarely convince.

The law, as anyone who teaches it knows, likes endings. And insofar as it presumes a measure of justice, it prefers its endings to be happy. But it is the ending the matters, the resolution, the certainty which ending brings. Life, however, is not that simple. It tends to be conflicted, full of dilemmas and ambiguities, and questions that defy determination, and full of people who are defined by their particular, necessarily contesting, 'frailties and excellences'.[47] This is not to dismiss the place of law in making society a better place within which to live. Law, as Nussbaum confirms, has a particular capacity to cultivate 'decent sentiments'.[48] The case for the better legal regulation of 'revenge porn' is unarguable. But justice requires something more than writing new law; just, indeed, as it will require more than writing new plays. Law is not, of course, the only discipline which craves resolution over ambiguity. The history of ethics is likewise full of 'comprehensive' theories. It is also full of disagreement, for what the same history also reveals is that the greater the attempt to impose resolution, the more reductive the endeavour becomes.[49] A 'poethical' jurisprudence is sceptical in precisely these terms.

It is also, as we noted before, expressly didactic in its aspiration, just as concerned with what happens in the classroom as it is what happens in the courtroom. The idea that the strength of a liberal political society depends upon the 'cultivation' of liberal sentiments in its schoolrooms is again familiar to readers of Martha Nussbaum's recent work. In *Cultivating Humanity* Nussbaum eloquently argued the case for an education that encourages students to 'think what it might be like to be in the shoes of a person different from oneself, to be an intelligent reader of that person's story, and to understand the emotions and wishes and desires that someone so placed might have'.[50] And there is no better way to nurture this 'compassionate imagination' than through the strategic didactic deployment of those whom

[47] See Nussbaum, *Emotions*, 383, and making much the same point *Cultivating Humanity*, 6.
[48] Nussbaum, *Emotions*, 315–16.
[49] Nussbaum, *Emotions*, 6, 118, 387.
[50] Nussbaum, *Cultivating Humanity: A Classical Defence of Reform in Liberal Education*, (Harvard UP, 1997), 10–11.

Richard Rorty famously termed the 'strong' poets.[51] More recently still in *Political Emotions*, Nussbaum has confirmed the importance of emotional education in the classroom. In words that enjoy an obvious pertinence in the context of *Girls Like That*, Nussbaum writes:

> The average high school is a veritable cauldron of envy. Adolescents are especially likely to be in a psychological condition of insecurity about their worth and their future. Everything that happens makes rankings salient: grading, the competition for college entrance, the visibility of sports in most places, the frequently cruel formation of cliques and groups and the related ranking of people by attractiveness. And the low-ranked often do feel hopeless about their situation.[52]

And a couple of months after leaving high school, a significant proportion arrives at law school. The environment might seem a little different, but the insecurities will have a certain familiarity, as will the cliques and the hierarchies. There will be lots of lusty Russells and lots of Tylers, and lots of Scarletts. And there will be a lot of pecking chickens, all trying to do that little bit better than everyone else, whatever it takes. There will be moments of shame and envy for sure; it is the natural consequence of grading papers and competing for placements. Hopefully, there will be moments when countervailing sentiments of compassion and empathy will come to the fore too. But it will not happen by chance. Nussbaum cites Walt Whitman's resonant metaphor; that teachers have a peculiar responsibility to 'plant companionship thick as trees'.[53] Reading Whitman would be a good start, of course. So would reading *Girls Like That*.

---

[51] Nussbaum, *Humanity*, 92, and R. Rorty, *Contingency, Irony, and Solidarity*, (Cambridge UP, 1989), 16–20, 60–1.

[52] Nussbaum, *Emotions*, 343.

[53] In Nussbaum, *Emotions*, 375.

Conclusion

There is an implication to a 'conclusion'. It supposes an end to something, and a resolution. Sometimes credible on those terms, sometimes not. There is an end to this book, but only in the most prosaic sense; in that there are no more chapters. But there is no thematic end, no argument finally resolved. Nothing definitive. And there is no final flourish either, no rabbit to be pulled out of the hat. What there is, though, is an opportunity to reflect. To revisit what has been ventured in the preceding pages, to identify perhaps some common themes, or maybe just play with some impressions.

Starting with something almost too obvious. As we noted at the very start, *The Play of Law* is a contribution to a strategic genre of inter or cross-disciplinary scholarship, variously termed 'law and literature' or 'law and humanities'. Principal amongst these strategies is the deployment of literary texts in order to reshape otherwise familiar legal tensions. Commonly, though not always, these will be relational tensions, most especially between law and morality, political or ethical. The kinds of tensions which Richard Weisberg terms 'poethical'. Tensions and relations. An interior irony approaches. The use of a various words which touch on the matter of engagement, distance, consonance, immediacy. Similar, but not the same. There are always nuances. Dealing with the relation between disciplines and ideas, can be a slippery business; as indeed can be using the right metaphors.

The relation of law, literature and morality has recurred throughout previous chapters. And we will contemplate it further very shortly. But there is something else, peculiar to *The Play of Law*, and which was also advertised from the very start; the relation of law, politics and history. History is always present. But here it assumes a slightly different shape; because we are looking at 'contemporary' drama. Indeed, the premise of *The Play of Law* is that 'contemporary' drama has been comparatively neglected, and for this reason warrants closer attention. A whole range of disciplinary relations then, constantly shifting. And not just from one text to another. But from one moment of reading to another, and one moment of performance. This book has tended to assume a greater textual direction, with comparatively less on the dimension of performance. But that does not stop us from venturing a few, relatively uncontentious, observations in regard to the latter. Audiences shift, as do actors. And whilst the author might add a certain stability, we might also be minded of the supposition that the author is anyway 'dead'. As for the text, stabilizing perhaps; until an actor or a director or a reader gets hold of it. And then, not so much.

We might, with this in mind, revisit what had gone before. To check out the precise, or imprecise, disciplinary relations. To contemplate resonances and dissonances. The first two chapters, if we recall, touched on species of 'documentary' drama. They seemed, as a consequence, more obviously legal. The first, David Hare's *Murmuring Judges*, was explicitly written into a legal setting, inside courtrooms, barrister chambers, Inns of Court, drawn variously from original material gleaned by the author. Quasi-documentary at least. The second chapter looked at plays which aspire to a still greater veracity by virtue of their 'verbatim', as well as 'documentary', form. Except that, in regard to the particular play upon which we focussed our closest attention, *Called to Account*, the scenario was actually fictitious. A different kind of veracity. The 'best court' we have, as Hare says of political theatre in general. In a sense perhaps. But it is a different kind of justice.

The second set of plays gestured more obviously towards history. There are, though, the same overarching questions, of reach and authenticity. The first two chapters in this set revisited seventeenth-century England, but did so, importantly, at different moments of composition. Caryl Churchill ventured back into the 'upside down' world of Civil War radicalism in order to cast some aspersions as to the state of left-wing, and gender, politics in the England of the 1970s. Raising a couple of very obvious 'others', 'true' Levellers and witches, in a confessedly 'combative' kind of writing, which is now set in its own historical aspic. Howard Brenton picks up the narrative, three decades on, revisiting the trial of King Charles I. In the hope that it might make his audience think rather more closely about the state of twenty-first England and its political institutions.

And something else; that even at its very 'highest' level, politics is described by personal engagement. The same insights that we find affirmed in the third of our 'history' plays, Mike Bartlett's *King Charles III*. Different though, for a very obvious reason. *King Charles III* is made up, like *Called to Account*, a species of what is sometimes called 'virtual' history; or 'what if' history. A more lyrical text too, reaching back in compositional terms to the 'histories' of William Shakespeare. And more spectral too. Haunted not just by the ghosts that stride the stage, the recently deceased Queen Elizabeth, a 'beshrouded' Princess Diana, but all those that flit about in recesses of the text. Shakespearean mainly, but not only; Prince Hal, Lady Macbeth,

Walter Bagehot. Different kinds of reality, and tangibility; all of which make us think again about the associated practices of historical writing, and reading.

And then, the final set of chapters, the 'tragedies'. Here, at first glance, more contemporary still, at least in terms of their setting. Not though otherwise. The crimes are ageless, rape, child murder and pornography. The sharpest expressions of what Sarah Kane terms the 'breakdown of human nature'. The technologies of violence may have changed, the mobile phones and the mortar bombs, but the experience is much the same. And the suffering. Kane's Kate suffers in the way that Aeschylus's Cassandra suffered, and Seneca's Strophe and Shakespeare's Lavinia. Rhona's mother in Lavery's *Frozen* is not the first to be devastated by the news that her daughter has been murdered. And neither is Placey's Scarlett the first women to be diminished on stage, in public or in private. A constant in one sense, but not of course in any other; for everyone feels differently. A simple point, which lies at the very heart of the 'law and literature' enterprise.

And which attaches to something else just as important. The capacity of literature, and performance, to humanise. By making us feel, not just as a response to things done to us, but as a response to things done to others. Empathy, the very essence of 'poethical' engagement. We might recall David Hume's supposition; that what makes us human is the 'propensity we have to sympathise with others'. It is here that Rorty's 'strong poet' assumes such a critical responsibility; facilitating that reach. Crafting 'sad and sentimental stories' which help us relate. We have come across plenty of these poets in the preceding chapters. Shakespeare, Marvell, Whitman; canonical each, for a reason. Sharing an aspiration, and a facility. We might pause for a moment of quiet reflection, on the words written by another 'strong' poet, who was forever urging us to do precisely this. In the Preface to his *Lyrical Ballads*, first published in 1798, William Wordsworth expressed a determination to write poetry that can 'speak a plainer more emphatic language', that is 'really used by men'. The gendered tone has not lasted well. But the broader point endures.

Which brings us to what is perhaps the defining aspiration of this book; which is to prove precisely that. Time strengthens the 'strong' poet, or at least it does their critical reputation. But it does not preclude their presence now, as then. For the aspiration is a constant. What compelled Shakespeare and Whitman and Wordsworth is precisely what now compels David Hare and Caryl Churchill, Bryony Lavery and Evan Placey, and each of the other writers whose work we have revisited in the preceding chapters. Determined still to toss their bombs through the proscenium arch; to make their audiences 'shake'. But determined also to write plays which, to repeat Bartlett's injunction, 'appeal to people who do jobs and have lives'. To use the imagination to reach into reality. It is what the 'strong' dramatist has always done. It is what they are doing now.

Index